Pelican Books
Geography and Environmental Stu
Editor: Peter Hall

GW01081403

Latin American Development

Alan Gilbert was born in London in 1944. He was educated at St Nicholas Grammar School, Northwood, and at Birmingham University, where he read geography, politics and economics. After a brief period in advertising he studied at the London School of Economics from 1966 to 1970. He made two extended visits to Latin America during that time, the first to collect data for his doctoral thesis, the second to work on a study of port expansion in Peru. In 1969 he became a research fellow at the Institute of Latin American Studies in London and the following year was appointed to a lecturing post created jointly at the Institute and the Department of Geography, University College, London. Since then he has visited Latin America several times, to participate in preparing an urban development plan for Bogota and to undertake research into the problems involved in health and education planning in Latin America.

Latin American Development

A Geographical Perspective

Alan Gilbert

Penguin Books

Penguin Books Ltd, Harmondsworth,
Middlesex, England
Penguin Books Inc., 7110 Ambassador Road,
Baltimore, Maryland 21207, U.S.A.
Penguin Books Australia Ltd, Ringwood,
Victoria, Australia

First published 1974
Copyright © Alan Gilbert, 1974

Made and printed in Great Britain
by Richard Clay (The Chaucer Press) Ltd
Bungay, Suffolk
Set in Monotype Times

This book is sold subject to the condition that it shall not, by way of trade or otherwise, be lent, re-sold, hired out, or otherwise circulated without the publisher's prior consent in any form of binding or cover other than that in which it is published and without a similar condition including this condition being imposed on the subsequent purchaser

Contents

List of Figures

List of Figures *cont'd*

Acknowledgements

This book is the result of seven years acquaintance with Latin America and with the spatial processes associated with developmental change. It is, however, much more than the sum of my own efforts. For during this period of familiarization a great many people have helped to stimulate my ideas, have provided me with information and have criticized my writing. Unfortunately, I cannot thank everyone by name, but I feel I must acknowledge the following for their special contributions.

Firstly, I should like to thank Professor Peter Odell for his patient supervision of my doctoral thesis while I was a student at the London School of Economics and for his continued interest in my work since that time. This interest has been reflected in a number of ways, not least by his careful comments on the text of this book.

Secondly, I am grateful to my employers over the past three years for their benevolent treatment. I have been completely free to develop any courses that I wished to teach and to follow research lines which I felt might be rewarding. In addition, I have been allowed regular leave to visit Latin America – leave that has been essential for me to maintain contacts and to obtain up-to-date information. For these reasons I would like to thank Professor R. A. Humphreys, Professor W. B. Mead and Dr Harold Blakemore.

Thirdly, I have also been fortunate to work in Latin America on a consultancy basis on two occasions. These trips have allowed me to visit parts of the continent which would otherwise have been impossible. On both occasions, too, I have had sympathetic employers who have allowed me time to don my academic hat and follow lines of my own choosing. Since these experiences have enriched this book I would like to thank Ian Harder and Jonathan Smulian.

Fourthly, I have been helped by an enormous number of people living in Latin America. Many have trusted me with information which I had no right to expect. Many others have provided the germs of ideas which have been developed in this book. Many others by their friendship have allowed me to enjoy and understand the continent more fully.

Fifthly, I have to thank friends and colleagues for helping in various ways. Thanks are due to Kenneth Duncan, David Goodman, Allan Lavell, Tony O'Connor, and David Robinson for reading sections of the manuscript. Valerie Cawley drew most of the maps and different members of the University College Geography Department's technical staff have helped in various ways.

Finally, I should like to thank my parents and my wife Jacqueline. The former by their many sacrifices provided me with the opportunity to write this book. The latter has been the person who has suffered most from its writing. To her patience, humour and above all her strength of character in not destroying the manuscript, I dedicate this book.

1: Orientation and Purpose

During the past thirty years most Latin American societies have experienced a number of fundamental changes in their economic, social and political structures. These changes have not been identical, nor have they occurred at the same rate or scale, but they have taken place in most parts of the continent. In terms of the occupational structure, larger numbers of people have become employed in industrial and commercial activities and a smaller proportion of the labour force now works in agriculture.[1] Improvements in health and sanitary facilities have removed the principal epidemic diseases and led to major reductions in infant-mortality and death rates.[2] Modifications in the social structure have resulted in the emergence of sizeable middle-class and working-class groups in most urban areas.[3] Political changes have modified the power bases of traditional elites and forced governments to pay greater heed to social and economic realities.[4]

These changes, of course, have not been confined to Latin America, but have characterized all countries which have experienced what is now generally described as the 'development process'. While such a term is open to misinterpretation and misunderstanding, it will be used throughout this book. Its use here, however, is not synonymous with the terms economic growth, westernization, modernization or progress. For, although development may clearly improve the position of large sections of society, there is not an inevitable association between the two. An expanding literature is emerging which points to the dangers and difficulties associated with particular forms of developmental change.[5] In this book, therefore, the word development will be used in a neutral sense to cover the general social, economic and political transformations which are affecting Latin

America and many other parts of the world. It will be used more in the sense of evolution than of progress, implying neither an improvement nor a deterioration in the quality of life, unless it is qualified by an appropriate adjective.

While this study is integrally concerned with the phenomenon of development, however, it is limited to specific aspects of that complex process. In particular, it concentrates upon those changes which involve some degree of spatial adjustment, that is changes which modify existing geographical distributions of social and economic activities or which affect the relations between different areas. While this emphasis limits the scope of the study considerably, it does direct attention to an important aspect of Latin American development. For, just as the industrial revolution in Britain led to the growth of cities, the decline of the old woollen and iron-founding areas, and the growth of industries in areas where water power and coal were available, so development in Latin America has meant that certain regions have benefited and others suffered. In Latin America, in fact, spatial changes have been many and rapid. The growth of manufacturing and commercial activities has encouraged metropolitan expansion and the comparative stagnation of rural areas. Transport development has produced major spatial changes, helping to integrate isolated communities into the economy and thereby accelerating change in those areas. In turn, these changes have affected the relationships between different social and economic groups, subtly influencing the interactions between rural and urban areas.

Such an approach represents a comparatively new trend in development studies. Until quite recently, several writers were complaining that the spatial component in development had been neglected in planning studies.[6] In particular, they claimed that it had been ignored by the technical literature on resource, manpower and investment planning. In recommending investment in the industrial rather than the agricultural sector, for example, planners had normally paid little attention to the consequences on regional income or employment levels.

During the past decade, however, a large multi-disciplinary literature has appeared dedicated to spatial problems. A number of studies have shed more light on changes in patterns of trade and commodity flows during development.[7] New work has appeared which has examined the spatial adjustments associated with sectoral developments such as the growth of manufacturing or transport networks.[8] These numerous studies have succeeded in demonstrating that different societies at different levels of economic development require spatial forms appropriate to their particular economic needs and value systems.[9] They have shown, for example, that primitive subsistence societies with limited commercial and exchange requirements do not require complex or highly specialized hierarchies of service centres. On the other hand, mass-consumption societies based on a capitalist system of production need highly developed transport and services systems to support the sophisticated advertising, marketing and retailing functions on which their economies depend.

As well as showing that different societies require different spatial forms, these studies have also demonstrated that spatial organization is frequently inflexible to changing developmental needs. At times the spatial structure may need modifying before development can take place. Failure to change this structure may retard or distort the whole development process. A transport network which evolved under colonial rule or which is geared to export shipments may slow development towards greater self-sufficiency. Similarly, the concentration of economic activities in particular areas may make the task of developing poor regions especially difficult. In short, therefore, these studies have shown that the spatial organization of an economy is as much a matter for planning as is the amount of investment to be directed into the different sectors of the economy.

In response to this awareness, a number of books are now appearing which concentrate upon spatial organization as an active factor in developmental change. Several writers have recently suggested forms of urban development which may be more appropriate to developing societies. Friedmann, Lewis, Miller, Berry, Pedersen and others have argued that integrated development may be more easily achieved in countries with a system of urban centres than in those with a single primate city.[10] Another writer, Johnson, has argued that a major requirement for agricultural change is the active development of a system of local market centres.[11] Other writers have argued that rapid economic growth is only compatible with the development of cities which are large enough to take advantage of economies of scale. An extensive literature has also emerged explaining how the spatial structure of less-developed societies may be modified. Methods of taxation, administrative control and licensing have been developed, and concepts such as the 'growth pole' have emerged as practical strategies for change.[12] Despite this cornucopia of ideas, however, there still seems little real agreement about the form of spatial organization most appropriate to different kinds of society. While most writers employ the same terminology, concepts and methodology, their attitudes to identical spatial patterns are very different. One example of these differences emerges in the debate over the most desirable spatial allocation of investment. Should investment be spread as widely as possible at an early stage of development or concentrated in a limited area where economic growth may be maximized? One group of writers and planners argues that a rapid rate of economic growth is the best solution for equity in the long run, as any attempt to spread investment *now* will result in a slower growth rate and a smaller product for division later.[13] On the other hand, a second group argues that a wider distribution of resources should be an immediate aim of less-developed societies. While rarely suggesting that such a distribution will maximize the rate of economic growth, they do ask whether an equitable society will ever be achieved through a growth-based strategy.[14] Naturally enough, this argument is the basis of great political controversy and represents one of the key questions in this book.

Having sketched something of the general approach of this study, a word should be said about the specific method of presentation. First of all, the topics included by no means exhaust the various aspects of spatial change in Latin America. Nothing is said, for example, about the internal structure of cities, nor has adequate attention been paid to the pattern of interregional commodity flows or to the difficulty of designing systems of public services to supply rural areas. Omissions of this sort are explained in part by personal interests and knowledge, but also by the fact that the literature on certain problems is very limited. The latter has been particularly important given that the primary purpose of this book is to summarize the extensive social-science literature relevant to the spatial problems of Latin America.

A second feature of the book is that it does not pretend to describe the spatial organization and characteristics of every Latin American country. Rather a systematic theme has been followed and illustrated

Fig. 1

with a liberal sprinkling of case studies. Such an approach gives undue weight to certain areas where particular spatial phenomena are more fully developed or better documented. Within these limits, case studies have been selected from as many of the twenty Spanish- and Portuguese-speaking republics as possible. No mention has been made, therefore, of British Honduras, the Guayanas or any of the Caribbean Islands with the exception of Cuba, the Dominican Republic and Puerto Rico.

Thirdly, while trying to summarize a large range of views and opinions equal weight has not been given to them all. The bias of omission has already been mentioned, but in addition it should be stated that I have not been reluctant to express my own feelings. In doing this I am assuming that a higher level of objectivity is achieved by debate between conflicting books and writers than by each individual writer trying to purge himself of his personal values, biases and prejudices.

Lastly, I should like to hazard a hope that this book, as well as providing factual information on Latin America, will also spark an interest in the wider social, political and economic issues challenging the continent. In particular, I hope that it will stimulate readers both to question the purpose of developmental change and to think about the alternative kinds of society which could be produced in Latin America. Even more, I hope that it will encourage scepticism about the automatic benefits to be derived from economic development and will constantly prompt the question – development for whom?

2: The International and Historical Setting

This book is concerned primarily neither with the history of Latin America nor with its international setting. And, since a number of excellent books have been written on these aspects, the interested reader is referred to these works in the bibliography.[1] Nevertheless, three specific questions would seem to merit attention in this chapter. Firstly, how far can Latin America be considered part of the Third World? This question is important because the past two decades have seen the growth of a considerable literature on underdevelopment. If Latin America's inclusion in the Third World can be justified, many of the solutions put forward in that literature may be relevant to the continent. Equally, the problems and growth experience of Latin America may prove useful to other poor areas in Africa, Asia and Australasia. Secondly, to what extent is it valid to study the problems of Latin America in isolation from the rest of the world? Does the continent form a sufficiently homogeneous social, cultural and economic area to justify this separation? How far, in fact, are the problems of Argentina and Cuba, Costa Rica and Brazil sufficiently similar to justify common treatment? Thirdly, how far does the legacy of the past impose difficulties for the future development of the continent? To what extent do the attitudes and institutions which emerged during the colonial and independence periods hinder necessary social and economic change? Without a brief answer to these questions I feel that many of Latin America's present difficulties will not be adequately understood.

Table 1: Measures of Latin America's Economic Position Compared to Other Continents

	Per capita income (US$) 1969	*Value of imports per 1,000 persons (US$) 1971*	*Consumption of energy (kWh.) 1971*	*Radio receivers per 1,000 persons 1970*	*Cars per 1,000 persons 1971*	*Tons of newsprint per 1,000 persons 1971*
South America	460*	68	832	134	31	3·6
Africa	170	47	343	46	10‡	0·8
Asia	240†	25	527	59	15	1·6
North America	4,090	223	8,080	1,009	294	29·7
Europe	1,850	405	3,996	265	238	11·8
Oceania	2,130	371	4,000	206	203	30·5

* Latin America.
† East and South-East Asia only.
‡ 1969.
Source: *UN Statistical Yearbook*, 1972.

The international context

Compared with Africa or Asia, Latin America appears to be quite highly 'developed'. By this I mean that its *per capita* income and other welfare indicators are much higher than those in other less-developed areas. At the same time, the continent appears far from developed if compared with Europe or North America. (See Table 1.)

Such generalizations, however, hide many important distinctions. Firstly, they assume that there is some easy way of measuring development and, by implication, that developed countries are in every respect 'better off' than the less-developed. Secondly, they ignore the vast differences that exist between the various parts of the continent. Thirdly, they do not explain why Latin America is traditionally, and I believe correctly, considered part of the Third World.

Latin America is in many ways heterogeneous. Many measures of development show that the differences within Latin America are larger than those between the continent's richest nations and the poorer countries of Europe. In terms of *per capita* income, Venezuela is as rich as Hungary or Ireland, and considerably richer than Greece, Spain, Portugal or Yugoslavia. In terms of the number of doctors per inhabitant, Argentina is better served than either the United Kingdom or the United States (one to every 700 people in 1966, compared with one to about 800 in the United States and one to every 1,000 people in the United Kingdom).[2] On the other hand, Bolivia, Ecuador and Paraguay, while not among the very poorest nations in the world, have measures of 'development' well below those of many less-developed nations in Africa and Asia.

If we confine our comparisons to the continent itself, the differences within Latin America are still clearer. (See Table 2.) In the late sixties, the *per capita* income of Puerto Rico was US$1,663, while that of Bolivia was US$179 and Haiti US$91. The number of persons per doctor in Argentina was 620 but 4,750 in Honduras. In Uruguay there were 59 tractors to every 1,000 rural people but less than one per thousand in Bolivia and most of Central America. Every 1,000 persons owned 164 road vehicles in Puerto Rico but only 6 in Paraguay. More than 55 per cent of all Argentinians, Chileans and Uruguayans lived in centres with more than 20,000 inhabitants,

Table 2: Measures of 'Development'

	1	2	3	4	5	6	7
Argentina	828	57	14·2	747	381	620	88
Bolivia	179	32	1·2	140	288	3,750	52
Brazil	337*	21	13·4	420	63	2,090	67
Chile	610	95	45·2	723	144	2,320	78
Colombia	360	29	17·5	327	111	2,220	53
Costa Rica	489	102	53·7	491	63	1,860	58
Dominican Republic	290*	39	10·9	168	38	1,940	44
Ecuador	251	36	22·7	144	204	3,030	50
El Salvador	279	63	31·1	172	118	4,340	44
Guatemala	328	46	14·5	107	115	4,140	57
Haiti	91*	8	0·8	24	17	13,150	46
Honduras	259	73	15·7	93	58	4,750	51
Mexico	566*	25	22·8	465	265	1,820	67
Nicaragua	380	82	32·6	206	56	2,570	59
Panama	647	82	24·1	411	—	2,060	62
Paraguay	236	22	2·4	78	—	1,660	63
Peru	291*	64	13·5	370	134	1,990	55
Puerto Rico	1,663	—	—	2,240	—	1,040	63
Uruguay	650*	63	104·0	683	379	880	112
Venezuela	944*	246	20·7	1,078	168	1,180	66

1 *Per capita* income, 1969 (1968 if marked by asterisk), in U S dollars (*UN Statistical Yearbook*, 1970).
2 Value of exports *per capita*, in U S dollars, 1968.
3 Fertilizer consumption, tons per 1,000 agricultural population, *c.* 1968 (*FAO Production Yearbook*, 1968).
4 Production of electricity, kWh *per capita*, 1968.
5 Radios per 1,000 people, 1968/9 (*UN Statistical Yearbook*, 1970).
6 Population per doctor.
7 Food supply, proteins g. per day.

Source: Blakemore, H., and Smith, C. T. (eds.) (1971).

compared to less than 20 per cent in Guatemala, Honduras or Paraguay. While some of these measures of development over-emphasize the differences, the gulf between many of the nations should not be understated. Latin America is a continent of major contrasts.

But, if this is so, why persist in regarding the whole continent as part of the Third World? Why, too, continue to imply that it represents a single entity, at least for the purpose of academic discussion?

My answer to both these questions is contained in the two words dependence and inequality. In the term dependence, I include a number of features which colour the relationship between the developed and the less-developed nations. For, like all other regions in the Third World, Latin America depends on the United States, Western Europe and Japan for trade, capital and technology. In terms of trade, Latin America's major markets and suppliers are limited in number: the United States supplies 40 per cent or more of Latin America's imports and Europe much of the rest. (See Fig. 2.) While, of course, international trade implies mutual dependence, Latin America finds itself in a fundamentally weaker trading position than its partners. Such a situation arises because Latin America imports mainly machinery and manufactured goods but exports agricultural and mineral products. Most Latin American countries, therefore, depend on a small range of export products, many of which face a difficult demand situation. Despite attempts to reduce this specialization, 63 per cent of Colombia's export revenue still comes from coffee, 72 per cent of Chile's from copper and 91 per cent of

Table 3: Principal Exports, 1971

	Value of total exports (US$ millions) 1971	*Principal products*	*Per cent of total export value*
Argentina	1,740	Corn & wheat	23
		Meat	24
Bolivia	222	Tin	49
		Tungsten	6
Brazil	2,904	Coffee	27
		Iron ore	8
		Cotton	5
Chile (1970)	1,247	Copper	73
		Iron ore	5
Colombia (1970)	732	Coffee	64
		Petroleum	8
Costa Rica	225	Coffee	26
		Bananas	28
Dominican Republic	243	Sugar	57
		Coffee	10
		Cacao	6

Table 3 (contd)

	Value of total exports (US$ millions) 1971	*Principal products*	*Per cent of total export value*
Ecuador	238	Bananas	51
		Coffee	15
		Cacao	11
El Salvador	228	Coffee	41
		Cotton	13
Guatemala	290	Coffee	34
		Cotton	9
Honduras	188	Bananas	51
		Coffee	12
		Wood	10
Mexico	1,502	Cotton	8
		Sugar	5
		Coffee	7
		Shrimp	5
Nicaragua	183	Cotton	23
		Coffee	16
		Meat	16
Panama	120	Bananas	56
		Petroleum (refined)	21
Paraguay	65	Meat	32
		Timber	16
Peru	892	Fishmeal	31
		Copper	19
		Iron ore	7
		Cotton	5
Uruguay	206	Meat	34
		Wool	31
		Hides	11
Venezuela	3,130	Petroleum	92
		Iron ore	5

Source: Ruddle, K., and Odermann, D. (eds.) (1972), Table 183.

Venezuela's from petroleum. This situation, depicted in Table 3, means that these countries are highly sensitive to world changes in supply and demand.* This situation would be less serious were it not

*Admittedly these changes can benefit primary producers – for example, the current situation favours petroleum exporters – but normally these fluctuations cause internal as well as balance-of-payments problems.

that Latin American imports come from these self-same countries. And, while demand for their exports tends to fluctuate, any reduction in their own demand for machinery and technical products is likely to harm the development of their agriculture, industry and economic infrastructure.

This dependence upon imports arises from a second facet of satellite status, their reliance upon imported technology. The majority of Latin American factories use technology developed in the United States and Europe and therefore import machinery from those areas. They do this because there is very little alternative.[3] Most of

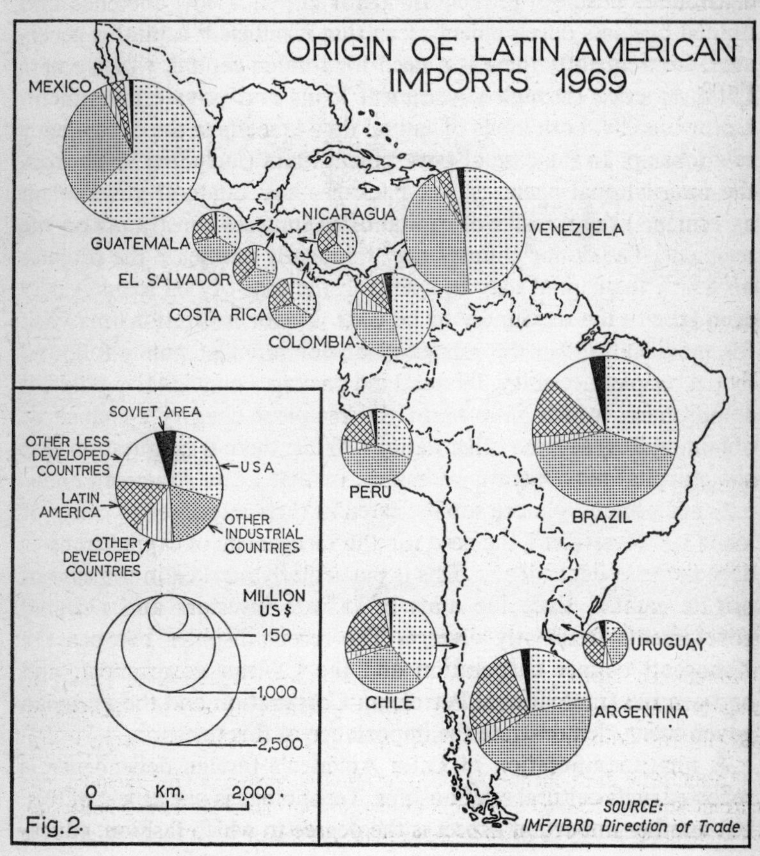

Fig. 2

the world's research and development work is carried out in the developed nations. Independent invention in Latin America is limited both in its success and by the resources available for it. Only by adopting more labour-intensive techniques and rejecting certain forms of material progress, such as the motor car, can the demand for foreign technology be reduced.

As it is, the need for technology and manufactured imports leads to the perpetuation of a third form of dependence, the need for injections of foreign capital.[4] In developed nations investment capital is normally generated through personal savings and through undistributed business profits. In Latin America low incomes and limited business development mean that insufficient capital is generated. Consequently there is a need for foreign capital, which enters Latin America through government loans and private investment. Unfortunately, both kinds of capital flow exacerbate the dependency relationship. In the case of government loans (including loans from the international agencies, aid packages and bilateral government agreements) the transfer of capital often imposes constraints on the recipient. The donor country may frequently nominate the projects on which the capital may be spent; in the case of tied loans it may even specify the machinery to be used. Donor institutions may ask for modifications in the monetary or development policy followed by the recipient country. Bilateral aid packages may involve political compromise, which may harm the recipient country's chance of obtaining finance from other nations. While there is no question that some capital movement is necessary, or that Latin American countries are becoming more sophisticated in their responses to offers of loans and investment, the need for and mechanism of capital transfer does increase dependency. This is particularly marked in the case of private capital, since the aims of private investors and national governments frequently diverge. The recent disputes between the Kennecott copper corporation and the Chilean government, and between the International Petroleum Corporation and the Peruvian government, demonstrate the importance of this question.

A final manifestation of Latin America's foreign dependence is reflected in its cultural relationships. Technology is one aspect of this, but another important aspect is the degree to which fashion, educa-

With the compliments of

PENGUIN BOOKS LTD

This book will be published on

28 November 1974

We request your co-operation
in not publishing any notice or review
before the date shown above
A copy of any notice would be appreciated
Blocks of illustrations available on request

Strad 22 08 Alan Tees.

Diana Craig - Northern Beach Stations

Philip Morgan.

81- 482.

tion and other forms of culture are influenced by what happens in the 'developed' world. To many Latin Americans, Paris, London and Rome still represent the only source of real culture. This external orientation means that many of the above forms of dependence are accentuated: imported products are valued more highly than local goods, foreign degrees more than local degrees, foreign consultants more than local experts. This cultural bias enhances and increases the total dependency relationship.

All these aspects of foreign dependence make Latin America part of the Third World. They also help to make it an entity, since every nation, except Cuba, depends upon similar trade partners and suffers

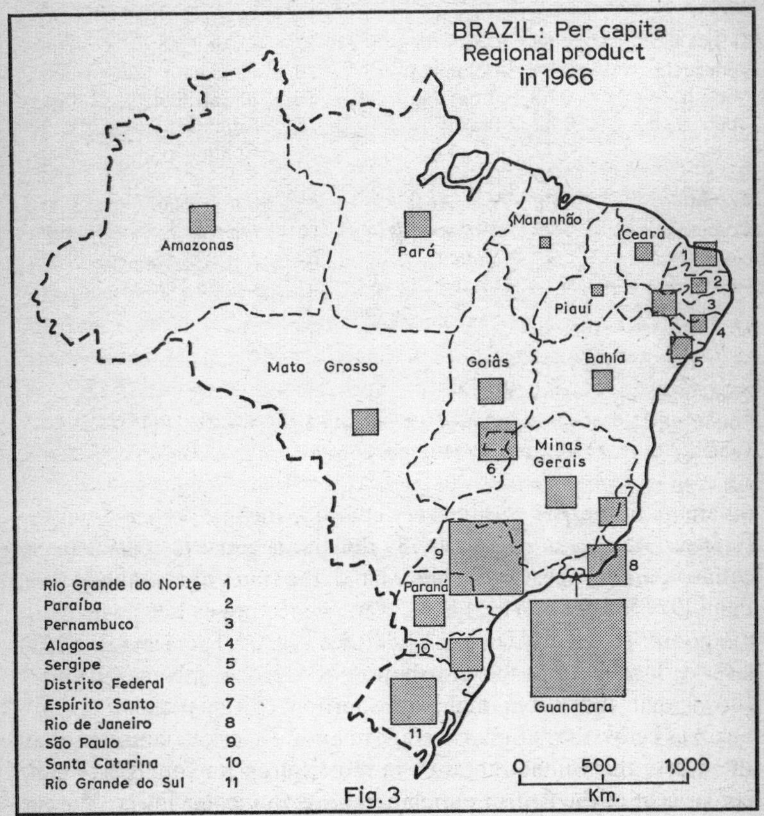

Fig. 3

from similar trade problems. However, they are not the only reason why Latin America should be included in the less-developed world.

An unfortunate characteristic of the Third World is that *per capita* incomes are not only much lower, but are less equitably distributed than in more-developed countries.[5] It has already been seen that there are major differences between Latin American nations, but a similar

Table 4: Comparison of Personal-Income Distribution in Latin American and 'Developed' Nations

Coefficients of concentration		*Per cent of total incomes below the national average*		*Incomes of top 5 per cent in nation compared with national average*	
Brazil	0·58	Panama	78	Brazil	790
El Salvador	0·54	Costa Rica	77	Costa Rica	700
Venezuela	0·54	Colombia	76	Panama	690
Mexico	0·53	Argentina	75	El Salvador	650
Costa Rica	0·52	Brazil	75	Argentina	620
France	0·52	Mexico	72	Colombia	610
Panama	0·49	El Salvador	70	Mexico	580
Argentina	0·48	Venezuela	68	Venezuela	520
Colombia	0·48	*Netherlands*	65	*France*	500
Netherlands	0·44	*France*	64	*Netherlands*	480
United Kingdom	0·40	*United States*	61	*United States*	400
United States	0·40	*United Kingdom*	60	*United Kingdom*	390
Norway	0·36	*Norway*	55	*Norway*	300

Complete equality 0·00 Arithmetical average = 100
Complete inequality 1·00
Source: ECLA, *Economic Survey of Latin America, 1969*, Tables, XXXIV, XXXVI, and XXXVII, pp. 365–7.

differentiation exists within every country. Income *per capita* in the state of Guanabara in Brazil (789 dollars) is equal to that of many countries in Europe. On the other hand, the states of Maranhão (90), Piauí (92) and Ceará (142) have average incomes as low as many of the poorer states of Africa or Asia. (See Fig. 3.) There is also a high level of inequality in the distribution of personal incomes. Table 4 shows that there is a higher proportion of the population with incomes below the national average in Latin American countries than there is in the United States or in most European countries. While 60 per cent of the British population have an income lower than the national average, as many as 75 to 80 per cent of the populations of Panama, Costa Rica, Colombia, Argentina and Brazil are in a similar position. These figures are typical of the Third World.

Inequality and foreign dependence, therefore, are two important characteristics of underdevelopment; on both counts Latin America can claim inclusion in the Third World.

Latin America as an entity

While there are parallels with other less-developed areas, Latin America's basic institutions, attitudes and problems are in many ways different from those of African and Asian countries. Equally, while strong differences exist within the continent, the many social, cultural and economic phenomena common to Latin American countries justify treating it as a single entity.

These common features arise from language, from the similar colonial experience, from the common fight for independence and from the fact that Latin America has been politically independent far longer than most other parts of the Third World. (Most countries in Latin America had achieved independence by 1830; the only real exceptions being the Dominican Republic (1844), Cuba (1902) and Panama (1903).) Since historical factors explain many of these similarities, they are worthy of a more detailed study, which will also shed more light on the region's present difficulties and show why economic growth is so unevenly spread. Why did some countries such as Argentina and Uruguay become relatively prosperous and others such as Ecuador, Bolivia and Honduras remain so poor? More importantly, historical perspective will provide a means of measuring the durability or flexibility of Latin American institutions and patterns of behaviour. Without such a perspective no assessment can be made of the extent to which fundamental changes may occur.

In studying the historical legacy I have not tried to be comprehensive but have selected particular characteristics relevant to the main interests of this book. Specifically, these include the origins of economic dependence and the land-ownership system, the evolution of administrative systems, and the emergence of the present structure and distribution of population. In making the following generalizations, however, it should be made clear that there were as many regional variations in the seventeenth as in the twentieth century and that the historical experience of different social classes was often quite distinct. As Gibson has suggested, 'the rate of historical change is modified, not simply as we move from city to country but as we move up or down the social scale'.[6] It is also necessary to define what is meant by the historical legacy. In some cases this is unnecessary, because the legacy is deep-seated and obvious. The physical legacies of the past such as language, architecture and race clearly fall into this category. In other cases, however, legacies are less marked because they 'appear in disguised forms'; traditions, values and patterns of behaviour are the most important examples.[7]

(I) ECONOMIC CHARACTERISTICS

The historical literature leaves little doubt that Latin America's principal economic difficulties owe much to the colonial experience. Lambert has argued that 'the colonial period, which started too early and lasted too long, gave Latin America an economic and social foundation, forms of ownership, and in many cases an élite psychology that fulfilled the needs of the home country instead of the colony; to some extent these factors linger on to this day'.[8] Similarly, the Steins have pointed out that 'in economic dependence and its syndrome of economic and social polarization we find the principal heritage of three centuries of subordination to Spain and Portugal'.[9]

This heritage was particularly important in the realm of trade, where the conquered lands were encouraged to export primary products to Spain and Portugal. In Spanish America silver and precious minerals were the main exports and were exchanged for manufactured goods from the mother country. In the case of the Portuguese Empire, where precious metals were not discovered until the eighteenth century, sugar was the largest export until it was replaced by cotton. The fundamental nature of this trade pattern changed little during the colonial period. (Major modifications did occur, of course, in the sources of exports during the colonial period. For example, Mexico gradually replaced Potosí as the principal source of Spanish silver.)

There were important modifications, however, in the destination of Latin America's exports during the eighteenth century. As Spain and Portugal became integrated into the world trading system, the Iberian peninsula imported increasing quantities of British manufactures and paid for them largely with colonial products.[10] This led creole groups during the late eighteenth century to ask why Spain and Portugal should be the principal beneficiaries of this trade. In addition, British commercial interests began to explore the possibilities for direct trade with Latin America. In time this situation led to accelerating demands for political independence throughout the continent.

One of the immediate consequences of political independence, therefore, was to allow the former colonies to trade directly with Britain. To encourage this exchange British and local entrepreneurs established import houses and commercial networks in these countries. In turn, the new Latin American states sought to provide Britain, and later the other industrialized nations, with the raw materials and precious metals which had previously gone via Spain and Portugal. To increase the production and export of these commodities, British and other foreign capital helped to develop Latin America's physical infrastructure. Railways, port installations and export-processing facilities were all built with the aid of British and North American technology and enterprise.[11] By the end of the nineteenth century, the present-day structure of economic dependence had been firmly established: Latin America was importing manufactured products, exporting primary goods and was heavily dependent upon foreign capital.

If foreign dependence is a direct outcome of colonial rule, so too are many forms of social and economic polarization. In particular, the inequitable system of land holding still present in many areas was strongly influenced by the past.

Control of the indigenous populations land was a key element in Spanish colonial rule. It was intended to reward the *conquistadores* for their efforts during the Conquest. It was used to control the indigenous populations. It was important for supplying the mining areas with food and working materials. Lastly, it was used in the subtropical areas as the basis for export-crop production. Naturally the balance of priorities varied from region to region, but there was relatively little variation in the process of control. In Spanish America the population and their land were normally divided up under one of two systems, the *encomienda* and the land grant. Under the former system, the Crown granted the *encomendero* certain privileges in return for a number of obligations. His principal benefit was permission to extract tribute from the indigenous population. In exchange, he contributed a proportion of this income – 'the royal fifth' – to the Spanish exchequer. In addition, he was expected to maintain law and order, to educate the local population and to convert them to Catholicism.

In many regions the *encomienda* was a very successful method of administration.[12] In those areas where the indigenous population could be persuaded to pay tribute to the new masters, the institution left the Indians their land while providing the *encomendero* with a sizeable income. On the other hand, where the local population was less docile or where an area was sparsely populated, it was less successful. In southern Chile, where the Araucanian Indians long remained a threat to colonial rule, the *encomenderos* faced major problems. And, in semi-tropical areas where there were few indigenous peoples, the limited tribute resulted in the land grant becoming more common than the *encomienda*.

Over time, however, both methods of control disappeared leaving behind a common legacy – the familiar *latifundio–minifundio* system (see Chapter Five). In the case of the *encomienda*, inadequate peninsular control led to a gradual chipping away of the communal lands and to the *de facto* acquisition of land by the *encomendero*. This tendency was accelerated by the decline and abolition of the *encomienda* in the early eighteenth century. In regions dominated by the land grant, the process differed but the results were similar. In plantation areas competition from other sub-tropical regions led to a fall in profits and to a diminution in the amount of land planted. With the decline in demand for the primary crop, land was left fallow and redundant labourers were forced to farm marginal scraps of land. Well before independence, the *latifundio–minifundio* system had developed in both kinds of area.

After independence this system became even more firmly entrenched. In some Spanish areas the final dissolution of peninsular control over the creole élites accelerated the tendency. In others the break-up of church lands had a similar effect. At the same time, however, other forms of land ownership were emerging in different parts of the continent. In the coffee areas of Brazil, large estates developed employing wage-earning labour, and in the southern states of Brazil a system of medium-sized farms evolved. Similarly in most colonization areas the worst consequences of the *latifundio–minifundio* system were avoided.

(II) POLITICAL LEGACIES

There can be little doubt that Latin American political systems are distinctive and that they owe many of their features to the historical experience. The most important of these features are the propensity for military intervention, limited political participation and centralism in the administrative system.

Few Latin American countries are as democratic as most nations in Western Europe. Of the twenty countries discussed in this book half have some form of military government – Bolivia, Brazil, Chile, Cuba, Ecuador, Honduras, Panama, Paraguay, Peru and Uruguay. Of the remainder, even some which hold elections cannot be considered highly democratic. In Colombia, presidential nominations between 1958 and 1974 were limited by a requirement that the successful candidate be elected in turn from the two principal parties – the Liberals and the Conservatives.[13] Similarly in Mexico, although there are regular elections and opposition political parties are allowed, it is no coincidence that the last fourteen presidents have come from the same party.[14] In addition, few elections take place in Latin America without accusations of fraud and corruption. Many of the charges are speculative and without serious foundation. On the other hand, there have been cases when such doubtful devices have kept a government in power (Colombia in 1970 and Guatemala in 1974).[15] Lastly, a fundamental weakness is that so few people participate in elections or in the political process in general. In Colombia, less than half the adult population normally vote in presidential elections, and in Peru and Bolivia the existence of literacy tests used to limit voting still further.

It is not really surprising that Latin America's democratic tradition is limited. For, as Humphreys has pointed out, 'there can be no political democracy without a measure of social democracy. And the social structure of the majority of the Latin American states is still profoundly undemocratic. The illiteracy and poverty so evident in most of the republics, the great cultural cleavages in the societies of the Indian and mestizo states, the glaring social inequalities, the land system which has concentrated political as well as social power in the hands of small minorities, these are not the foundations on which the structure of democratic government is built. And they have been combined with a tradition of authoritarianism in church and state on the one hand, and on the other, with a highly personalist interpretation of politics.'[16]

Many of these social characteristics can be adequately explained only in a historical context. The *encomienda* system and the later evolution of *latifundios* led to the emergence of powerful landowners who controlled most aspects of rural life. With the coming of independence, different groups of these rural *caciques* competed for power. In many countries this led to military strength becoming the final arbiter of political power and to a succession of civil wars and military *coups*.[17] Such was the pattern in Venezuela, for example, where military rulers governed the country almost without break from the time of independence to 1958.

The historical legacy, however, is not only manifest in the way that governments acquire and keep power. It is also reflected in the way they use it. In particular it has led to the centralization of administrative power and the weakening of local government. As Borah has said, 'whatever the legal fiction of local autonomy, the province captures power and revenues from its local units, and the national government in turn strips states and provinces of sustenance and vigour'.[18] To an extent centralism is a direct result of a centralist constitution, for in all but a few of the republics the state is organized under a unitary system.[19] Under most of these systems regional governors are appointed directly by the president and under some even local mayors are presidential appointees. Even in the four federal countries centralism is strong. In Venezuela and Argentina, state governors are appointed by the president, and a similar situation existed in Brazil before the institution of the military régime. Functions and finance are also centralized – few local areas in Latin America exercise important functions and even fewer have the funds to perform them efficiently.[20]

Centralization is not a new problem in Latin America. It was a principal issue in the conflicts between conservatives and liberals during the nineteenth century.[21] For, as Lambert has said, the liberals 'wanted to repudiate not only Spanish rule, but anything that smacked of absolutism – centralization, hegemony of the executive power, and above everything else clericalism'.[22] These differences between conservative and liberal factions were fanned by conflicts between city and rural élites. In Argentina there was frequent strife between groups in the city of Buenos Aires and those in the rural interior. In Uruguay, battles often occurred between rural and urban groups which are still reflected in the strength of the two main parties – the *Colorados* in the cities and the *Blancos* in the country.[23]

A further political legacy lies in the inefficiency of the administrative system. In the Spanish Empire government jobs were often merely posts of prestige.[24] As such, payments and efficiency were low and recruitment maintained by the promise of future betterment. In many places such a system still survives: government salaries are frequently poor and responsibility weak, decisions are passed upwards through the bureaucracy, and months pass while menial requests await the signature of the president. This system in turn breeds corruption, as individuals try to circumvent the bureaucracy. It also encourages patronage on the part of governments, as official posts can be created for political supporters and as a sponge for unemployment. Another aspect of this inefficiency is the difference between the functions which governments are legally entitled to perform and the powers they actually exert. The legislation which has been passed in Latin America is sufficient to give government control over most aspects of economic and social life. Legislation usually covers social security, minimum wages, compulsory education and political suffrage. Government decrees exist which cover transport, import tariffs, how the education and health system should be administered and trade-union activity. However, there is an important difference between theory and practice; for, while the laws and decrees exist, they are seldom effectively implemented.* As will be seen in Chapter Five this situation is particularly true in the rural areas, where minimum wages, land reform, social security and health provision are invariably aspirations rather than realities.

While not every aspect of government operation evolved before the turn of the century, many legacies of the colonial and independence periods have been passed on. Today many Latin American governments are centralized, bureaucratic and unimaginative. And, if governments are expected to accelerate the rate of development in the region, these negative characteristics will have to be overcome.

(III) THE POPULATION LEGACY

Iberian rule left an indelible mark on Latin America's population. During the colonial period enormous changes occurred in its racial structure, its spatial distribution and the dynamics of its growth. The impact of these changes is apparent to this day.

The colonial influence on racial structure was especially important. Firstly, because there was a heavy predominance of males during the early colonial period and, because there were few social or religious sanctions against miscegenation, sexual relationships between Indians and Spaniards were common. The progeny of these unions formed the basis of what is today Spanish America's most common racial type – the mestizo. Secondly, the Indian strain was severely weakened by the decimation of the indigenous population. The joint forces of warfare and disease are reputed to have reduced the population by 1650 to one-twentieth its pre-Conquest size. Thirdly, the slave trade introduced a strong Negroid element into many areas' racial structure.[26]

The effect of colonial rule on racial composition was dramatic, therefore, although its nature varied from area to area. It is still visible today. In highland Ecuador, Peru and Bolivia, where important indigenous civilizations were located, large Indian populations still survive. In the old Caribbean and Brazilian plantation areas, the

* Myrdal suggests that such a situation is typical of many nations in the Third World. He calls countries with such governments 'soft states'.[25] Lambert calls laws that are not implemented '*lois bleues*'.

majority of the population are Negro or mulatto. Over the rest of the continent, the population ranges from European through mestizo or mulatto to Indian or Negro.

Not all the continent's racial differences are explained by the colonial experience, however, for during the nineteenth and early twentieth centuries Argentina, southern Brazil and Uruguay received large numbers of European migrants. Millions of Italians, Spaniards, Portuguese, Germans and others migrated to these areas, altering both the size and the racial structure of the population. The impact of these migrations can be judged by the fact that, between 1869 and 1919, 2·5 million people moved to Argentina, a country which had only 1,800,000 inhabitants at the earlier date.[27] As a result, the populations of these areas are very European in comparison to those of north-east Brazil, Mexico or Peru.

In many parts of the world racial mixture leads to racial discrimination and conflict. Many writers, however, have suggested that race relations in Latin America are more harmonious than in most other regions. The ability of the Brazilian population to live, work and play together is commonly cited as evidence of this racial harmony. Unfortunately this is too simple a view, for, while there is certainly less racial bitterness than in parts of Africa or in the United States, severe forms of discrimination do exist. Although different racial types do live side by side throughout the continent, nowhere are all races considered equal. Although talented Negroes or mestizos have succeeded in these societies, their racial origin has made social progress more difficult. A reflection of this situation is the fact that nearly every Latin American country has a predominantly European ruling class or an Indian or Negro lower class. In places this racial differentiation is directly associated with material deprivation. The 'Indian problem' of Bolivia, Ecuador, Mexico and Peru, the relative poverty of the Brazilian north-east and the racial gradation in cities from the poorest to the richest *barrios* can be cited as obvious examples. Throughout Latin America, race, poverty and class are highly correlated.

The continent's present pattern of settlement has also been influenced by the past. The high population densities in certain Andean countries and Central America reflect in part the pre-

Conquest settlement patterns. In addition, the distribution of major urban settlements was determined largely by Spanish and Portuguese colonization. By the time of independence, Mexico City, Buenos Aires, Bogotá and Lima had become the capitals of the four Spanish Viceroyalties, and Rio de Janeiro was the capital of the Portuguese Empire. In addition, Caracas, Guayaquíl, Quito, Santiago and Salvador de Bahía had all developed into major regional capitals. The conquests also had an important effect in introducing large numbers of people into underpopulated areas such as the Brazilian north-east. Further, they implanted a stronger urban tradition than had previously existed, as a result of which an important prejudice against rural life has developed in many parts of the continent.

Lastly, Spanish and Portuguese rule bequeathed a religious and cultural attitude which now influences the rate of population growth throughout the continent. While certain nations experience less rapid growth, the continent as a whole has the fastest rate in the world. Its annual growth of 2·9 per cent compares with 0·9 per cent in Europe, 1·5 per cent in North America, 1·4 per cent in East Asia, 2·3 per cent in Africa and 2·5 per cent in South Asia.[28] If the same growth rate should continue in the future, the population of 206 millions in 1960 will grow to 362 millions by 1980.

The causes of this rate of growth are of course clear. The improvements which have taken place in health and medicine through the continent have lowered the death rate dramatically. In particular, they have reduced infant mortality, so that more children are surviving their early months. But, while the death rate has been cut, the birth rate continues at a high level. While the crude birth rate in Europe in the middle sixties was 19 per 1,000 people, in Latin America it was 44 per 1,000.

What is less obvious is whether such growth represents a problem and, if it does, what to do about it. As regards the first difficulty there are many people, public institutions and political parties in Latin America who view rapid population growth with approval. Gradually, however, a change in attitude is occurring and more people are accepting that there is a need for population policies. This change has been particularly marked during the past decade in the southern nations, where birth-control practices, including abortion, have become widespread. This regional difference in attitude is reflected in the substantially lower fertility rates in the southern nations. (See Table 5.)

Table 5: Population Characteristics of Latin American Nations, 1970

	Population (thousands)	*Annual growth rate 1963–8*
Argentina	23,400	1·5
Bolivia (1969)	4,804	2·6
Brazil	92,200	3·0
Chile	9,780	2·4
Colombia	21,100	3·2
Costa Rica	1,740	3·3
Cuba (1969)	8,210	2·2
Dominican Republic (1969)	4,174	3·6
Ecuador	6,090	3·4
El Salvador	3,530	*
Guatemala	5,190	3·7
Haiti (1969)	4,768	3·1
Honduras	2,580	2·0
Mexico	50,670	3·5
Nicaragua	1,980	3·6
Panama	1,430	3·3
Paraguay	2,386	3·2
Peru	13,590	3·1
Puerto Rico (1969)	2,754	*
Uruguay	2,989	1·2
Venezuela	10,400	3·5

* No data available.
Source: *UN Demographic Yearbook, 1971.*

In the rest of the continent a major obstacle preventing the wider adoption of population policies is the position of the Church. The influence of the 1968 Papal Encyclical, which expressed disapproval of the use of mechanical methods of birth control, is still being felt by birth-control agencies throughout the region. It is probable, too, that the Church plays an important role in delaying individual acceptance of birth-control practices, despite the efforts of many priests in the opposite direction. The role of the Church should not be overstated, however, for birth control has been adopted in Argentina, Chile and Uruguay despite the fact that these are Catholic countries. In addition it is clear that the factors which influence the acceptance of control practices are complex. High birth rates are related not only to religious beliefs but also to levels of income, education and social class.[29] Inability to read, material poverty and lack of alternative opportunities are as important in encouraging high fertility as the attitude of the Church. Even so, the rate of population growth could be slowed more quickly if the Church were to play a more positive role.

Latin America is wedded firmly to its past. There are innumerable characteristics, institutions and sets of values which testify to this fact. In many cases these institutions represent problems for those who wish to press for rapid economic and social change. The social structure, for example, while showing some signs of change, still reflects many of the characteristics of the colonial period. The relationships between classes in rural areas still show many links with the situation that had evolved by the time of independence. Similarly the power of the Church, the system and practices of government and the land-tenure situation are obvious and pervasive survivals of the colonial period. Nor, of course, is the heritage of the past confined to the internal situation. The whole dependency relationship between Latin America and the developed world was laid during the colonial period.

But in stressing the influence of the past, we must not forget that enormous changes have taken place during the twentieth century. The vast increase in population due to natural increase and in places to international migration, the massive migration of people from rural to urban areas, the growth of industry, the great improvements in transport networks and technology, the introduction of mass social-service schemes and the institution of national planning all represent recent major adjustments on the Latin American scene. And, while each has been moulded by the influence of the past, each testifies to the ability of the continent to change in the future.

3: The Process of Industrial Change

Industrial change in Latin America has been extensively documented during the past fifteen years and by now its principal characteristics are well known. Consequently no attempt will be made here to describe the industrialization process in detail. Rather the emphasis of this chapter is on describing the spatial changes that have taken place in the sector and to relate such changes to the total process of industrial growth. In this context several specific questions should be answered. How far have geographic changes been related to modifications that have taken place in industrial technology, in the structure of industrial production or in the pattern of ownership? How far has the general process of development altered the factors considered by industrial managers in locating their plants? Lastly, how far have governments tried to influence the distribution of industry, what methods have they used to accomplish this end and how successful have they been? The answers to these questions, it is hoped, will provide some help in determining the future trends in industrial location and the opportunities open to governments to change them.

Industrial development before 1929

With the exception of Chile, Argentina, Brazil and Mexico, sustained industrial growth did not begin in most Latin American countries until the world depression of the 1930s. In certain places, such as Bolivia, Venezuela and Central America, it was delayed until after the Second World War. The reasons why industrial expansion came late are complex, but the following factors seem to have been important.

Competition from foreign manufactured goods certainly stifled many early attempts at industrialization; a process accentuated by many foreign companies' deep commercial involvement in Latin American economies. Frequently British or other foreign interests controlled local commercial outlets and were able to encourage the consumption of imports at the expense of local production.[1] This process was helped by the increasing efficiency of foreign production, the gradual decline in shipping costs, and by local incentives to foreign enterprise.[2] Only factories processing exports, or plants making highly perishable goods or products with low value-to-weight ratios,* were likely to be successful.

Given the inability of local industry to compete under these circumstances, one solution would have been for national governments to have provided artificial protection through import tariffs or quotas. Until the 1929 crisis, however, it seems that few Latin American governments were willing to provide this kind of protection, frequently because such intervention would have prejudiced the interests of the local ruling élites. Such a situation was true in Brazil, for example, where the reforms of 1889 strengthened the ruling agricultural classes and thus led to the adoption of policies contrary to the needs of industrial activities.[3] Similarly in Argentina the weak political and social positions of industrial groups permitted them few concessions from the national government.[4] Only in Mexico, during the Porfiriato (1876–1910), and in Peru, during the Leguía administration (1919–29), was this experience not general to the whole continent. This view is supported by Grunwald, who has argued that 'contrary to the positive development policies of the United States during the period when she was an "emerging" country, Latin American policies, in so far as there have been any, have been largely passive until comparatively recently. It is, of course, impossible to generalize for some twenty nations, but, looking at the century before the 1930s, one is struck by the relative absence of anything that could be called policies for economic development in most of the countries of the region.'[5]

Some countries, however, notably Argentina, Chile and Mexico,

*A low value-to-weight ratio means that the cost of transport will be high relative to the final sales price, as for example in the soft drinks industry. This affords such products a high level of protection against imports.

did succeed in breaking the industrial monopoly of the USA and the European nations. Why did they achieve this breakthrough and others not? Furtado believes that the difference depended on five factors:

'(a) the nature of the export activity: this determined the relative amount of manpower to be absorbed by the expanding high-productivity sector;
(b) the type of infrastructure required by the export activity: temperate agriculture creating an extensive transportation network; tropical agriculture, concentrated in smaller areas and often in mountainous regions, being able to make do with a more modest infrastructure; mining production requiring a specialized infrastructure, in most cases scarcely producing external economies for other economic activities;
(c) ownership of the investments made in the export economy: foreign ownership reducing the proportion of the flow of income generated by the expanding sector that remains in the country; given the greater prevalence of foreign ownership in the export mining economies, their negative aspects were aggravated;
(d) the wage rates prevailing in the export sector during the initial phase, these being dependent largely on the relative size of the manpower surplus;
(e) the size of the expanding sector, in most cases reflecting the country's geographical area and population size.'[6]

In the case of Argentina, export revenues were sufficiently large to generate a high national income, and one, moreover, which was not highly concentrated in the hands of the few. At the same time, rapid immigration from Spain, Italy and other European countries led to the development of Buenos Aires, to the emergence of an industrial labour force and to the establishment of an entrepreneurial élite who were capable of making full use of these industrial opportunities. This combination of factors led to industrial growth and the employment of 150,000 industrial workers by 1895. A similar expansion, based upon export earnings and foreign immigrants also affected Chile, and, at a later date, Brazil, where coffee earnings and the massive influx of

European labour into the south-east enabled industrial employment to increase to 310,000 workers by 1920.[7]

Other nations, however, despite earning substantial export revenues, did not overcome the problems posed by the availability of cheap manufactured imports and the inability of governments to protect local industry. Bolivia failed to develop an industrial sector despite the importance of the tin industry. Furtado attributes this to the small fraction of the nation's labour force employed in the export sector.[8] Since the tin miners were also employed at low wage rates, the national market did not expand as a result of export generation. Other factors were also important. The export-oriented infrastructure created by the mining sector was not conducive to industrial expansion; similarly the major dislocations caused by the loss of the nitrates and the port of Antofagasta in the war with Chile (1879–83) also dampened local initiative.[9]

The role of foreign immigrants has been mentioned on several occasions already and there can be little doubt of their importance to the industrial expansion of Latin America. This is true not only of the southern nations, where large numbers settled, but of all parts of the continent. In Chile, their influence was far greater than their numbers would suggest: in 1914, 863 out of 1,750 industrial enterprises were owned by immigrants.[10] Farther north, most breweries, such as Bavaria in Colombia, the Kopp company in Ecuador and the Cervecería Cuauhtémoc in Mexico, were established by Dutch and German immigrants. In textiles, leather and clothing, their influence was particularly marked, an influence which has remained important to the present day.

By 1929, therefore, industrial development had occurred in a number of nations, but only in four countries had it developed to any marked extent. At that date industrial production represented 22·8 per cent of Argentina's gross domestic product, 14·2 per cent of Mexico's, 11·7 per cent of Brazil's and 7·9 per cent of Chile's, but less than 7 per cent in all of the other nations of the continent.[11]

Industrial location before 1929

Industrial development before 1929 was characterized by three kinds of activity. Firstly, there were plants associated with export production, secondly, artisan plants catering for local markets and, thirdly, a certain number of manufacturing plants producing for the domestic market. Each of these activities tended to follow a distinctive locational pattern, so that the distribution of industry in each nation depended upon the relative importance of each activity in the total industrial structure.

Export-based industries tended to be established in one of two locations. A few activities, and particularly those associated with mineral production, were located near export centres, but the majority tended to be concentrated at break-of-bulk shipment points such as the major ports.* Those nations where export-oriented industries were particularly important, therefore, tended to exhibit a highly concentrated industrial distribution. In Argentina, for example, 89 per cent of its industrial employment in 1914 was concentrated around the River Plate estuary in the three provinces of Buenos Aires, Entre Rios and Santa Fé.[12]

Artisan industries, however, exhibited a different pattern, one which was more closely associated with the distribution of population. By their nature artisan industries tended to produce goods for local markets in fields such as clothing, foodstuffs and leather. Therefore, relative to the distribution of export-oriented industry, artisan production was widely dispersed. Only in those areas where the urban population was highly concentrated did the distribution of artisan production also become concentrated: such was the situation in Argentina and Uruguay, where the large numbers of foreign immigrants in Buenos Aires and Montevideo provided a market and entrepreneurial enterprise. In most countries, however, where the markets were less highly concentrated, artisan industries were evident

*A break-of-bulk shipment point exists where goods have to be transferred from one mode of transport to another. Location at such a point eliminates additional loading charges and may occur where road meets rail, land transport meets water transport or very occasionally where land transport meets air transport.

in most provincial cities and even in some rural areas. In Brazil a widely dispersed industrial distribution existed at the turn of the century, and a similar, though less marked, pattern could be seen in most parts of the continent outside Argentina, Chile and Uruguay.[13]

By contrast, domestically-oriented manufacturing tended everywhere to favour market locations and especially the larger cities. These centres were normally, but not always, the national capitals; the exceptions include the industrial complexes which had developed by the end of the period in Monterrey (Mexico), Medellín (Colombia), and São Paulo (Brazil).

Industrialization after 1929

'It is often said that the world depression of the thirties initiated a phase of radical changes in the rate and patterns of development in Latin America, and that these changes particularly affected the region's industrialization process. Until the end of the twenties, the Latin American economies were characterized by their "outward-directed" development; since then the new world trade conditions caused a change towards "inward-directed" development.'[14]

By 1929 there were increasing signs that something was going wrong with the industrialization process in Latin America. Although several nations had developed an industrial sector based upon export-oriented growth, the vast majority of countries had not. Even in the continent's most industrialized nations, the rate of industrial growth was beginning to slow down. Consequently, the series of external shocks which began with the 1929 monetary crisis and ended with the termination of the Second World War could not really harm industrial growth in Latin America. In fact, despite the problems faced by Latin American exports, it was soon apparent that these shocks were actually assisting industrialization in certain countries.

The first result of the depression in most Latin American countries was to cause a fall in export earnings and in foreign investment. Such a result might well have led to deflation had it not been for the action of many governments to maintain the internal level of demand. In Brazil the government maintained demand by instituting internal price-support programmes for the major export commodities, notably coffee. The industrial consequences of this action were that foreign products could not be purchased owing to the shortage of foreign exchange, but domestic industry was stimulated to produce adequate substitutes. This process was particularly marked in those nations where industrial production could expand without major new investments. But, in countries where there was little industry, the effect of these events was merely to redirect investment into the agricultural and commercial sectors.

This stimulus to industrial growth in the continent's more developed nations was given a further boost by the Second World War. During this period, manufactured imports from the developed nations became scarce and the prices of Latin America's primary export commodities rose. As a result, Latin America's industrial expansion and foreign-exchange reserves were given a strong boost. By the end of hostilities several Latin American nations possessed sufficient funds to modernize their industrial plant and were poised to expand rapidly in the future.

Such a process was especially marked in the larger countries. In Brazil, for example, 'the low financial capacity to import of the 1930s was followed by the disruption of trade due to the Second World War, and industrial production grew about 5 per cent per year from 1930 to 1940, and about 5·5 per cent per year from 1940 to 1945'.[15] Between 1929 and 1947 industrial output as a percentage of GDP increased from 23 per cent to 31 per cent in Argentina, from 12 to 17 per cent in Brazil, from 8 to 17 per cent in Chile, and from 14 to 20 per cent in Mexico. Simultaneously, the propensity to import had declined, total imports as a per cent of GDP falling during the same period from 31·2 to 12·6 per cent in Chile, and from 17·8 to 11·7 per cent in Argentina.[16]

During this period, too, several national governments became closely involved in guiding and initiating economic change for the first time. In Brazil, the Vargas administration was operating export price-maintenance schemes and was establishing the National Steel Company (1940), which built the Volta Redonda plant. In Chile, the government established the Corporation for the Development of Production (CORFO) in 1939, which founded steel, oil, sugar and other industries during the 1940s. In Colombia, the Institute for Industrial Development was established in 1941 and in Mexico the National Finance Corporation in 1939.

It was not until after 1945, however, that these different actions began to coalesce into a deliberate policy of import-substituting industrialization. Until then 'these policies were not co-ordinated, nor was there at first a conscious attempt to industrialize through import substitution. Manufacturing emerged haphazardly, based upon import restrictions and exchange-rate controls. Protective tariffs were awarded almost at random.'[17] After the Second World War, however, co-ordinated attempts began which culminated in the first overall economic plan: Brazil's Target Plan of 1956–60. Although formal economic planning did not become general in the continent until the 1960s, import-substitution policies were being implemented in most nations during the 1950s.

The rationale behind these policies of import substitution was quite simple. If industrial expansion had received such a boost from the external shocks from 1929 to 1945 why could this impulse not be continued through government-inspired monetary, fiscal and foreign-exchange policies? Such policies would have the advantage of reducing further the dominance of foreign and especially North American interests. It would also encourage the development of the country's own national resources and their manufacture within the nations themselves. Also underlying the policy was the basic assumption that Latin America's infant industries would be unable to export manufactured goods for many years ahead. Not only were they high-cost producers serving a small domestic market, but in addition, the developed nations controlled the shipping services which exports would use. The developed nations were also likely to apply restrictive tariffs upon Latin America's exports if they did become competitive. (Both these factors pose restraints on the development of exports at the present time.) The only effective means by which industrialization could be fostered was by building industry to supply the home market, and by protecting this market from foreign imports. This was the principal strategy underlying industrial growth in all Latin American nations at least until the 1960s.

The import-substitution process

There can be no doubt that the import-substitution policy has led to a faster rate of industrial growth than would have occurred otherwise. In turn, industrialization has led to fundamental transformations in every Latin American economy. It has led, for example, to changes in the composition of industrial production, in the structure of ownership and in the size and efficiency of manufacturing plants. In addition, it has led to the development of a large body of economic infrastructure. In the course of these changes it has profoundly affected the regional concentration of economic activity in most Latin American nations. However, before discussing changes in the regional distribution of industry, certain problems inherent in this form of industrialization must be examined.

The principal problem with the import-substitution policy has been that in most countries it has failed to sustain industrial expansion. The reasons why are best explained by describing the four stages through which industrial expansion was expected to pass:

(1) Consumer goods such as textiles, foodstuffs and pharmaceuticals. At this stage all materials and machinery would be imported.
(2) Consumer durable products, which would be assembled in local factories using imported parts. Typical goods at this stage would be electrical products such as radios and refrigerators.
(3) Intermediate industries which produced the inputs for companies set up during stages (1) and (2). Typical industries at this stage would be chemical plants making paint, dyes and acids, and engineering works.
(4) Capital-goods industries, which would produce the machinery and plant for all industries in the country.

The difficulty with this progression has been that while the first two stages have been comparatively easy, the third and fourth have required complex technological knowledge and the creation of a large market. If, as has frequently occurred, the national market for consumer-durable products has been small, then there has been insufficient demand for the next stage of intermediate- and capital-goods industries. Only where a large market for consumer goods has been generated, as in Argentina, Brazil and Mexico, has a sustained process of industrialization been achieved.[18] Where this has not occurred the third and fourth stages of industrial growth have been stunted.

Another problem has been that Latin American industrialization has depended almost completely upon imported machinery and technology. This has caused two kinds of difficulty. Firstly, it has continually caused problems for countries with weak balances of payments. Secondly, it has had major repercussions on the efficiency of Latin American industry. In the case of Argentina 'the manufacture of light consumer goods developed fast in a period in which revolutionary change in productive techniques for these commodities was well under way in the industrialized countries. Within a lapse of a few years the technological gap between the techniques used in Argentina and those of the more efficient countries was quite marked. Such a disadvantage forced the administration to protect domestic industries by increasingly heavy import duties.'[19] Imported technology caused other problems. One was that the internal market for many manufactured products was frequently far smaller than a moderately efficient imported plant could produce. As a result a series of plants were set up which produced at less than full capacity. In Ecuador, Bottomley found that only four plants out of the sixteen he had studied were operating at more than 60 per cent capacity.[20] More generally, Scitovsky has stated that 'the few Latin American statistics available on the subject, for Argentina, Chile, Colombia, Ecuador, all confirm this [over-capacity], ranging from a capacity utilization of 46 per cent in Chile to about 65 per cent in Argentina. Such figures must be contrasted to capacity utilization in the United States, where it ranges from the low to the high 80s, and in Western European countries, where the overall average is almost always above 90 per cent.'[21]

The problem was frequently aggravated by the fact that governments did not restrict the number of entrants into particular fields. As a result, there was a proliferation of plants each with severe problems of over-capacity, a notable example being the car industries of Chile and Peru. In 1964 the situation in Chile was that eighteen different plants were producing twenty-five different makes of car in a total industrial production of only 7,558 units – an average production of 302.[22] By 1968, this situation had improved somewhat, but there were still as many as fourteen plants producing only 26,000 cars. In Peru, too, there were thirteen producers making only 16,680 cars in 1968.*

Among other things, such over-capacity led to Latin American industries becoming high-cost producers. This in turn led to high prices, and, in the absence of effective competition, to high average profits. A comprehensive survey of this problem was made some time ago by the Economic Commission for Latin America when they compared the costs of sixty-two products made in Latin America with those of the same products made in the United States.[23] They found that, while 31 per cent of products were cheaper in Latin America, 58 per cent were cheaper in the United States and 11 per cent the same in both places. When the degree of difference in costs was examined, however, the evidence supported the contention that relative costs of manufactured goods in Latin American countries were generally higher than those in the United States. (See Table 6.)

Table 6: Comparison of Manufacturing Costs in Latin America and the United States

(Percentages of the total products considered)

I Lower costs than in the United States	31
(a) Lower than 55 per cent	3
(b) Between 55 and 84 per cent	18
(c) Between 85 and 94 per cent	10
II The same costs as in the United States	11
III Higher costs than in the United States	58
(a) Between 106 and 115 per cent	8
(b) Between 116 and 145 per cent	26
(c) Over 145 per cent	24
Total	100
Number of products	62

Source: UN ECLA (1966).

Naturally the situation within Latin America varied from country to country, and Bergsmann has claimed that the majority of firms

*The Velasco government in Peru has since acted to reduce the number of car manufacturers.

making producer goods in Brazil were operating at prices within 20 or 30 per cent of the cost of imports at the free exchange rate (1966).[24] In that country most cases of extreme inefficiency could be attributed to attempts by the government to maintain employment in certain supply industries such as the Santa Catarina coal mines. Such a justification could not explain the high costs of the Chilean car industry, however, where Johnson has claimed 'that two, three, or even four dollars of local resources are being consumed for each dollar of foreign exchange being saved through the [import-substitution] programme'.[25]

Import-substitution programmes also led to other forms of inefficiency. In particular, government involvement frequently led to the emergence of highly bureaucratic administrative procedures. These procedures occupied large numbers of people in negotiations between government and industry. In Mexico many people were employed by individual companies to negotiate for import licences.[26] And in Ecuador foreign companies had to face the Kafkaesque situation of dealing with forty government or semi-official offices before they could even begin production.[27]

Perhaps the most surprising feature of import-substitution policies, however, was that they frequently neither reduced imports nor created a large amount of employment. The cause of the first problem is illustrated by the Argentinian experience, where 'the substitution of imports of consumer durables had a negative effect on the balance of payments. The domestic production of consumer durables brought about a rapidly increasing demand for basic raw materials, fuel and heavy capital equipment.'[28] The second problem has been caused principally by the extent to which most industrial companies have employed capital-intensive techniques. As a result, industrial value-added has increased far more rapidly than industrial employment. This situation has sometimes been worsened by government and trade-union attempts to improve the working, pay and tenure conditions of industrial workers. Dismissal payments aimed at countering industrial companies' hire-and-fire policies have been particularly effective in encouraging the introduction of labour-saving machinery.

It should not be suggested, though, that every aspect of the import-substitution process has been unsatisfactory. It has increased employment and created strong multiplier effects. It has also led to industrial growth in most Latin American countries, as is shown by Table 7. However, the point has now been reached where import-

Table 7: Share of Industrial Product in the Total Gross Domestic Product, 1950, 1960, 1967

Country	*1950*	*1960*	*1967*
Argentina	29·4	32·2	34·1
Bolivia	11·9	10·2	10·8
Brazil	15·1	21·4	21·6
Chile	21·2	23·7	25·8
Colombia	14·2	17·0	18·2
Costa Rica	9·5	11·1	14·0
Dominican Republic	11·9	14·0	14·6
Ecuador	15·7	15·6	16·8
El Salvador	12·0	13·6	17·2
Guatemala	10·1	10·5	12·9
Haiti	11·1	12·2	11·8
Honduras	8·4	12·1	14·8
Mexico	19·9	23·2	25·6
Nicaragua	9·4	11·1	12·3
Panama	8·2	12·8	16·0
Paraguay	19·4	17·3	18·2
Peru	14·1	16·7	19·3
Uruguay	17·3	21·2	21·0
Venezuela	8·0	10·6	13·4
Total	18·7	21·7	23·1

Source: ECLA, 'Industrial Development in Latin America', *Economic Bulletin for Latin America,* XIV, no. 2, second half of 1969.

substitution policies are unlikely to maintain existing industrial-growth rates. Some alternative strategy is therefore required.

Some writers believe that the recent Brazilian 'miracle' provides the guidelines for such a strategy. This is unlikely, however, if only because the problems faced by Brazil were far less serious than those now encountered by the smaller nations of the continent. Brazil's situation was helped by a number of factors. Firstly, the capital-goods sector continued to expand owing to the major investments being made by the federal government in the Amazon, the north-east and in other areas. Secondly, Brazilian industry was able to develop major export lines; manufactured exports increased from US$21 million in 1960 to US$400 million in 1970. It managed to develop export lines mainly because its companies were sufficiently large to compete with industries in the developed world. Industry was also helped by the government's attempts to make exporting more profitable by manipulation of the foreign-exchange rate.[29]

Neither of these factors appears to apply to the smaller, less-efficient nations of the continent, nor even to some of the larger ones, such as Peru and Venezuela. Even so, various governments still believe that export production can provide a solution to this impasse. Their argument is that if their nations are not sufficiently competitive to export to the developed nations then they must export to one another. This 'second-best' position can be achieved by establishing a free-trade area or common market. It will maintain protection against the imports of the developed nations while encouraging the expansion of continental trade.

Such an argument has been the basis for a number of agreements between different groups in the past thirty or so years. In 1939, Argentina and Brazil came to an industrial-complementation agreement, and the 1940s saw the signing of several bilateral integration agreements, all of which eventually foundered on the rock of economic nationalism. The first real signs of success, however, came in 1958, when four Central American countries (El Salvador, Honduras, Nicaragua and Guatemala) agreed upon a multilateral free-trade agreement. This treaty led to the foundation of the Central American Common Market (CACM) in 1960, a grouping which also included Costa Rica.[30] In the same year, Argentina, Brazil, Chile, Uruguay, Mexico, Paraguay and Peru signed the treaty of Montevideo, which established the Latin American Free Trade Area (LAFTA).*

Unfortunately, the initial euphoria stimulated by these agreements began to evaporate as it became obvious that severe imbalances were emerging in the distribution of trade. In LAFTA, for example, the trade between Argentina, Brazil and Chile accounted for 74 per cent of the total in 1968, and in CACM the trade between Guatemala and El Salvador accounted for 60 per cent of the total. It was also obvious that owing to the lack of reciprocal agreements total intra-continental

*Colombia and Ecuador joined in 1961, Venezuela in 1966, and Bolivia in 1967.

trade was not increasing quickly enough. In 1966, for example, it still accounted for only 10 per cent of the total trade of the member countries, as compared with 6 per cent five years previously. In addition, it was clear that the more powerful countries in each community were gaining the major benefits from industrial development.[31]

As a result of these and other problems, major political difficulties arose in both communities, exploding sensationally in the case of CACM with the 'Football War' between Honduras and El Salvador in July 1969. The conflict led to the departure of Honduras from CACM in 1972 and to a decline of the market as an effective economic force. A similar decline in effectiveness has also affected LAFTA, a problem highlighted by the formation of the Andean Pact in 1969. The latter consists of six nations which hope to achieve more rapid integration than that being achieved through the larger grouping.* Its founding, together with the establishment of the River Plate Group, suggests that there is still basic faith in the idea of international economic integration as a route towards industrial development. And, to judge from the early experience of the Pact, this faith may be well-placed. Certainly the entry of Venezuela and the agreement made over the treatment of foreign investment encourage optimism about the Pact's future.

Faith in the idea of integration, however, is by no means universal. Some writers feel that it is no solution to the fundamental problems afflicting the continent. This is certainly the view of Araujo, who has written about the great Venezuelan 'paradox' whereby industrialists complain of 'narrow markets' when most people are poorly fed, clothed and housed.[32] The solution to this paradox, he feels, lies not in the construction of a continental-wide market but in attempts to increase internal demand within Venezuela. This can be achieved only by encouraging a wider distribution of income within the country, thereby expanding the industrial market and helping cure poverty. Such a policy is also implicit in Furtado's claim (1968) that 'the basic cause of Brazil's industrial stagnation would seem to be excessive concentration of income in the hands of a small minority,

*Bolivia, Colombia, Chile, Ecuador, Peru and since 1973 Venezuela are the members of the Andean Pact.

due to the traditional way of life of a society with an agrarian and semi-feudal base.'[33]

Manufacturing distribution changes since 1929

Manufacturing activity in many Latin American nations had become highly localized in the period up to 1929. As a result of the import-substitution process induced by the world depression, the Second World War and later by government planning, this spatial concentration became more marked as industrial growth continued. This pattern may be seen in Table 8, where data have been collected for a number of countries for the period since 1929. Unfortunately, industrial statistics by city or department tend to be scarce for the early part of the period, but in most cases the figures shown do demonstrate a general tendency to greater concentration. Of the six countries where data are available for twenty years or more, only one, Argentina, does not exhibit increasing spatial concentration. In all of the others, Brazil, Chile, Colombia, Mexico and Peru, the figures show that the level of industrial centralization has increased over time. The trend has been most marked in those nations where industry was less concentrated at the earlier dates, notably in Peru and Colombia.

Even where dispersal has taken place, notably in Argentina and later in Ecuador, the number of centres benefiting from industrial expansion have been few. In the former case, the only centres to have obtained industry have been Córdoba, Mendoza and the cities close to Buenos Aires. In the case of Ecuador, only Riobamba and Cuenca have really gained from the dispersal of industrial activity.

The figures in Table 8, however, also show a separate tendency. This is the tendency, common in most developed nations, for industry to locate increasingly outside the major city centres but remain within the city-region (see Fig. 4). The figures for Argentina show this quite clearly: the proportion of industrial employment in the Federal Capital declined markedly from 47·0 per cent in 1935 to 26·0 per cent in 1965 while contiguous states grew in almost inverse proportion. This tendency has been manifest in the development of major

Table 8: Spatial Concentration in Manufacturing, 1930–68

Argentina	*Per cent of industrial workers*			
	1935	*1946*	*1954*	*1965*
Federal Capital	47·0	40·2	32·2	26·0
Buenos Aires	25·2	29·5	33·2	39·9
Córdoba	4·3	4·8	6·2	8·0
Santa Fé	9·6	9·2	9·5	9·7
Total employment	467,315	1,107,829	1,498,115	1,370,500

Brazil	*Per cent of industrial employment*			
	1940	*1950*	*1960*	*1968*
São Paulo	35·0	38·6	45·6	50·2
Guanabara (Rio)	15·8	13·2	9·6	9·3
Minas Gerais	9·5	8·8	8·0	*
Rio Grande do Sul	7·8	7·9	7·4	7·3
Rio de Janeiro	5·8	6·1	6·4	*
Pernambuco	7·3	6·0	4·2	*
Total employment	781,185	1,256,807	1,425,886	2,218,278

*Not available

Chile	*Per cent of manufacturing employment*		
	1940	*1952*	*1960*
Central region	68·5	70·6	71·8
Concepción & La Frontera	14·9	15·0	14·3

	Per cent of industrial employment		*Per cent of manufacturing employment*	
	1952	*1960*	*1957*	*1964*
Santiago	49·3	52·3	51·5	60·3
Valparaiso	10·4	9·9	18·1	11·8
Concepción	8·5	9·2	12·6	11·8
Bío-Bío	1·0	1·3	1·1	2·3
Valdivia	3·6	2·4	2·5	1·8
Tarapacá	1·0	1·4	0·6	4·0
Total employment	408,700	428,900	160,900	241,700

Colombia	*Per cent of manufacturing employment*	
	1945	*1967*
Bogotá and Soacha	16·7	25·3
Medellín complex	21·9	22·8
Cali	7·1	12·5
Barranquilla	10·5	8·3
Total employment	135,400	293,825

Ecuador	*Per cent of manufacturing employment*		
	1950	*1955*	*1965*
Guayas (Guayaquíl)	38·9	42·0	38·8
Pichincha (Quito)	38·3	36·8	30·7
Total employment		30,370	47,629

Mexico	*Per cent of industrial employment*		
	1930	*1950*	*1965*
México D.F.	24·6	30·3	33·9
México	2·9	4·9	12·1
Jalisco (Guadalajara)	6·4	4·4	5·4
Nuevo León (Monterrey)			7·1
Total employment	197,091	808,561	1,409,489

Peru	*Per cent of industrial employment*		*Per cent of manufacturing employment*	
	1940	*1961*	*1955*	*1963*
Lima/Callao	13·7	38·1	65·5	70·2
Arequipa	3·8	5·0		4·4
Cajamarca	13·0	5·1		0·2
Cuzco	10·4	6·0		1·6
La Libertad	5·4	5·2		2·9
Junín				4.9
Total employment	380,281	410,981		164,930

Source: Respective industrial and economic censuses.

new industrial plants, such as petro-chemicals, iron and steel, along the Santa Fé–La Plata axis. A similar but less marked trend can be seen in Mexico, where, although the Federal District increased its share of industrial employment between 1950 and 1965, expansion in the contiguous state of Mexico was much more rapid.* This growth was concentrated, in fact, in a series of smaller centres on the edge of the conurbation and in several other centres up to 250 kilometres from Mexico City, notably Toluca, Puebla, Cuernavaca and Querétaro. Such a tendency has also been experienced in Brazil and Colombia, although the figures do not reflect the change. In the case of Brazil, manufacturing industry has tended to disperse from Rio de Janeiro to nearby cities such as Niterói and Petrópolis, and the same

*Both the nation and the state bear the same name.

phenomenon has taken place around São Paulo. Even in the smaller industrial concentrations in Colombia there has been a similar trend, with several industries leaving Medellín to move to Rionegro, 38 kilometres away.

There have been, therefore, two synchronous changes taking place

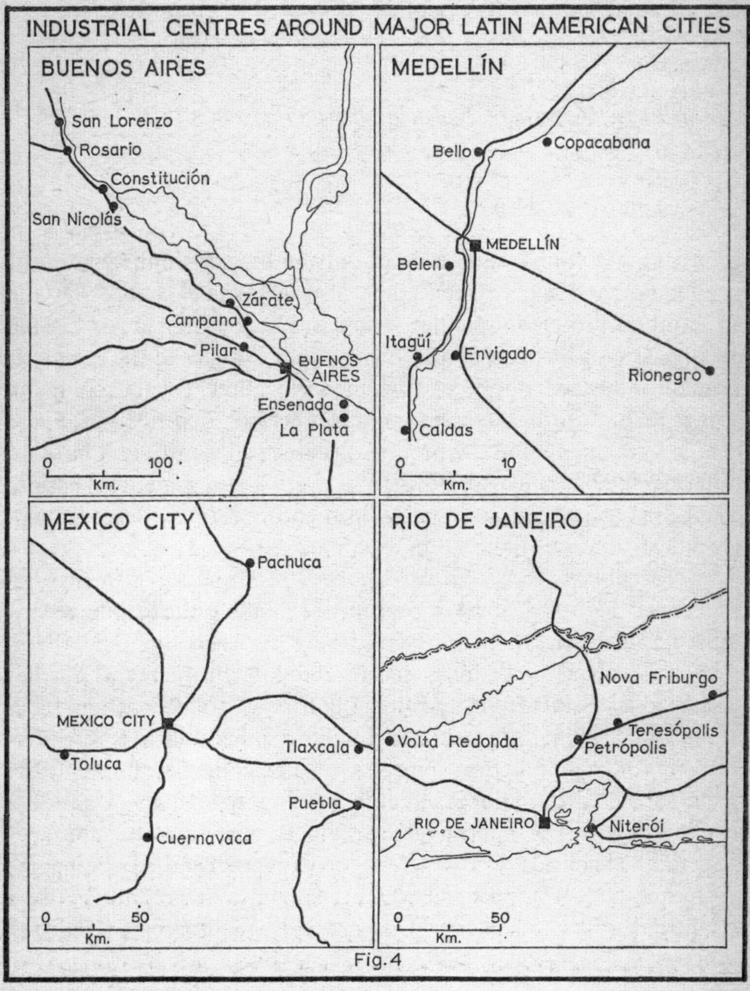

Fig. 4

during the post-1929 period. On the one hand, a higher proportion of companies have been established near to the existing industrial centres, thereby increasing spatial concentration in the nation as a whole. On the other hand, a smaller proportion of companies have been prepared to establish themselves in the central cities and have chosen, often with government assistance, to settle in smaller cities elsewhere within the city-region.

The processes governing industrial distribution since 1929

(I) TECHNOLOGY AND THE SECTORAL COMPOSITION OF PRODUCTION

Industrial growth has involved not only an increase in the volume of production and employment, but also wholesale changes in the structure of production. It has been associated with increases in the average size of companies and plants, with changes in the composition of industrial output, with 'modernization' of the company structure and with increases in inter-sectoral dependence. These changes are inherent in the process of industrial growth and have, to differing extents, affected industry in every Latin American nation. Their spatial impact has usually been to increase the level of geographical concentration within each nation.

(a) *The composition of production.* As a result partly of the natural process of industrial growth and partly of the policies pursued by most Latin American governments, there has been a gradual alteration in the structure of industrial production. In the main, this has consisted of a shift from traditional consumer goods, such as foodstuffs and clothing, to consumer-durable products such as refrigerators, motor cars and television sets. In some countries, this shift has gone further and national manufacturers have begun to produce larger quantities of intermediate products such as metal products, paper and chemicals. And in a few, such as Brazil and Argentina, the stage has even been reached where companies are producing large quantities of capital goods. This process can be seen in Table 9,

Table 9: Structure of the Gross Value of Industrial Production by Groups of Industries, 1950, 1960 and 1968

Industrial group	*1950*	*1960*	*1968**
Food	27·8	22·8	20·5
Beverages and tobacco	8·1	6·1	5·8
Textiles	16·6	12·2	10·0
Footwear and clothing	6·6	5·0	3·7
Wood and furniture	3·4	3·0	2·7
Paper and paper products	2·4	2·5	3·4
Chemicals and petroleum products	10·2	13·9	16·7
Non-metallic minerals	4·5	3·8	4·0
Basic metals	4·3	5·9	6·6
Metal transforming	9·4	18·6	20·7
Leather, printing, rubber and miscellaneous	6·7	6·2	5·9
	100·0	100·0	100·0

*Estimates

Source: UN ECLA (1969a.)

where temporal changes in the composition of production in Latin America as a whole are illustrated.

These temporal changes have affected the spatial distribution of industry in a variety of ways, most of which have tended to increase the degree of concentration. The situation has arisen, in part, because the newer industries have been more dependent upon supplies from other factories than were traditional companies. They have tended to buy partially processed inputs from other companies rather than employ raw materials directly, and have sold their products to other companies rather than directly to consumers.[34] As a result, they have been inclined to locate nearer to other industries than to either the sources of raw materials or the consumer market. This, in turn, has assured them of good communications with the managers of other companies and of reliable supplies of inputs.

The trend can be detected in the development of several industrial complexes in Latin America, notably in the petro-chemical industry in Argentina, and in the textile industry in Brazil (São Paulo) and Colombia (Medellín). It is also reflected in Table 10, which shows that the modern industries are more highly concentrated than the traditional and less-integrated sectors. As the industrialization pro-

Table 10: Regional Concentration of Manufacturing Industry by Sector
(Percentage of industry in each sector located in named cities)

Sector	*Average**	1 *Lima/ Callao 1963*	2 *Santiago 1962*	3 *São Paulo 1968*	4 *Bogotá 1969*
Foodstuffs	18	52·9	27·4	33·6	20·9
Drinks and beverages	15	57·8	44·3	32·9	26·5
Tobacco	16	100·0	—	19·9	15·1
Textiles	12	79·5	71·9	49·8	18·6
Footwear and clothing	8	92·6	83·2	48·2	24·3
Wood	19	34·8	63·9	13·2	16·9
Furniture	7	85·6	86·3	45·0	45·1
Paper and paper products	13	90·8	46·7	57·2	18·2
Printing and publishing	10	78·7	81·4	28·5	42·6
Leather	11	61·8	86·0	40·9	26·8
Rubber	4	95·0	100·0	75·0	20·9
Chemicals	6	86·7	66·6	59·6	33·9
Petroleum derivatives	20	20·3	0·6	—	8·6
Non-metallic mineral products	14	81·5	50·6	46·5	19·2
Basic metals	16	8·6	25·2	49·5	25·1
Metal products	2	94·1	90·8	75·7	34·4
Machinery	9	86·5	57·0	75·5	19·7
Electrical goods	2	92·2	93·2	75·5	53·0
Transport products	5	78·3	50·2	75·9	45·4
Miscellaneous	1	98·4	94·0	71·7	57·4
Total		70·2		50·9	27·4

* Average of the ranks of the four sets of percentages.

Sources: 1. 1963 Censo Nacional Económico, Peru, Manufacturing Employment.
2. F. S. Weaver, *Regional Patterns of Economic Change in Chile 1950–1966*, Cornell University, Dissertation, Table 11-7, 'Industrial Production'.
3. *Anuario Estatístico do Brasil,* 1969.
4. *Boletín Mensual de Estadística.* Manufacturing Employment.

cess in each country continues, stronger inter-industry links are likely to develop. In the absence of countervailing forces, therefore, the propensity for industrial concentration will increase and the ability of governments to influence industrial location will decline.*

(b) *Increased efficiency and plant size.* A further characteristic of industrial growth in Latin America has been the general increase in plant size and in labour productivity. The principal result of these changes has been to reduce the number of plants in each of the traditional sectors and to increase the number of plants in all sectors producing for a national, rather than a local, market. The locational consequences of the two processes have been marked, although slight differences exist in the manner in which they have affected the newly expanding industries and the traditional sectors.

In the former industries, the general tendency has been for new plants to be established which produce goods not previously manufactured. Since the majority of these factories distribute to a national market, they have tended to locate in the largest population and industrial concentrations, thereby maximizing sales and minimizing transport costs. The result has been to produce an absolute and relative concentration of production in those centres.

The effect of these changes has been far greater in the traditional sectors, however, for increases in plant size and labour productivity have exerted even more competitive pressures upon existing plants in those sectors. The result of this competition has normally favoured the larger, more-efficient plants, which have tended to be more highly concentrated in the major cities. In the traditional sectors, therefore, not only has there been an expansion of production and employment in the major cities as new companies became established, but, in addition, redundancy has been caused in the smaller cities where the less efficient, local-market industries have been forced to close. Such a situation has characterized most of the countries in the continent, but was especially marked in Peru between 1940 and 1961. At the earlier date, the major industrial centre, Lima/Callao, held only 13·7 per cent of the country's industrial workers but by 1961 this share had increased to 38·1 per cent. In some of the inland departments, meanwhile, the effect of manufacturing growth on the coast was taking its toll, with industrial employment between the two dates

*See the discussion below (pp. 77–8) on the distribution of the Chilean car industry for one example of the effect of this process on government location policies.

falling from 49,379 to 20,794 in Cajamarca, from 32,260 to 20,082 in Puno, and from 39,525 to 24,668 in Cuzco.[35] (See Fig. 5.)

(c) *Company structure.* A general tendency of the industrialization process in most countries has been to induce fundamental changes in company structure. These changes have included a general increase in share participation, an expansion in the number of joint-stock companies (*sociedades anónimas*) and a decrease in the number of partnerships and private companies. Such changes in turn may well have influenced the manner in which Latin American companies choose their locations – a possibility which will be discussed later.

(d) *Economic infrastructure and agglomeration economies.* In Europe and North America the emergence of electricity and oil as sources of power freed many industries from their previous dependence upon coal and water.[36] The new fuels permitted a wider choice of locations than before because of the large number of cities where both were available. In Latin America, however, the effect has frequently been to pose yet one more restriction upon locational flexibility. The main problem has been that adequate supplies are commonly available only in the larger cities and many smaller towns in the poorer nations do not possess them. Thus industry, which might be considered 'footloose' in the developed world, is limited in its choice of location by the availability of power supplies.

However, it should not be thought that the availability of power need always impede the wider dispersal of industry. For, in some cases, companies have been prepared to establish their own electricity generator to supplement existing supplies. Such an example was provided during the 1950s by companies in Cali (Colombia), where the city's other locational advantages such as proximity to agricultural raw materials and the Pacific coast more than compensated for the unreliable electricity supplies.[37] Even so, power supplies do pose a major problem, although the situation is improving in most countries.

The concentrating tendency of electricity provision is only one example of the way infrastructure has influenced industrial location in Latin America. Another is the effect of transport networks. In many Latin American nations transportation facilities are heavily concentrated in and near to the largest cities – a lasting heritage of European neo-colonialism. The effect upon industrial location, of

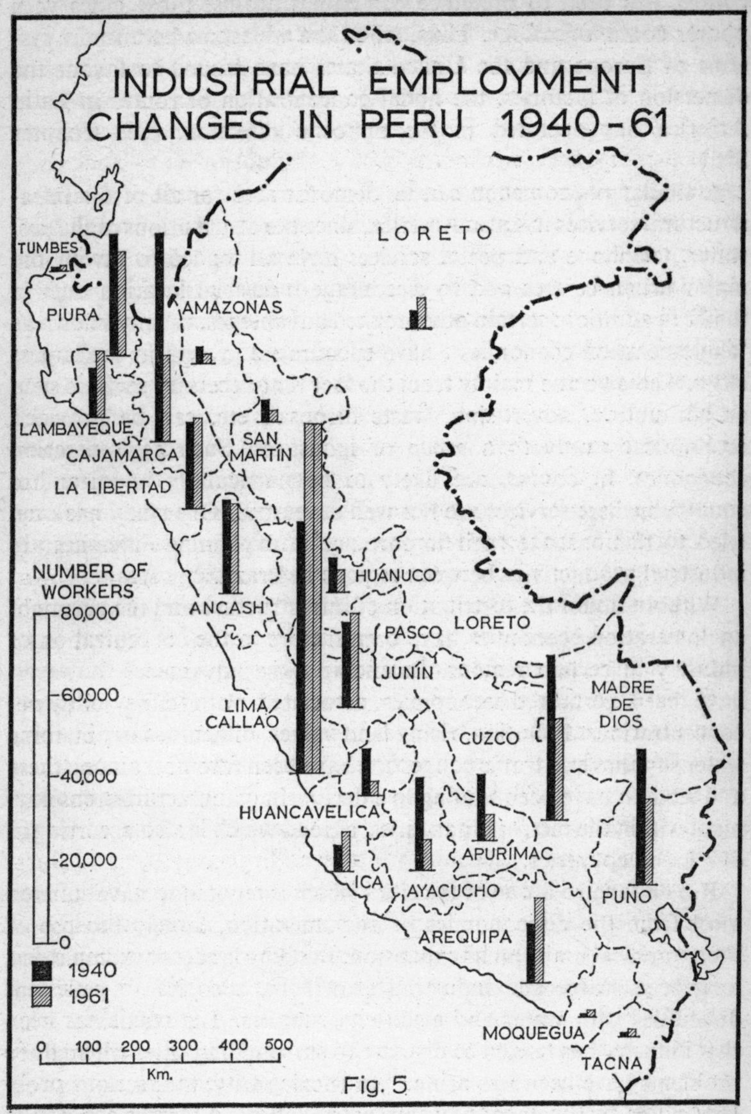
INDUSTRIAL EMPLOYMENT
CHANGES IN PERU 1940-61
LORETO
TUMBES
PIURA
AMAZONAS
LAMBAYEQUE
CAJAMARCA
SAN
MARTIN
LA LIBERTAD
NUMBER OF
WORKERS
80,000
60,000
40,000
20,000
0
ANCASH
HUÁNUCO
PASCO
LORETO
JUNÍN
LIMA/
CALLAO
MADRE
DE
DIOS
CUZCO
HUANCAVELICA
APURÍMAC
ICA
AYACUCHO
PUNO
AREQUIPA
1940
1961
MOQUEGUA
0 100 200 300 400 500
Km.
TACNA
Fig. 5

course, has been to prejudice companies against those cities with poorer communications. Thus, while the widespread transport systems of Europe and the United States have tended to favour the dispersion of factories, the nodal concentration of routes in Latin America has operated in the opposite direction. (See Chapter Six.)

A similar phenomenon can be demonstrated for all of the infrastructural services in Latin America, since the distributions of the gas, water, telephone and postal services have all tended to favour the major urban centres and to discourage industrial location outside them. In addition, certain other related advantages, usually known as 'agglomeration economies', have encouraged growth in the largest cities. These accrue mainly from the fact that necessary services such as accounting, advertising, waste disposal, etc. can be provided economically only to a *group* of industries. Such agglomeration economies, of course, are likely to be particularly important in countries where services are not well developed. One study has even tried to demonstrate their importance in explaining differences in industrial productivity between regions in Brazil.[38]

Without doubt the distribution of infrastructure and the nature of agglomeration economies have been factors in the concentration of industry in certain regions. Balancing these advantages, however, have been certain diseconomies associated with large industrial concentrations. Pollution, rising land values, difficulties in obtaining water supplies and traffic congestion have been foremost among these and seem to have been leading to a decline in manufacturing employment within the metropolitan cities, a trend which is also occurring in developed countries.

Rio de Janeiro is one of the cities which is reputed to have suffered most from the diseconomies of agglomeration, largely because of topographical limits on its expansion. Building land, for example, has long been scarce and industrial growth has also led to persistent difficulties with water and electricity supplies. The result has been that industry has tended to disperse to surrounding cities where these problems have been less acute.[39] In Mexico City, too, serious problems posed by shortages of water, air pollution and traffic congestion have helped to persuade many companies to establish plants outside the Federal District.[40] Another city in a semi-desert area, Lima, has also been beset by water problems as a result of industrial and population expansion, even if, in this case, industrial dispersal has not been marked.

(II) THE INFLUENCE OF THE MARKET

Proximity to the market represents an influential factor in the choice of location of industrial companies in most parts of the world.[41] In Latin America this attraction has been particularly strong owing to the fact that *per capita* incomes are so much higher in the larger urban areas. Market attraction represents one of the major forces leading to the concentration of industry. It also represents a force that may have been intensified by the changes that have taken place in the manufacturing sector in recent years.

As explained above, the establishment of plants based upon the technology of developed countries has produced many factories which can adequately supply the whole national market. Increasingly, therefore, the 'average' plant has changed from one which supplied only a local market to one that supplied the whole nation. In terms of location, such a tendency has tended to encourage the establishment of companies in the primate cities, that is in those cities which usually constitute the nodal centre of the transport network and the highest concentrations of purchasing power. Even in the few cases where consumer markets have been relatively widely spread, modern commercial and wholesale techniques have led to a reduction in the number of sales outlets. The growth of supermarkets and department stores in many countries has permitted centralized purchasing arrangements, so that many industrial companies now sell a high proportion of their products to a handful of distributors. Since these centralized purchasing agents are also likely to be placed in the major cities the dominance of these centres is further emphasized. The general trend, therefore, has been towards a higher degree of concentration in the consumer market. And, since similar tendencies have also been affecting the intermediate- and capital-goods industries owing to the growth of inter-industry linkages, there has been a general inclination towards concentration in the largest cities.

(III) ACCESSIBILITY TO INPUTS

The pull exerted by labour and especially by a 'skilled pool of labour' has always been surrounded by an aura of unassailable logic. Geography books, industrial managers and planners have always stressed its importance in determining the location of industries, whether the area concerned be Lancashire or the state of São Paulo.[42] In many cases, however, it would seem that managers have used this factor more as a *post hoc* rationalization than as a motive for location. And, in the few cases when it has influenced managers, it has usually been to justify their existing prejudices against particular areas and labour forces.

It is certain that the average Latin American plant is more labour-intensive than that in North America or Europe, and on average the employment structure of each plant tends to be of lower quality in skills, education and general experience.[43] Many companies, in fact, employ a labour force which consists of a handful of engineers and administrative personnel, and a large proportion of workers who have been trained in a period of less than three months. In theory this should allow industrial companies more flexibility. Since there is general underemployment among low-skilled professions in most Latin American countries, an unskilled but literate work-force will be available in any medium-sized urban centre. The only real limitation, therefore, will be the need to attract the skilled personnel. But, given the limited numbers required, this should rarely prove an insuperable obstacle.

The fact that few companies appear to have taken advantage of this flexibility probably reflects one of three possibilities. Firstly, that labour costs in every manufacturing centre are so low that the labour element in the total cost structure is very small. Thus companies are more concerned with other factors concerned with location than with the need to search for even cheaper supplies of labour. Secondly, that neither managers nor the skilled personnel have any real desire to live outside the major industrial centres even if profits or salaries are much higher. Finally, that managers do not share the view that work-forces are equally adaptable in every area. This view would certainly be supported by Colombian experience, where many managers expressed an antipathy to the largely Negro work-force on the

Caribbean coast, even though the companies which were operating in that area seemed highly satisfied.

A second location motive, accessibility to materials, has probably had a stronger effect on industrial location than accessibility to labour. This influence has been especially strong in those industries where the production process has involved a high level of weight-loss during processing, or has used a perishable raw material. Both factors have been important in determining the location of several industries associated with sugar cultivation. Sugar mills, for example, have normally been located near to the cane fields because the sugar content in the cane declines rapidly after cutting, and processing must take place as soon as possible. Similarly, factories making paper out of the sugar bagasse are built close to the areas of cultivation because the final product is cheaper to transport than the raw material.

Another example of an industry which has frequently been located close to raw-material supplies is the iron and steel industry (see Fig. 6). In Mexico, for example, the early establishment of this industry near Monterrey is explained by the availability of coal in the Sabinas basin and iron ore in Durango. Similarly the location of several Brazilian steel plants in Minas Gerais can be explained largely by accessibility to local iron ore, and the location of the Paz del Río works in Colombia by the availability of local coal and iron ore. However, there are also examples of iron and steel works situated not on inland supplies but close to a port, so that they may take advantage of sea-borne material supplies. The Huachipato plant near Concepción in Chile depends on imported coal from the USA, on iron ore from northern Chile and on limestone from the south of the country. Similarly the new integrated steel works near Santos in Brazil will also depend largely on imported supplies of materials. There are, of course, other plants which are located close to their principal markets, for example, the Volta Redonda works between Rio de Janeiro and São Paulo.

(IV) THE ROLE OF GOVERNMENT

During the past twenty years or so most Latin American governments have become actively involved in guiding economic growth and

Fig. 6

development. They have produced national plans, instituted controls upon activities affecting the balance of payments, encouraged industrial development and engaged in the construction of physical infrastructure. But, in the process of becoming more involved in planning, they have introduced a new dimension into the question of industrial location.

This new dimension has been the desire on the part of industrial companies to be situated near the source of government decisions, that is in the capital city. For, with the growing importance of government actions upon the day-to-day operations of companies, these companies have had to negotiate more and more frequently with government agencies. Managers have been required to visit the capital more often, and new companies aware of this problem have often decided to move to the capital to cut down managerial travel time.

In part this factor has become important because of the way Latin Americans do business. They tend to operate on a more personal basis than many European or North American managers, especially when their negotiations are with the state bureaucracy. Thus, as the number of government activities has increased, so have the number of meetings between businessmen and government officials. Of course, the need to be in the capital city could have been avoided if the state had established regional offices or if more companies had employed lawyers to work on their behalf in the capital. However, this has not been the case, and more and more companies have been attracted to capital cities so as to ease negotiations with the government.

The effects of this preference for direct personal dealings upon industrial location have been noted in several places. King has commented that 'one consequence of the frequent need to obtain an individual decision from a government ministry having few branches located outside Mexico City is an additional incentive to industrial location in the Valley of Mexico'.[44] In Colombia, too, many industrial managers from the provincial centres are forced to make frequent trips to Bogotá for the purpose of negotiating with government agencies, especially over the matter of import licences. This factor has partially explained why some companies have moved their head offices to Bogotá, separating their production and administrative functions. Whether, of course, companies located in the capital gain any real advantage is a difficult question, but some figures available for Colombia provide at least *prima facie* support for this view. Between 1953 and 1964 the share of Cundinamarca (the department in which Bogotá is situated) in the total imports of the country increased from 35·5 per cent to 49·3 per cent, while the share of the two other major industrial departments remained virtually stable.[45] Even having considered the faster growth rate of Bogotá, particularly in the sectors with high-import propensities, one is led to the conclusion that such a large increase must depend on proximity to the government.

This factor should not be over-stressed, however, for the pressure upon companies to negotiate directly with the government varies from industry to industry and from country to country. Industries which require few import licences are freed from a great deal of bargaining, as are companies which operate in a country where administrative controls are relatively relaxed, such as Brazil. Even so, the number of occasions when companies are required to negotiate with governments is increasing and certainly in some cases this factor has encouraged industrial concentration.

The location of industry in and near the capital cities has also been associated with other government policies largely unconnected with industry. In Mexico City, for example, government measures to hold down the prices of foodstuffs, especially maize, and to restrict rises in bus fares may have reduced pressure for higher wage rates.[46] Indirectly, therefore, these policies have reduced the costs of industrial companies operating in Mexico City below the level they might otherwise have reached. The final result has probably been to increase the attractiveness of the capital.

The locational effect of Latin American integration

The various attempts at Latin American economic integration have already shown that successful schemes will fundamentally change the spatial pattern of industry both within countries and in the continent as a whole. And, with the rise of sub-groups such as the Andean Pact which are attempting to accelerate the pace of integration, it is important to consider what form the new patterns of industrial distribution will take. One feature, already clear from the experience of LAFTA and CACM, is that freer trade favours industrialization in the most advanced nations within a community. As a consequence, the smaller nations such as Bolivia and Paraguay will find that their attempts at industrial growth are made more difficult, even though they have been granted special trade dispensations.[47]

In addition, economic integration is likely to effect the spatial distribution of industry within each nation. As Odell has pointed out, successful integration will encourage companies to favour cities with access to port facilities, where they may more easily export their products.[48] Such a tendency will lead to further concentrations on or near the coast, where most of the existing 'cores of economic activity' are already situated. As a result, the position of Santiago, São Paulo, Rio de Janeiro, Buenos Aires, Guayaquíl and other similarly placed cities will be improved *vis-à-vis* inland industrial centres. Such a tendency will certainly complicate attempts to disperse industry more widely.

The nature of the location decision

Before going on to discuss government attempts to influence industrial location, it is important to examine briefly how Latin American companies make this kind of decision. How far do they make rational decisions based upon detailed analysis of the alternative sites? How far do they look for a site where they can maximize their profits rather than one which will grant them acceptable levels of profit? And, how far does the business environment in which they operate affect the relative importance of these decisions *vis-à-vis* other managerial decisions?

In many ways, it may be suggested that industrial location is not a matter that is decided on the basis of detailed investigation. Most new companies, excepting some of the large foreign corporations, seem not to make studies of alternative sites, and base their decisions on more subjective grounds. One of these grounds is the preference among many managers to remain in their home cities, a decision which has determined the location of many industries. Of course, such a preference has been common in developed countries, too – how else can Henry Ford's choice of Detroit or Lord Nuffield's choice of Oxford be justified? – but it would appear that this tendency is particularly strong in Latin America. In my study of Colombian industry, for example, I found that only twenty-seven out of 224 large national companies had been established in cities other than the one in which the manager or owner had been born. And, in this example, the only alternative location which managers seemed prepared to consider was the national capital.[49]

The changes that are occurring in the ownership structure of industry in Latin America, however, may tend to reduce the frequency of this kind of 'subjective' decision. As the number of companies controlled by single individuals declines relative to the number of joint-stock companies, there may be a stronger tendency towards more objective reasoning. This may serve to concentrate companies even more in the capital cities. On the other hand, and especially if governments encourage decentralization, it may well result in a gradual reduction in the degree of industrial concentration, as companies are forced to consider alternative locations more carefully.

Government policies on the distribution of industry

In several Latin American countries, political conditions have allowed governments to implement policies aimed at the regional dispersal of industry. But, in general, these policies have employed rhetoric rather than action, and only in Chile, Brazil, Cuba and Puerto Rico have any major changes been made in the regional distribution of industry. Even in these countries government action has only slowed the tide towards a highly localized spatial distribution and not reversed it. Such a situation has not arisen because governments lacked suitable tools for dispersal, for a variety of methods have been employed. Rather, it seems as if the political will to implement these methods is the element that was lacking.

(I) FINANCIAL MECHANISMS FOR INDUSTRIAL DISPERSAL

Financial incentives seem to have been the main mechanism used by Latin American governments to tempt industry towards the less-developed regions. They have taken a variety of forms, such as exemption from profit-taxes, the waiving of import duties and the reduction of rents in government-built factories. The first country to adopt such incentives was Mexico when, in the 1930s, several states bordering on the United States were granted concessions from import duties.[50] The main motive behind this policy was to improve the competitive position of these areas *vis-à-vis* the rest of the country, mainly because transport links with these areas were still very poor. Later, several other border areas were exempted from certain import duties. In addition, since 1966, firms in these areas have been allowed to import duty-free raw materials provided that the final manufactured goods were re-exported. Largely as a result of these policies several cities have experienced rapid industrial growth, notably Mexicali, Tijuana and Ciudad Juárez (see Fig. 7). However, it is doubtful whether these concessions would have had the same result, or even that the concessions would have been offered, had

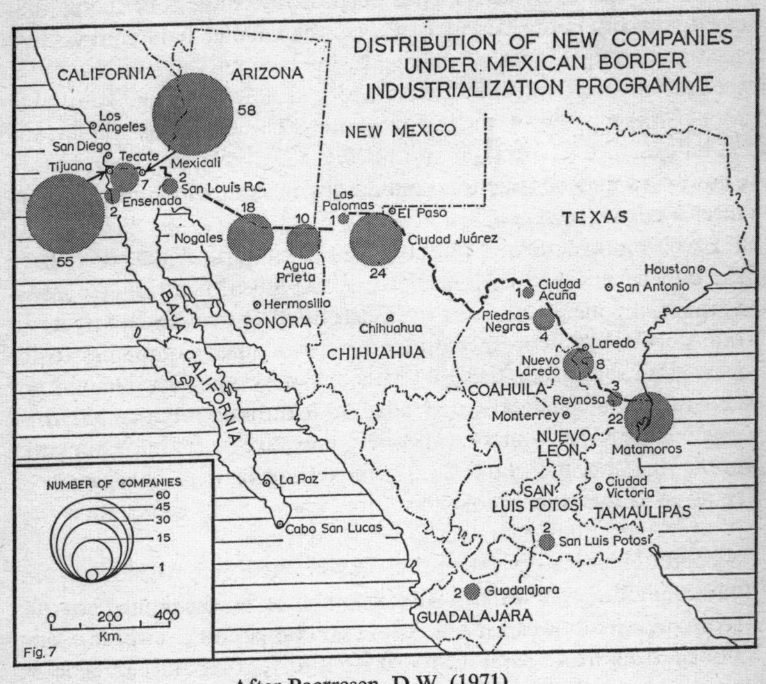

After Baerresen, D.W. (1971)

it not been for the proximity of the United States border. Without the interest of American corporations in the cheap supplies of Mexican labour, and the access to the United States market for Mexican manufacturers, these policies would probably have failed.

Tax concessions have also been employed for many years in other parts of Mexico but with less apparent success. Under one scheme the different state governments tried to attract industry by exempting companies from local taxes – some states such as Zacatecas having begun as early as 1939. The main problem has been, however, that as more and more states adopted this scheme, the relative differences between the taxes levied in each state have become very small. Since the tax levels were in any case very low, these concessions have had little effect upon the location of industrial companies.[51]

Further tax concessions to new industries were announced in July 1972 in a renewed effort to encourage industrial decentralization. The country has been divided for this purpose into three zones consisting essentially of (1) the largest cities, (2) the smaller industrial centres such as Lerma, Toluca, Cuernavaca, Puebla and Querétero, and (3) the rest of the country. Large benefits will now be available to most Mexican companies in the last two zones. These benefits will include major exemptions from import duties, vastly accelerated depreciation allowances and considerable reductions in company and manufacturer's sales taxes.

Much more successful than the Mexican efforts to date have been the policies adopted by the Puerto Rican government. Since 1955 a number of concessions have been permitted to companies setting up outside the San Juan metropolitan region.[52] For companies in the least desirable areas these concessions were considerable, but the actual level of benefit also depended upon the amount of employment generated by each plant. The first incentive was that companies occupying factories built by the government were charged lower rents in the less desirable locations. These rents could vary from 95 cents per square metre in the San Juan region to 50 cents elsewhere. Secondly, income-tax exemption was granted differentially to companies in different areas, with companies in the San Juan area receiving exemptions for ten years and companies elsewhere exemptions lasting up to seventeen years. Thirdly, companies outside San

Juan could claim capital grants which were unavailable to companies within the metropolitan area. These grants varied with the number of workers employed by the company but in unpopular areas could be as high as 50,000 dollars for every 100 workers. Lastly, the government also offered an indirect financial incentive by improving the economic infrastructure in various parts of the island.

Such a barrage of schemes had a marked effect, for the share of new industrial employment being created in San Juan fell from more than one half in the early 1950s to one third by the middle 1960s. It has also been claimed that these concessions have been cheap to administer. This is because the tax revenues lost by the government have been less than the costs it would have incurred had it improved the roads and other urban services in San Juan to accommodate continued industrial concentration.[53] Despite this success, however, it is unlikely that such a scheme is applicable to other countries with larger areas and less-developed infrastructures whose governments would have had greater difficulty in persuading companies of the advantages of peripherally located areas.

A financial scheme which could be more easily applied to most Latin American countries is that presently being operated in Brazil. Since 1961 Article 34/18 has permitted all companies registered in Brazil to halve their income tax on condition that they invest this money, together with fresh funds, in approved projects in the north-east, and the scheme has recently been extended to cover the Amazonas region. A considerable saving can be made in this way, since income is taxed at the rate of 30 per cent. The amount of fresh funds required may be quite low, and in projects given a high social-desirability rating they may represent a mere 25 per cent of the total cost of the project. In addition, projects under this scheme are entitled to state loans at advantageous rates of interest and to various tax and import-duty exemptions during operation.

Several writers have suggested that this scheme has brought considerable benefits for the north-east. Hirschman, for example, has shown that 'by the end of May 1967 total investment represented by industrial projects taking advantage of the Art. 34/18 mechanism amounted to NCr 1,811 million. When this figure is compared to an estimate of the industrial capital stock existing in the Northeast just before the Art. 34/18 mechanism became effective, it is found that 34/18-induced investment will double the industrial capital stock in the Northeast.'[54] Not only has industrial investment risen, but the structure of production has been diversified, 'with sharply increased representation of industries that are both dynamic and rich in linkage effects'.[55]

Other views of the 34/18 mechanism, however, have been less favourable. Goodman, for example, has made a number of detailed criticisms of the scheme.[56] Firstly, he has argued that it is failing to create sufficient jobs to satisfy the demand for industrial labour in the region. Just to maintain the manufacturing sector's 8 per cent share of total employment, for example, 274,000 new jobs need to be created during the 1970s: up to June 1967, however, approved projects were expected to create only 67,800 jobs (compared to a 1959 labour force of 176,800 workers). Worse still, Goodman argues that this figure records the gross, as opposed to the net, increase in employment. The distinction is important because at least half of the direct employment created by the scheme will be in modernization projects which will cause unemployment in existing plants in the region. In the textile sector, for example, up to 50 per cent of the sector's pre-modernization labour force could soon be laid off.[57] In addition, it is probable that the increase in employment has been overestimated since the data were provided by the industrial companies themselves. And, since the number of jobs created is one criterion of determining eligibility for 34/18 funds, companies are known to overestimate the direct employment impact of their investment.

Secondly, a related problem with the scheme is that much of the 34/18 investment has been directed towards highly capital-intensive projects. This not only means that employment is created at a high cost but also that it is expensive in terms of foreign exchange. One reason for this tendency is that the 34/18 mechanism effectively subsidizes the cost of foreign exchange and, therefore, encourages investment in foreign machinery.

Thirdly, the scheme has been criticized because its principal beneficiaries are concentrated in the industrial south-east. In 1965, 55·4 and 22·7 per cent of all 34/18 deposits came from the states of São Paulo and Guanabara respectively.

A fourth area of criticism concerns the concentration of investment within certain areas of the north-east. By the end of 1968, for example, 38·4 per cent of the investment in new projects had been planned for the state of Bahía and 35·7 per cent for Pernambuco (see Fig. 23, p. 252). These states had 26·5 and 18·1 per cent respectively of the north-east's estimated population in 1967. And within these states it was the capital cities, Salvador and Recife, which were gaining most of the new employment. In order to counteract this tendency, SUDENE increased the benefits available to companies locating outside these cities (1969).*

Finally, a fundamental criticism made of the scheme has been that it is creating an inefficient manufacturing sector. Rather than creating a series of industries based on the north-east's resource or labour advantages, it is claimed that it is duplicating the import-substitution process that has only recently been completed in the country as a whole. One symptom of this process has been that most of the new industries are highly dependent upon supplies from, and markets in, the south-east. Rather than creating a highly integrated industrial complex in the north-east, industrial decentralization is merely leading to the development of inefficient plants and to the generation of inter-regional transport flows.

While these criticisms appear to be valid, few critics have recommended that the scheme be discontinued. While Hirschman over-praises the mechanism's effectiveness, more jobs have been created than would otherwise have developed. At the very least the scheme represents a very interesting method of tempting industry to move to depressed areas in a mixed economy.

Chile provides another example of a government using financial incentives. Unlike the Brazilian scheme, however, it has been claimed that this policy has 'had little or no effect' upon industrial location except in the case of Arica in the far north of the country.[58] Taking this one more successful example, the main financial incentive to location in Arica was its establishment as a free port in 1953. This lifted import duties and disembarkation taxes from materials used in locally based industrial production. The same privilege was granted

*This action, in turn, has been criticized for encouraging the inefficient diffusion of companies and infrastructure throughout the north-east.

to the provinces of Chiloé, Aysén and Magallanes in 1955, although there was no exemption from disembarkation taxes. Partially as a result of these policies, the amount of manufacturing industry in Arica increased, especially in the chemical, electrical-machinery and motor industries, which depended largely on imported materials.

More important than these tax concessions, however, was the fact that after 1958 the national government virtually compelled all car manufacturers to locate in Arica. As a result of this measure some nineteen companies were operating in the city in 1964, even though the free-port privileges had been rescinded. This ban on car-plant location in the Santiago area was lifted in 1967 and immediately four major industrial companies – Fiat, Ford, Renault and Chrysler – decided to move to the central region of the country. (The tax concessions still available in Arica were 90 per cent exemption from income taxes for a fifteen-year period and exemption from the 7 per cent sales tax on inputs from Santiago used in the production of vehicles in Arica.) New investment of US $10 million plus a further US$20 million in subsidiary plants was committed in the Santiago area during 1968, in an industry whose fixed capital in 1966 was only US$10 million. The major reasons for this shift, which occurred even though considerable tax concessions were still available in Arica, were quite straightforward. Firstly, the managers of the car companies claimed that it was very difficult to operate a production plant in Arica when their administrative offices were in Santiago. Secondly, the major market was concentrated in the Santiago area. Lastly, 90 per cent of the 220 auxiliary plants were located in Santiago and its environs. The supply problems of the car industry had become particularly acute during the period because of the growing importance of national suppliers based in Santiago. While the majority of materials had been imported, plants in Arica could be supplied directly by sea. Once the majority were supplied from Santiago however, a very expensive double transport haul became necessary.

(II) ADMINISTRATIVE CONTROLS

The policy of the Chilean government with respect to car manufacturers represents one example of administrative controls upon location. In general, though, this kind of control has been used but rarely. The Mexican government also applied some controls on industrial location but did not implement them vigorously. A more typical method was the attempt to influence industrial location by threatening to refuse companies additional water, fuel and gas supplies. Although there are cases where they have been effective, in Mexico controls upon location would seem to have had comparatively little effect. In general more companies have set up in Mexico City, to gain access to the government bureaucracy, than have dispersed as a result of location controls.[59]

(III) INDUSTRIAL ESTATES

Another strategy which has frequently been used by Latin American governments is to establish industrial estates in backward areas. These estates provide the basic services required by industry, such as electricity, drainage, water and communications, thereby saving individual companies considerable expense. On occasions, governments have even built factories on the estates and rented them to companies.

The Mexican government has opened industrial estates on several occasions, the most ambitious attempt being at Ciudad Sahagún, where a whole new city was developed. In this case the National Finance Corporation opened the estate in the middle 1950s with the aim of attracting heavy industry. Unfortunately the two original state-operated industries, set up by the National Finance Corporation itself at the time the estate was established, were joined by very few private industries, even though the estate is only 100 kilometres from Mexico City. Other estates were less ambitious but did encourage industrial development, notably in Puebla, Toluca and Cuernavaca. During 1972, greater efforts in this direction were announced and industrial areas are being developed at Durango, Carrillo Puerto (Querétaro) and El Framboyán (Veracruz).

The policy of establishing industrial estates has also been followed in Peru. The most successful has been the estate in Arequipa, where, in addition to financing certain industries of its own, the local development corporation succeeded in attracting several private companies. In this effort the corporation was assisted by considerable tax exemptions granted by the national government, but even so the establishment of a variety of industries making radios, dehydrated foodstuffs, pencils, adhesive tape and aluminium products represented a major success. In addition to this industrial estate, the development corporation also established a park for artisan industries (1968). Also effective was the establishment of a park in Tacna, near to the Chilean border, where a photographic company, a toy factory and a jewellery works had been set up by 1968. Three other estates were developed in the less prosperous cities of Cuzco, Juliaca and Puno. The intention behind all these parks was to attract industries oriented towards local skills and the processing of local resources.

Lastly, in Brazil, SUDENE have recently established an industrial estate at Aratu, on the outskirts of Salvador.

(IV) DIRECT STATE ENTERPRISE

The most effective method of achieving industrial decentralization has been for national governments to establish companies in less-privileged areas. The iron and steel industry has been a common candidate for such a policy, in large part because it depends on bulky raw materials. The siting of the state-owned plants at Huachipato (Chile), Volta Redonda (Brazil), Paz del Río (Colombia) and Chimbote (Peru) was influenced in each case by material availability.

The influence of material orientation has not been confined to the iron and steel industry: in Chile CORFO set up a paper mill and sugar-beet refineries in the south and a sulphuric-acid plant and a copper foundry in the north between 1950 and 1955.[60] In Colombia, too, various material-oriented enterprises were established by the Industrial Development Institute (IFI). Among these companies were a coconut-oil factory in San Andrés, a tanning plant in Riohacha, a caustic-soda plant in Cartagena and a sisal plant in Popayán.

Such a dispersal strategy would seem to be effective in as far as it combines three basic aims. Firstly, it allows governments to establish industries which private enterprise is unable or unwilling to provide. Secondly, it helps to develop unused raw-material resources. And, thirdly, it is a policy which can be directly effective in establishing industry in less-privileged areas. In the synchronous combination of several national and regional priorities this method represents an effective regional-development instrument.

For many years, industrial growth has been the main hope for rapid development in Latin America. It was hoped that industrialization would provide a major source of employment and would permit a gradual improvement in the average standard of living. In addition, it would release most Latin American countries from their dependence upon the developed world, by reducing their requirements of manufactured imports and thereby improving their balances of payments. Industrialization, therefore, represented a means by which the twin aspirations of nationalism and modernization could be achieved.

In most countries, however, the growth of manufacturing has not been sufficiently rapid to satisfy these aims. It has not generated adequate employment opportunities nor has it reduced the demand for imported goods. In part this failure has been due to the inability of Latin American industry to compete with established companies in the developed world. It has also been the result of many unwise policies adopted by the respective national governments. In many ways, however, industrialization has been a failure only because too much was expected of it. In terms of growth, individual countries such as Mexico and Brazil have experienced dramatic increases in the level of manufacturing production and employment. The problem has been that industrial growth has occurred too slowly to resolve the problems created by the rapid increase in population.

In spatial terms, the most important effect of industrial growth has been its tendency to concentrate in the largest cities. In turn, and as will be shown in succeeding chapters, this has led to an accentuation of regional-income differentials, and to highly concentrated distributions of social infrastructure.

Several national governments have attempted to modify this tendency and have made strong policy statements in favour of industrial dispersal. In Chile, the actions of CORFO between 1940 and 1955 led to a wider distribution of manufacturing, and in Brazil efforts are presently being made to develop industry in the north-east. In general, however, the problems facing governments have proved too great, and very few have persevered with decentralization policies. Many of these problems have been due to the fact that industry was in private hands. This meant that unpopular policies of dispersal, such as forcing companies to move outside the major centres, might be achieved only at the cost of slower industrial growth. Few governments have been prepared to face this possibility. Even where governments have attempted to control industrial location they have frequently been faced by unexpected problems. Chilean attempts to establish the motor industry in Arica, for example, were made more difficult by the growth of industries producing car components in the Santiago area. The growth of these plants, which had been deliberately fostered by the import-substitution process, eventually made Arica an unviable location for car manufacturing. This kind of difficulty has made most governments reluctant to compel companies to move to specific areas. Increasingly, therefore, they have relied upon indirect methods, such as the granting of income-tax concessions and the provision of basic physical infrastructure. On occasion, these incentives have been quite sophisticated, as in the 34/18 mechanism in Brazil. In general, however, the success of governments in persuading private companies to move to less desirable places has proved both expensive and unsuccessful. As a result, the tide towards the existing industrial complexes has increased year by year in most countries.

Only where governments have themselves established companies in the poorer regions has any real success been achieved. For, not only have these attempts resulted in higher employment in the poorer areas, but the industries thus established have been in sectors where the private sector had shown little interest. The policy, therefore, has managed to combine two objectives, one the regional one of decentralizing industrial activities, the second the national aim of encouraging industrial growth.

4: The Pattern of Urbanization

During the past twenty years social scientists have devoted a great deal of attention to the relationship between urbanization and developmental change. Unfortunately, this wealth of literature has failed to answer a number of critical questions. In particular we still know very little about how urban growth contributes to economic growth, about the most appropriate form that urbanization should take in a less developed country, or whether the acceleration of urban growth is a phenomenon which should be encouraged or discouraged. Such a situation is particularly serious in countries where urban growth is occurring rapidly and where governments are attempting to plan the course of development. Most Latin American nations fall squarely into this category.

Urban growth

During the past two decades the rate of urban growth throughout Latin America has been very rapid. By 1980, the share of the population living in urban areas is likely to have increased from 39·1 per cent in 1950 to 60·7 per cent[1]. Not surprisingly the urban population in most countries is increasing several times faster than that of the rural areas. Such accelerated urban growth, however, is of recent origin; before 1930 it was characteristic only of the southern regions, Argentina, Chile, Uruguay and southern Brazil. This growth pattern is clear from Table 11, where it can be seen that the number of people living in cities with more than 20,000 inhabitants was higher in Argentina, Chile and Uruguay at the time of the First World War than it is in most of the other nations today.

The early urbanization of the southern nations is explicable largely

Table 11: The Pattern of Urban Growth

Country	*Date*	*Per cent of population living in cities with:* *20,000 inhabitants or more*	*100,000 inhabitants or more*	*Per cent of population living in largest city*
Argentina	1914	38·0	31·5	25·8
	1947	49·3	40·0	29·7
	1960	57·7	47·5	33·7
Bolivia	1950	19·6	10·6	10·6
Brazil	1920	11·3	8·7	3·8
	1940	15·3	10·7	3·7
	1950	20·2	13·2	4·4
	1960	28·1	18·8	4·5
Chile	1920	28·0	18·4	13·6
	1930	32·5	20·7	16·2
	1940	36·4	23·1	18·9
	1952	42·8	28·5	22·7
	1960	54·7	33·3	25·9
Colombia	1938	13·2	7·5	4·1
	1951	23·0	15·4	6·2
	1964	36·6	27·5	9·7
Costa Rica	1927	19·3	—	19·3
	1950	22·3	22·3	22·3
	1960	24·0	24·0	24·0
Cuba	1919	24·3	14·7	14·7
	1931	27·6	18·5	16·0
	1943	30·7	19·9	17·4
	1953	35·5	22·9	18·3
Dominican	1920	3·5	—	3·5
Republic	1935	7·1	—	4·8
	1950	11·1	8·5	8·5
	1960	18·7	12·1	12·1
Ecuador	1950	17·8	14·6	8·1
	1962	26·9	18·9	11·2
El Salvador	1930	9·0	—	6·2
	1950	12·9	8·7	8·7
	1961	17·7	10·2	10·2
Guatemala	1950	11·2	10·2.	10·2
	1964	15·5	13·4	13·4
Honduras	1940	6·1	—	4·2
	1950	6·9	—	5·3
	1961	11·6	7·1	7·1

Table 11 (cont.)

Country	*Date*	*Per cent of population living in cities with:* 20,000 inhabitants or more	100,000 inhabitants or more	*Per cent of population living in largest city*
Mexico	1940	18·1	10·2	7·4
	1950	24·1	15·1	8·7
	1960	29·6	18·6	8·1
Nicaragua	1950	15·2	10·3	10·3
	1963	23·0	15·3	15·3
Panama	1930	22·3	—	15·8
	1940	26·5	19·4	19·4
	1950	28·6	22·1	22·1
	1960	33·1	25·4	25·4
Paraguay	1950	15·6	15·6	15·6
	1960	15·9	15·9	15·9
Peru	1940	14·2	8·4	8·4
	1961	28·9	18·4	14·5
Uruguay	1908	30·0	28·0	28·0
	1963	61·3	44·7	44·7
Venezuela	1936	17·0	11·1	7·8
	1941	18·7	12·4	9·2
	1950	32·7	20·6	13·8
	1961	47·3	30·0	17·8

Source: ECLA, *Economic Survey of Latin America*, 1967, pp. 41–2.

in terms of their different patterns of economic growth. As we saw in Chapter Three, economic expansion in Argentina and Uruguay was associated with the development of agricultural products catering for a rapidly increasing world demand. This economic growth generated high *per capita* incomes among a relatively large proportion of the population, as well as creating a large number of jobs in industry and commerce. In turn this pattern led to urban development. Similarly the development of the Chilean export sector created opportunities for non-agricultural enterprises and led to urban expansion in the north as well as in Santiago and Valparaiso.[2]

The early urban expansion of the southern nations was not matched elsewhere because export production created little direct or secondary employment. By the 1930s, however, additional countries had begun to experience rapid urban growth based in part on the expansion of exports; in Venezuela, for example, it was associated with the development of the petroleum industry. Urban growth was also stimulated throughout the continent by a general fall in the death rate and by attempts to industrialize through import-substitution. Naturally, these two processes did not have the same impact in every country or occur at the same time; industrialization in particular took much longer to begin in Central America than in Mexico or Colombia. But by the 1950s urban growth was occurring in most countries.

To a great extent, therefore, different levels of urban development

Fig. 8

today are related to past differences in growth. Urban development is most advanced in nations where rapid economic growth took place during the late nineteenth and early twentieth centuries. In nations where it began later, the major part of the population still lives in rural areas.

Different levels of urban development, however, are also a reflection of the distribution and density of population that existed before economic expansion began. In the southern nations, for example, population was sparsely settled compared with the relatively dense clusters of rural population found in Central and Andean America. Consequently, when economic growth occurred in the south,

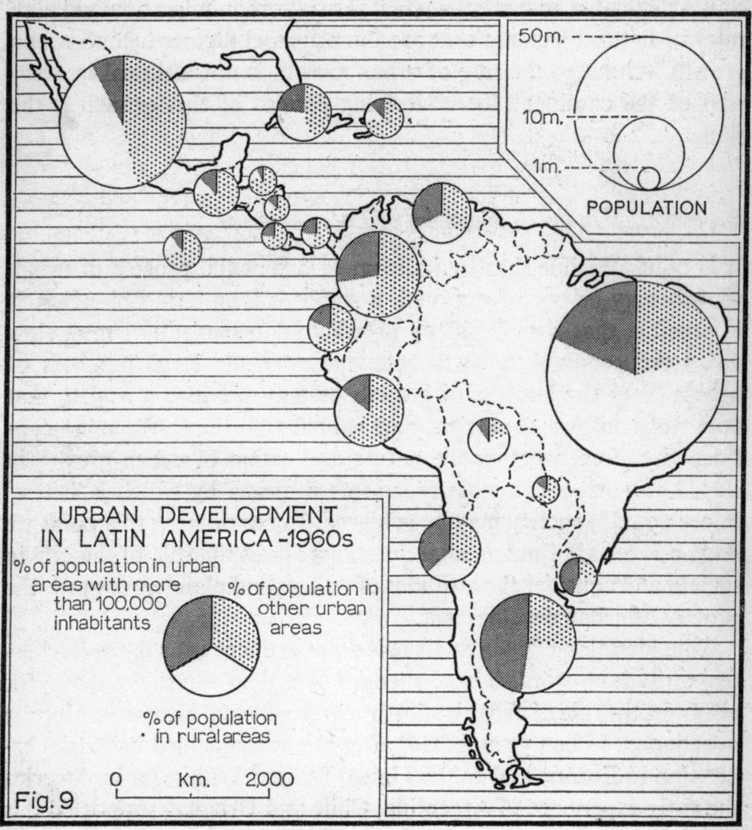

Fig. 9

urbanization was fed less by rural-urban migration than by immigration from Europe. This influx increased the total population of the area considerably, and as a result the share of the population living in urban areas increased quickly. When urbanization began further north, it was superimposed on a population concentrated mainly in the rural areas. Therefore, even though rapid rural-urban migration took place, the share of the population living in urban areas increased more slowly.

While the degree of urban development in the different countries differs widely, over time the process of urbanization has become increasingly similar throughout the continent. Today foreign immigration is negligible, and everywhere it is rural-urban migration and high rates of natural increase that are the principal factors behind urban growth. Although the rate of urban growth is not identical in every part of the continent the underlying pattern of that growth is the same.

Urbanization in the development of Latin America

It is quite possible that by its form or extent the process of urban growth may be out of step with a society's long-term objectives. It is possible that over-rapid or unbalanced urbanization may slow down the economic growth rate, may exclude large numbers of people from the benefits of growth or may produce a society that does not conform to ancient and valued traditions. We must consider, therefore, whether the nature and extent of urban growth in each Latin American state represents a means by which a 'better' (more equal?) society may be achieved. In considering this point we must ask certain fundamental questions about the role of the city in society and consider the attitudes of writers and planners towards the process of urban development.

Consideration of such an issue is very pertinent in as far as intellectual attitudes towards it have changed over time. Up to the 1950s, for example, the role of urbanization in developmental change was hardly questioned. Urban growth had, after all, accompanied industrial expansion in Europe and in the United States.[3] Within Latin America the early experience of Argentina, Chile and Uruguay supported this favourable interpretation. In addition, urban development in itself was seen as a further stimulus to the modernization of society. Through exposure to urban institutions, traditional attitudes to work, leisure, politics and family life would be modified; these changes would help people adjust to the needs of today. Hand in hand with urbanization would emerge a more prosperous and happier society.

Unfortunately the post-war experiences of Latin America and other less-developed areas did not seem to support this view. Various studies began to appear showing that urban growth was associated less with development than with the growth of shanty-towns, crime, unemployment and petty services. Seminars were held on the problems associated with urban growth and the conclusions were often highly pessimistic. Lerner, for example, summed up many of the 'benefits' of urban growth as follows: 'Every student of development is aware of the global spread of urban slums – from the "ranchos" of Caracas and "favelas" of Rio, to the "geceköndu" of Ankara, to the "bidonvilles" and "tin-can cities" that infest the metropolitan centres of every developing country from Cairo to Manila. The point that must be stressed in referring to this suffering mass of humanity displaced from the rural areas to the filthy peripheries of the great cities is that few of them experience the "transition" from agricultural to urban-industrial labour called for by the mechanism of development and the model of modernization. They are neither housed, nor trained, nor employed, nor serviced. They languish on the urban periphery without entering into any productive relationship with its industrial operations. These are the "displaced persons", the DPs, of the developmental process as it now typically occurs in most of the world, a human flotsam and jetsam that has been displaced from traditional agricultural life without being incorporated into modern industrial life.'[4]

Less emotively, but equally pessimistically, a UN/UNESCO seminar concluded that 'urban misery and rural poverty exist side by side, with the result that the city can hardly be "dynamic" as social historians of developed countries generally described the process'.[5] Authors such as Hoselitz began describing cities as being 'parasitic' and many others raised doubts about the idea that urban development was beneficial to the modernization of less-developed nations.[6]

These views were supported by findings from a number of statistical analyses of underdeveloped countries. One of the most pervasive of these findings was the concept 'over-urbanization'. This concept, which was based on cross-section studies of the relationship between *per capita* income, industrialization and urban development, suggested that the less-developed societies were deviating from the 'normal' path of modernization.[7] In particular, it was claimed that 'countries in the early stages of industrialization suffer an imbalance in both the size and distribution of their urban populations implying primarily that they have a higher percentage of people living in cities and towns than is "warranted" at their stage of economic growth'. The inevitable consequence of such a situation is the 'excessive migration of un- and under-employed folk to the cities in advance of the adequate expansion of urban employment opportunities'.[8]

This shortage of employment opportunities was tied in turn to the observation that the tertiary sector* was expanding rapidly in most developing countries. Unlike tertiary growth in developed societies, however, it represented a negative tendency, being typified by a proliferation of petty services such as boot-blacks, lottery salesmen and street vendors. The contribution of this tertiary growth was felt to be so limited that some writers even suggested that its output should be excluded from the national accounts.[9]

During the late sixties, however, new writing began to appear which questioned the over-urbanization concept.[10] Firstly, doubt was expressed about the association between urban and tertiary-sector growth. A recent study in Mexico, for example, showed that when urban growth in that country was at its fastest the tertiary sector was expanding less rapidly than industrial activities.[11] While this study did not disprove the hypothesis, it did generate additional doubts about the validity of the concept.

Secondly, the concept was criticized for failing to distinguish between tertiary growth *per se* and the growth of petty services and unemployment. This meant that it drew no distinction between the growth of useful services such as improved medicine, education and

*The tertiary sector normally includes: trade, finance, real estate, personal, business, domestic and professional services and government.

sanitation and the growth of the less-desirable boot-blacking and lottery sales. It also failed to take account of what the people performing petty services would have been doing otherwise. If the alternative was unemployment in rural areas and a life without access to social facilities, then the role of petty services in providing a limited opportunity for employment and for children to go to school might be seen as a positive force.

Thirdly, a major criticism of the over-urbanization thesis was that it failed to examine the structure of urban development. It implied that all urban growth takes place in primate cities and failed to recognize that the population of many provincial and intermediate cities also grows. This is important in that many of these smaller centres grow not on a basis of industrial expansion but for administrative and commercial reasons. In such centres, therefore, tertiary growth may represent a source of prosperity rather than a symptom of underemployment.

Partly as a result of such doubts, and partly as a result of the positive findings emerging from detailed studies of the urban poor (see below), urbanization is once again being seen as a process favourable to development. Writers are again stressing the value of urban economies or scale, particularly in the provision of infrastructure for industry, while others are pointing out that urban growth permits the more effective dispensation of social services. Currie has argued that services can be provided effectively only in urban areas and suggests that there is no real alternative open to democratic governments than to encourage greater numbers of people to move to urban centres.[12] Others point to the beneficial effects of urban growth on social and political attitudes. Friedmann, for example, has claimed that hyper-urbanization in Chile brought about 'a crisis of inclusion in which the majority of the Chilean people who had largely been excluded from the benefits of economic growth clamoured with increasing insistence for a drastic change in the structure of the social order'.[13] Similarly, Kahl has shown how urban facilities in Brazil and Mexico help families to realize long-held ambitions concerning family size and education.[14] Some writers have even suggested that urban growth should be accelerated as a deliberate developmental strategy.[15]

The size-distribution of urban centres

While urban growth is again seen in a more favourable light, one strand of the over-urbanization concept has persisted. This concerns the question whether the *form* of urban growth distorts the process of development; in particular, whether development is harmed by the fact that a large proportion of the urban population lives in one metropolitan centre.

Such a question is particularly important in Latin America, since 'no other major world region displays so consistently the pattern in which the primary or first city is many times larger than the second city'.[16] For, if we accept Browning's simple definition of primacy, it is clear that every Latin American country with the exception of Brazil, Colombia and Ecuador exhibits a primate distribution. In many cases, the degree of primacy is acute and shows signs of increasing. (See Table 12.) In Peru for example, Lima/Callao was thirteen times larger than Arequipa/Miraflores in 1961, compared to 'only' eight times larger in 1940. In Chile, Santiago was seven-and-a-half times larger than Valparaiso in 1960, compared to four-and-a-half times larger twenty years earlier. In Venezuela, Caracas was more than three times as large as Maracaibo in 1961, compared to more than twice as large in 1936. If we widen Browning's definition of primacy to include cases where two cities are many times larger than the third city, even Brazil and Ecuador cease to be exceptions. Of all the countries in the continent in fact, only Colombia demonstrates the 'rank–size' hierarchy which many writers deem to be desirable. In that case Bogotá is approximately twice as large as Medellín, three times the size of Cali and has four times the population of Barranquilla.

Unfortunately, while the pattern is clear, explanation of the phenomenon is not, even though many theories have purported to explain it. Linsky, for example, has suggested that primacy is associated with six general conditions. It is negatively associated with the areal extent of dense population, negatively associated with *per capita* income, positively associated with the economy's dependence on foreign trade, either positively or negatively associated with ex-colonial status, positively associated with the proportion of the work-force en-

Table 12: City-Size Distributions 1940–70
(thousands of persons)

	Argentina		*Brazil*		*Chile*		*Colombia*		*Ecuador*	
Position	*1950*	*1970*	*1940*	*1970*	*1940*	*1960*	*1938*	*1964*	*1950*	*1962*
1	4,500	8,400(1)	1,764	5,979(2)	952	1,907(1)	326	1,662(1)	259	511(1)
2	570	803(2)	1,326	4,316(1)	210	253(2)	150	911(3)	210	355(2)
3	426	791(3)	348	1,255(6)	86	148(3)	144	618(4)	40	60(3)
4	325	573(5)	290	1,084(3)	66	115(4)	88	493(2)	31	53(4)
5	256	556(4)	272	1,027(4)	50	88(6)	73	218(5)	30	42(5)
6			211	903(5)	49	84(10)	51	217(7)	19	34(6)
7			206	873(8)	43	72(8)	42	190(6)	16	33(11)
8			180	643(7)	42	68(5)	37	148(9)	15	32(7)
9			140	624(9)	38	65(7)	31	147(8)	14	29(17)
10			106	546(–)	36	61(11)	30	125(12)	14	28(10)

	El Salvador		*Mexico*		*Nicaragua*		*Peru*		*Venezuela*	
Position	*1950*	*1961*	*1940*	*1970*	*1950*	*1963*	*1940*	*1972*	*1941*	*1961*
1	162	256(1)	1,757	6,874(1)	109	235(1)	614	3,317,648(1)	354	1,336(1)
2	52	73(2)	236	1,196(2)	31	45(1)	77	304,653(2)	122	422(2)
3	27	40(3)	190	830(3)	21	29(1)	41	241,882(4)	55	199(4)
4	18	27(4)	148	522(4)	17	23(4)	37	189,685(6)	54	164(3)
5	18	24(6)	115	545(8)	13	22(5)	32	159,045(–)	33	135(5)
6	13	24(5)	104	436(21)	10	15(6)	32	126,702(10)	32	98(6)
7	10	15(7)	104	390(24)			27	120,881(3)	26	90(9)
8	10	15(12)	103	364(13)			21	115,693(7)	20	76(10)
9	10	13(10)	98	359(10)			21	111,327(5)	18	70(7)
10	10	13(8)	93	335(–)			19	73,883(9)	16	63(8)

Figures in brackets show each city's rank at the earlier date.
Source: Respective national censuses.

gaged in agriculture and positively associated with a rapid rate of population growth.[17] Unfortunately few of these hypotheses are applicable to Latin America, where primacy is found simultaneously in the richest and largest countries and in the smallest and poorest.

Equally unsuccessful were the two sets of hypotheses put forward by Berry to explain primacy on a world scale.[18] In the first group he tested whether high primacy was associated with high levels of urbanization and with economic development. In neither case was the hypothesis valid – a situation which would also have been true had Latin America been considered alone. In the second group, he argued that primate patterns were most likely to occur in countries which were smaller than average, had a short history of urbanization and were politically or economically simple. He also suggested that over time a primate-city distribution was likely to move towards a rank–size distribution. Unfortunately, there seems to be little validity in this second group of hypotheses either, at least as far as Latin America is concerned.

One of the major drawbacks of Berry's and Linsky's ideas was that they were both making static analyses of pattern rather than considering the underlying processes working towards primacy. More recently, however, another theory has been suggested which does employ a deductive framework to explain the processes which govern city-size distributions through time.

In this theory, Vapñarsky argues that the key variables affecting city-size distribution over time are 'interdependence' and 'closure'.[19] 'Interdependence' is concerned with the strength of inter-regional linkages within a national economy, while 'closure' refers to dependence upon international trade. His hypothesis is that societies tend to move in time from a situation of low interdependence and high closure, as in peasant societies, through low closure and high interdependence, as in modern Argentina, to a situation akin to that of the USA, with high interdependence and high closure. Associated with this transition are changes in the urban-size hierarchy (Table 13) – from a primate distribution, through a rank–size distribution in all centres below the primate centre, to a final position where a complete rank–size hierarchy is achieved.

There are, though, many problems associated with this model, the

Table 13: Variables Determining Urban Primacy and Rank–Size Distribution

		CLOSURE	
		high	*low*
INTERDEPENDENCE	*high*	rank–size rule applies to all cities (United States)	largest city or cities show primacy; rest follow rank–size rule (modern Argentina)
	low	no primate city nor clear rank–size pattern (underdeveloped, isolated areas)	primate city linking with outside world; no clear rank–size pattern for other cities (nineteenth-century Argentina)

Source: Adapted from Vapñarsky, C. A. (1969), 585.

most important being that, although it tentatively fits the Argentinian experience, it is less consistent with that of other Latin American nations. The rank–size hierarchy of Colombia, for example, emerged during the post-colonial period and had developed fully by 1918. At this time, however, there was little regional interdependence, as is suggested by the fact that the three largest cities of the country were not connected by road until 1940. In Peru and Chile, the city-size distributions would be expected to conform to the stage of high interdependence and low closure. But, although low closure is characteristic of both countries, high interdependence hardly describes the Peruvian situation, where a poorly developed road network, low volumes of interregional trade and its isolated *sierra* communities make it a good example of what Berry calls a 'poorly articulated economy'.[20]

While the Vapñarsky model does not explain the full range of circumstances which have encouraged primacy in Latin America it does explain part of the process. It also fits quite closely with the simple generalization of Davis that primacy is associated with the 'small size of the country, political centralization (including the combination of political, economic and ecclesiastical power), a "tributary economy", and location of the government in the primate city'.[21]

Though the first condition – small size of the country – is not valid in Latin America, most of the others are supported by a number of writers on Latin America. In particular, Romero, Liévano, Quijano, Mariátegui, Lieuwen, Furtado and others have all suggested that primacy has been closely associated with economic dependence and political centralism.[22] In Peru, for example, Lima's incipient primacy became an actuality only when political independence had been achieved and the nation became more fully integrated into the world trading community. The development of guano as a principal export led to the centralization of export revenues in the hands of the Lima government and weakened the provincial economies. Similarly, the growth of primacy in Venezuela during the past years has been closely associated with the development of the petroleum industry. The revenues from this industry not only made Venezuela highly dependent upon world trade but allowed the Pérez Jiménez régime (1950–58) to plough enormous sums of money into motorways, and government and residential buildings in the national capital.[23] On the other hand, Colombia, the only country where primacy did not develop, was also characterized by political centralism and export dependence. In that case, however, the national government did not manage to control the revenue generated by the principal export products, gold and later coffee. Rather the city of Medellín, through its monopoly over gold, and the main trade artery, the river Magdalena, prevented the national capital from controlling all parts of the economy.[24]

Primacy, therefore, has depended on a complex of factors associated with foreign trade and political and economic centralism. It has developed strongly in Latin America mainly because foreign dependence was established at an early date and was normally channelled through the largest and capital city.

Primacy – an aid or hindrance to development?

The question still remains unanswered whether it really matters if the majority of the urban population live in a primate centre. What are the economic costs and benefits related to this urban-size distribution, and the social and political associations which might make another form of distribution more desirable? To some extent, of course, the whole question is part and parcel of the arguments about equity versus efficiency and regional versus national development that are developed in other parts of this book. However, within this wider controversy there is a great deal of argument about the desired characteristics of a city-size distribution. Some writers see the primate city as a parasitic element in a developing nation. Others see it as the only true growth sector in a generally stagnant economy, while a third group feel that it is a transitional feature which is found only in countries at an intermediate stage of development.

On the benefits of the primate city there is a copious literature. In general, however, this literature emphasizes the economic advantages of primacy at the expense of the social. Bird, for example, referring to the Mexican situation, suggests that 'the growing urban centre is the leading "growth pole" in a developing country and should be encouraged not hampered'.[25] Taking up a complementary argument Wingo has asked whether primacy is not an excellent means by which capital resources can be preserved in a capital-scarce nation.[26] Since urban services and other infrastructures are expensive, primacy ensures that economies of scale are achieved. The alternative to primacy is to disperse services widely, with consequent losses of efficiency and *per capita* coverage. Such an argument has been supported by Browning with reference to geographically restricted nations with small populations such as Uruguay.[27] Lastly, Sjoberg has argued on a world-wide basis that 'very large urban concentrations (in contrast to medium-sized ones) permit groupings of scarce specialists (teachers, scientists, managers, and so on) in sufficient numbers to engage in effective pursuit of particular organizational, notably scientific, activities. The function of cities in heightening interpersonal communication – as a necessary condition for sustaining various kinds of social activity – is usually ignored by those who perceive the large metropolis as a hindrance to economic development.'[28]

Ranged against this set of opinions, however, are those of a growing number of writers who see primacy as a major handicap to the balanced development of poor nations. These writers argue that many primate cities have grown far beyond the point where economies of scale accrue, and have reached the position where there are increasing numbers of diseconomies. The evils of traffic congestion, water shortage, population overcrowding and air pollution are all symptoms of this excessive growth. And the costs of remedies which are being put forward to remove these evils, such as underground railways, expressways and popular-housing schemes, are far in excess of the budgets of developing nations. Related to these diseconomies are other economic costs emanating from primacy. In the first place, most primate cities are characterized by large concentrations of foreign diplomats, businessmen and consultants. These people live and work in a manner which enables the inhabitants to observe the products and way of life of the developed world and encourages high-level consumption patterns, the importation of 'superior' foreign products and has other deleterious effects. While this tendency is not confined to primate cities, Hoselitz and Spengler have suggested that 'universalistic, achievement-oriented social values' are more pronounced in primate cities.[29] Secondly, the concentration of private and public investment and expenditure in the primate city deprives other areas of funds. In many cases, this means that resources are not exploited which could be of great assistance to the economic growth of the nation. Lewis, for example, subscribes to this view and argues that there are many cases where 'the population of the town or region grows far beyond its proper economic size, at the expense of other regions where, from the economic point of view, investment of resources would be more productive'.[30] Most commentators, however, emphasize the economic less than the social consequences of primacy. To some writers, such as Griffin or Frank, primacy is a manifestation of the neglect suffered by rural areas.[31] The primate city is a symbol of the affluence of the few and of the poverty of the many. To them the primate city assists the development of a culture which is alien to the needs of the majority since it is strongly associated with capitalism, imperialism and exploitation. To others who desire the end of primacy, such as Odell and Friedmann, it is simply a question of human neglect and of the creation of a socially-divided society.[32]

Of course, the validity of these arguments varies from nation to nation and from ideology to ideology. The costs and benefits in a small socialistic state like Cuba may be very different from those in a large capitalist state like Brazil. It is possible, therefore, that either situation may suit the needs of particular societies. What has to be remembered, however, is that there can be no simple solution expressed only in terms of economic gains or losses. There is an important economic component in the debate about primacy, but the decision in favour or against can be made only in terms of social and ideological values.[33] Any simple solution that attempts to lay down generalizations for all societies will almost certainly be wrong.

Even so, there are circumstances where a strong case can be made for backing a decentralization policy. The primacy exhibited in Peru, Chile, Venezuela, Mexico and Argentina seems excessive. It has been fostered by artificial policies and strong elements of parasitism. Government policies to reduce city transport costs, maintain food prices and build up their services have helped these cities to expand at the expense of other regions. The workings of the world trading system and monopolies associated with it have concentrated the benefits of international commerce into these national centres. Primacy has developed not because of its suitability to the society but because it has been financed by poorer regions within the nation.

But if we accept that primacy may in some circumstances be an artificial form of urbanization, what kind of city-size distribution would be better? The one most frequently advocated is a distribution which accords to the rank–size rule (see p. 92), where the first city is twice the size of the second, three times that of the third and so on. However, despite some ingenious explanations of why such a distribution represents an 'ideal' pattern, the most convincing explanation for its frequent advocacy is that it is the distribution found in the United States of America. As a result, many claim that it demonstrates the position which many nations will eventually reach and that it would be advisable to strive for this position as soon as possible. To my mind this is no justification either for or against primacy.

What is needed is to examine not only city-size distributions but also their spatial patterns. There is some evidence to suggest that innovations, ideas, techniques, etc. diffuse from cities into rural areas as some function of accessibility.[34] If this is true, and a great deal of work is needed to substantiate or reject it, then an optimum distribution would involve not just one major city, but a series of intermediate centres supplying and stimulating the rural areas.[35] *

What also has to be demonstrated, before a more widely spread distribution of centres can be proposed, is that cities can stimulate their surrounding areas rather than simply exploit them. It may be that in one society widely dispersed cities may exact some innovative response from the surrounding areas, while in another this network of cities will serve merely as a more efficient means of exploitation. If the social structure is élitist and the government not dedicated to egalitarian ends, there is no reason to favour a widely dispersed any more than a primate distribution. The distribution of cities is secondary to the social situation. General suggestions, such as Lewis's that 'a workable approach to regional balance is to treat suspiciously all proposals for development in towns whose population exceeds 500,000, or has not yet reached 5,000', are simply irrelevant.[36]

Modifying the urban pattern – the importance of migration

Having suggested that there may be good reasons for modifying the pattern of urban growth, it is pertinent to ask whether such a policy can be effectively implemented.† In particular, it is necessary to understand how and why the present cities are growing and whether the present pattern of demographic growth lends itself to serious modification.

To the question why Latin American cities are growing, one expects the traditional reply that it is because people are moving in large numbers from the rural areas. In this case, it could be assumed that the most effective means of modifying the size and areal distributions of urban population would be to control migration. Un-

*Such a series of centres is not necessarily the same as a rank–size distribution. This can be shown by the example of the department of Antioquia in Colombia where the city of Medellín and its suburbs dominate a rural area with some two million inhabitants. Within a 200-kilometre radius there is no other city with more than 25,000 inhabitants.

† Methods of achieving a more balanced distribution will be discussed in more detail in Chapters Eight and Nine.

fortunately, the conventional wisdom reflects only part of a more complex truth. It is true that there are large numbers of migrants moving to the cities, but the most important element in city growth is no longer in-migration but natural increase within the cities themselves. According to Arriaga, for example, natural increase during the fifties accounted for 58·7 per cent of population increase in cities with more than 20,000 inhabitants in Mexico, Chile and Venezuela. In addition, the same author has even suggested that it is unlikely that internal migration is 'now greater than that observed at any time in the industrialized countries – it may even be smaller'.[37]

The cities have now reached a second stage of growth where the population is being accelerated by the natural increase of the migrants who arrived during the 1950s and 1960s. This process is demonstrated hypothetically in Table 14, where conservative parameters have been assumed regarding the rate of natural increase of the migrant population. Despite this conservatism and the assumption that migration continues as a constant proportion of the rural population, the role of natural increase in city growth can be seen to grow over a period of time.

In terms of urban planning, of course, the phenomenon makes any major modifications in city distributions that much harder to achieve. For, although it is *possible* to dissuade migrants from moving to particular cities, it is very difficult indeed to persuade the inhabitants of large cities to move elsewhere. This shift in migrant/natural-increase ratio towards the latter will make it far more difficult to influence the city-size hierarchy and distribution. Such a statement assumes that migrants to the largest cities can be dissuaded from moving there in the first place. Of course, this assumption is not necessarily correct, and the next section will be concerned with testing its general validity through an examination of who the migrants are, where they originate and why they move. Such an understanding is particularly important given the inaccuracy of so many of the beliefs about migrants.

Table 14: Hypothetical Relationship Between Natural Increase and Migration in City Growth

	Year t				
	1	*2*	*3*	*4*	*5*
Population beginning year (t)	100,000	109,000	118,450	128,369	138,776
Natural increase year (t)	3,000	3,270	3,554	3,851	4,163
Migration during year (t)	6,000	6,180	6,365	6,556	6,753
Population end year (t)	109,000	118,450	128,369	138,776	149,692
Share of growth from natural increase (%)	33·3	34·6	35·8	37·0	38·1
Share of growth from migration (%)	66·7	65·4	64·2	63·0	61·9
Growth of urban population (%)	9·0	8·7	8·4	8·1	7·9

Assumptions: Ratio in year one between migration and natural increase equals 2:1.
A constant and equal rate of natural increase in the city and the rural areas – 3 per cent per annum.

The migration movement

A popular stereotype of the migrant is that of a peasant who has been pushed out of the rural areas by an inability to support his family. In the rural areas the inequitable land-tenure system forced him to farm marginal land and eventually to quit the land altogether. He moved with his family to a nearby town, where he remained for a while searching for regular employment. Eventually, the shortage of work and the appeal of the 'bright lights' of the city attracted him to the largest metropolitan centre in the country. Even there his aspirations were thwarted by a lack of education, by widespread underemployment and by his lack of contacts. As a result he was forced to live in a shanty-town on the edge of the city, to work as a bootblack or a newspaper vendor, and seriously to consider returning to his original home.

This stereotype is an accurate picture not of the average migrant, but of the least fortunate. Certainly, it does not conform to the empirical evidence which now depicts the average migrant as being better educated, better informed and from a higher occupational background than many of his fellows in the rural areas. Perhaps the most important conclusion to be drawn from this evidence is that migrants are drawn from all classes and all kinds of environments, and move for varying reasons with different levels of aspiration and different chances of success. Most important of all, however, is the fact that migrants do not move out of ignorance but make rational decisions based upon information supplied by family and friends already living in the cities. In short, they are not victims of their environment as much as active participants in developmental change.

The origins and destinations of migrants

(a) *Rural versus urban origins.* A number of studies made in different countries show that few generalizations can be supported regarding the origins of migrants. Certainly, there are large numbers who move from rural areas to cities, but there are also many who move from one city to another. This confused pattern, made worse by the

Table 15: Migrant Origin: Rural or Urban Places

City	*Pattern*	*Author of Study*
São Paulo	51% urban areas	
São Paulo	75% of semi-skilled and unskilled from agricultural areas	Morse (1971)
Recife	76% from towns, 9% from villages, 16% from rival areas	
Santiago	28% from settlements with less than 5,000 inhabitants	Elizaga (1966)
Guatemala City	60% males from settlement with more than 2,000 inhabitants	Roberts (1970)
Rosario (Argentina)	12·8% from rural areas, 12·4% from cities with more than 100,000 inhabitants	Testa (1970)
Monterrey (Mexico)	56% from settlements with less than 5,000 inhabitants	Browning & Feindt (1969)
Barranquilla (Colombia)	60% from settlements with less than 1,500 inhabitants	Havens & Usandizaga (1966)
Bogotá	71% from settlements with less than 1,500 inhabitants 12% from settlements with more than 20,000 inhabitants	Flinn & Converse (1970)

diversity of measures used to define urban settlements, is demonstrated in Table 15, where empirical evidence from a number of studies and countries is presented.

(b) *Geographical proximity*. A number of studies have come to the conclusion that accessibility affects the likelihood that a person will migrate. In general, it has been found that the farther a person lives from a city the lower the probability that he will move. Herrick, for example, found that there was a close linear relationship between migration and distance in Chile.[38] In the case of several Bogotá slums, Flinn and Converse found that 'a majority of the residents of the barrios were born and/or moved to Bogotá from within a 100-mile radius of the city'.[39] Similarly, in Guatemala City, Roberts found that 57 per cent of the males had originated from contiguous departments, and in Barranquilla (Colombia) 90 per cent of the inhabitants of three *barrios* had originated in the same or in the two neighbouring departments.[40]

Some studies have also appeared which cast doubt on this relationship. Adams' study of several *municipios* in Colombia, for example, led him to believe that distance was less important in determining migration flows than local opportunities. In addition, Schultz's multiple-regression analysis of population movement in the same country led him to the view that 'young men and women living in remote towns are more likely to migrate from their community than are those living close to a big city'.[41] Unfortunately, there are certain statistical deficiencies in both of these studies which may have encouraged false conclusions. (Adams' analysis did not take account of class, education or income differences. Schultz's regression analysis took insufficient account of multicollinearity.) What they do both show, however, is that distance is only one factor among several which affect the pattern of migration.

Among these other factors is one that is very important, namely the size and power of attraction of individual cities. While large numbers of migrants from all parts of Brazil are to be found in Rio de Janeiro, nearly all migrants found in Niterói, across the bay, have come from the surrounding state. A similar pattern has been found in Peru, where the frictional effect of distance is important for the smaller cities and towns, but had a lesser effect upon migration to Lima.

These findings about the effect of distance and city size on migration suggest that analysis would be better served by combining these two elements into a simple model. Such a model does in fact exist and has been used in several geographical and sociological studies to analyse movements of people, traffic, telephone calls and other kinds of flows.[42] It is known as the gravity model and hypothesizes that the probability of interaction between two centres is a positive function of their combined size (mass) and a negative function of the distance between them (frictional effect). These elements are expressed in the following formula:

$$\frac{P_i P_j}{d_{ij}} = M_{ij}$$

where
M_{ij} is the predicted volume of migration between i and j
$P_i P_j$ is the product of the population of settlements i and j
d_{ij} is the distance between the two centres

A more sophisticated model may be obtained by weighting the different elements. The population of the cities may be weighted by *per capita* income, or distance by an empirically derived exponent as in the following form:

$$R \cdot \frac{r_i P_i . r_j P_j}{d_{ij}{}^b} = M_{ij}$$

where
r_i = regional income
b = empirically derived exponent
R = constant

The application of such a simple model would not explain the processes underlying migration, but it would provide a more effective method of testing the roles of distance and city size. (To the author's knowledge it has been employed only in Colombia and then more as a tool of regionalization than for predicting migration flows.[43]) In addition, the results would be very useful in establishing which areas were producing higher than average and which lower than average flows of migrants. Subsequent analysis could then concentrate upon establishing the reasons behind such anomalies.

(c) *The societal contest.* In interpreting why some areas attract migrants and others are subject to heavy out-migration, there is little evidence to rely on. However, one can generalize fairly safely about why people migrate to certain centres – the normal motivation being to gain access to employment opportunities and social facilities available only in the cities. One can almost generalize that any city with 100,000 inhabitants is likely to attract migrants, and many other cities with less than this number will be centres of attraction under certain circumstances. The key variable seems to be the general dynamism of the centre relative to the rural areas, a feature that can be present even in migration to small towns. There are, for example, many instances of small towns which have grown rapidly owing to the presence of new employment opportunities. One example is Chimbote in Peru, where the population grew from 4,243 in 1940 to 159,045 in 1972, owing to the opportunities created by the foundation of the fish-meal and iron and steel industries. Similarly, in Colombia the *municipio* of Turbo grew from 14,434 persons in 1951 to 69,420 in 1964 as a result of the expansion in banana production and increased land colonization in the area. A third example of such towns are two *municipios* in Pernambuco (Brazil), which act as 'catchment towns' for migration to Recife, the nearest large city. They became centres of attraction owing to the employment offered by two large textile mills.

These are all specific examples of towns which have attracted migrants. They do not provide a basis on their own for an explanation why certain areas are centres of out-migration and others of in-migration. One attempt, though, has recently been made to do this in terms of the nature of the local society.[44] Forni and Mármora suggest that levels of migration are determined by the socio-economic structure. This is filtered through the pervading social climate, which in turn governs the level of out- or in-migration. This social climate can be depicted on two axes (Table 16). The first is the level of acceptance of innovation in the community, a variable that runs from open to closed. The second depicts the social norms in the community, a variable that runs from integrated to disintegrated. The hypothesized flows which emerge from this framework are as follows. Open, integrated communities, which tend to be associated with 'dynamic

Table 16: Community Types and Migratory Tendencies in a Rural Zone of Argentina

SOCIAL NORMS	ACCEPTANCE OF INNOVATION *open*	*closed*
integrated	DYNAMIC DEVELOPMENT standards of business and consumption changing; cumulative investments create new jobs; gross and *per capita* production rising; new technology adopted; IMMIGRATION ATTRACTED	REGRESSIVE standards of business and consumption unaffected; technology and gross product unchanging; *per capita* consumption falling; natural population growth; NO EMIGRATION
disintegrated	SUBORDINATE DEVELOPMENT standards of business and consumption changing; investment fails to create new jobs; gross product study; *per capita* income rising; EMIGRATION	STATIONARY business norms unaffected; no investments; technological change variable; gross product steady; consumption patterns changing and *per capita* consumption falling; EMIGRATION

Source: Adapted from Forni, F., and Mármora, L. (1967), 23.

development' will generally attract migrants, while open, disintegrated communities which are associated with 'subordinate development' will normally produce emigration. The heaviest out-migration, however, will be from those communities where there is a closed but disintegrated society and where the economic situation is 'stationary'. Lastly the fourth type of community, the integrated, closed community, which is characterized by 'regressive development', will neither lose nor gain population.

These hypotheses have been tested only for rural Argentina, but they are intellectually appealing and seem to fit the evidence of other studies in that country where no correlation has been found between rural poverty and the tendency to migrate.[45] *Prima facie*, they also seem to provide a reasonable explanation for other areas. In Peru, they may explain why the department of Puno, although it is 'the most densely populated [department] in the country and has suffered . . . severely from repeated drought and subsequent famines . . . [has] produced the least number of migrants'.[46] Has this reduced rate of out-migration been associated with the local kind of society and economy? Have the problems of language and culture reduced the attractions of Lima and other large towns for the Indian peasants? Research along these lines, together with investigations through gravity models, may lead to greater understanding than we have today.

How the migrants move

One aspect of the migration process that has received a great deal of documentary attention is concerned with the way in which migrants move. Theoretically, there are three ways: by direct movements, by step migration and by fill-in migration. Direct migration is the process whereby a migrant moves from his original home to his final destination in a single stage. Step migration differs in that the migrants stop in one or more other places while moving from the original home to the final destination. (On occasions, of course, these steps may be rapid and the difference between step and direct migration less important.) Lastly, fill-in migration describes the process whereby migrants move from one home to another, and their children or even younger brothers and sisters move on to new destinations. Fill-in migration, therefore, takes place over a longer period of time, with one generation making the first set of moves and another generation the final steps.

There are a variety of reasons why these distinctions have been analysed in great detail. In the first place, many writers have been interested to compare the migration process as manifest in Latin America with that in Europe during the industrial revolution. In the latter, most population movements seemed to fit into the step-migration pattern, especially where there were strong expulsion factors, such as the enclosure movement. In Latin America, however, there seemed to be a greater number of direct migrations, permitted perhaps by the cheaper transport available in twentieth-century

Latin America compared to nineteenth-century Europe. In the second place, attention focused on the nature of the movement because it was likely to affect the social, cultural and political attitudes of the migrants. The migrant who moved directly from a rural environment to a major city was likely to have less sophisticated or 'urban' attitudes compared to the migrant who had moved in stages. The latter might have moved from the countryside to a small town, where he would experience many changes in his life pattern. When he finally moved to the metropolitan centre he would be more accustomed to city life than would the person moving directly from the rural areas.

Table 17: The Evidence for Step Migration

Country (*City*)	*Experience*	*Author*
Bogotá *barrios*	58·3% went directly to Bogotá 30·4% made one or two stops *en route* 11·3% made three steps or more	Flinn & Converse (1970)
Bogotá	54% made one or more stops *en route* but of these 66% completed migration in one year	Flinn & Cartano (1970)
Guatemala City	73% of migrant sample moved directly to city	Roberts (1970)
Cali	76% moved directly to the city	Valencia (1965)
Colombia	In general rejects step migration	McGreevey (1968)
Buenos Aires	At least one third made one or more intermediate steps	Germani (1958)
Bogotá	70% of rural sample moved directly to the city	Reyes (1964)
Barranquilla	50% made stops between home and the city	Havens & Usandizaga (1966)
Santiago	Migrants moved generally in stages	Herrick (1965)
Santiago	50·8% of males arriving at the age of 14 or more moved directly to the city	Elizaga (1966)

On the basis of abundant documentary evidence, some of which is listed in Table 17, Morse has summarized the Latin American experience as follows: 'Without forgetting regional discrepancies, one can plausibly generalize that (1) only one quarter to one third of the migration to large cities occurs in stages, (2) direct migration from rural and semi-rural places to large cities, while not unusual, cannot account for the balance of the migratory movement.'[47] He therefore accepts that fill-in migration is very important. Certainly this last kind of movement has been documented for Argentina (Margulis), Colombia (McGreevey) and Chile (Herrick).[48]

Despite the arguments in support of this kind of analysis, it serves less purpose than studies which split up movements into social, educational and class elements. For without detailed analysis of this kind, few conclusions can be drawn about the reactions and attitudes of people on reaching their final destinations, or the reasons why they failed to stay in their original homes. Highly aggregated analyses are also negligent in that they fail to examine whether people from different social, occupational and educational backgrounds move in different ways. Intuitively, at least, one would expect those migrants with good educational and class backgrounds to move directly from origin to destination in one move. On the other hand, the poor and less-educated migrant would be expected to move in stages, gradually accumulating experience and income on his way to his final destination. And yet studies using highly aggregated populations do not investigate these differences and thereby contribute little to our knowledge of the migration process.

The characteristics of migrants

(a) *Education levels.* According to our popular stereotype of the migrant, the average person who moves to a large city has received little in the way of formal education. The evidence at hand, however, suggests that this is not true of all migrants, and the average migrant would seem to be better educated than his fellows who fail to move. In Colombia Adams found that 'in each of the seven out-migration areas studied, the average level of education of non-migrants was significantly lower than for the migrants'.[49] He does, however, draw a major distinction between different kinds of migrants. While those who moved to cities had relatively high education levels, those who moved to nearby villages had 'education levels as low or lower than non-migrants'.[50] The case of Guatemala City provides additional support for the idea that cityward migrants are relatively well educated. Roberts found that 'of all migrants to the city who are seven and over, 31 per cent have no formal schooling as compared with approximately 74 per cent of the total provincial population of that age. Of migrants, 15 per cent reached secondary education or higher while 1 per cent of the total provincial population aged seven and over attained these levels.'[51] Lastly, in a sample drawn from the *barriadas* of Lima, Lowder comments that the educational level of migrants' fathers was much higher than that of the nation as a whole.[52] (See Table 18.)

Table 18: Education Levels of Migrants

(per cent of interviewed sample)

	Guatemala City migrants[1]	*Bogotá barrios*[2]	*Lima barriadas*[3]	*Santiago migrants*[4]	*San Salvador migrants*[5]
No formal education	34	27	20	6	10
Some primary education (1–3 years)	41	51	11	52	36
Primary education (4–5 years)	10	15	4		20
Some secondary education		3	50	6	24
Secondary	15		11	29	
University		0	4	8	10
Unknown		4	0		
Total interviewed	118	319	432		

1. Roberts, B. R. (1970).
2. Flinn, W. L., and Converse, J. W. (1970).
3. Lowder, S. (1970).
4. Herrick, B. H. (1965).
5. Balan, J. (1969).

(b) *Class background.* The social background of most migrants, like their educational background, does not accord with popular myth. The average migrant comes from a higher class than the average non-migrant.[53] Naturally, there are large numbers of peasants from impoverished rural areas who do migrate. But, as Lowder has pointed out as regards Peru, 'what has been overlooked is that such migrants are rare in Lima – barely 10 per cent of the CISM sample obviously came from such humble and desperate backgrounds'.[54]

(c) *Family and marital status.* The empirical evidence suggests that there is greater regional variation in whether people move before marriage or after than in other aspects of population movement. In some studies the greater number have moved while single, especially where women moving to the cities to undertake domestic work make up a large proportion of the sample. An interesting aspect of the migration of families concerns whether they move together (simultaneous migration) or separately (split migrations). The object of the split migration is to allow the head of the family to move to the city to obtain work and shelter before his family's arrival. In the only study which has specifically examined this question, 20 per cent of the migrations to Monterrey (Mexico) were solitary (that is without dependants), 38 per cent were simultaneous and as many as 42 per cent were split migrations (with the dependants following the head of the family at a later date.)[55] These figures are likely to be very different for other regions and nations, and no general tendency can yet be observed.

(d) *Age composition.* There seems little doubt that the majority of migrants are young. Certainly the average age of migrants has normally been less than that of resident populations and most migrants have been concentrated in the younger working-age brackets, although this tendency has probably now been affected by the large numbers of children growing up in the cities. Several studies have indicated that the majority have arrived before the age of thirty. In Colombia, for example, Adams found that 90 per cent of the migrants who had left seven rural *municipios* had done so before they reached that age.[56] Similarly, in the case of Santiago, Herrick found that six out of ten migrants arrived before their twenty-sixth birthday.[57]

(e) *Sexual composition.* Even more than its comparative youth, the migrant population is characterized by its large female component. According to Lowder there were 111 migrant women in the age group 15–45 in Lima to every 100 residents in that category.[58] In the case of

Guatemala City, 'female migrants exceed male migrants and create an imbalance in the urban sex-ratio (the urban sex-ratio is 767 with a heavy imbalance in the age groups 10–29)'.[59] In Argentina, Germani suggested that it is the women who are most likely to move.[60] And in Santiago among migrants between 15 and 24 there were only 64 men to every 100 women.[61]

This predominance of females is in marked contrast to most other parts of the less-developed world where more men migrate than women. The difference probably rests in the differing social and economic structures in the different areas. There is, however, some evidence leading to the suggestion that geographical proximity may differentially affect the number of men and women who migrate. In Colombia, for example, Adams found that 'in remote areas it was generally more difficult for females to migrate long distances than for males. Entrance into the military service was a method for young men to migrate from remote areas. On the other hand, the girls who lived near large cities could more readily obtain employment as domestics, clerks and industrial workers'.[62]

To summarize this general evidence, the migrants appear, in comparison with non-migrants, to be quite well educated, to come from a higher class background and to be quite young. Other characteristics are that they are as likely to be married as single, more likely to be female than male, and are likely to have relations in the city and to have visited the city before arrival. However, in order to prevent a new stereotype emerging, a warning is necessary – there are major regional and temporal variations. The patterns are not identical in Brazil and Mexico. Nor, as Browning and Feindt point out, 'can we assume that in a fast-changing society . . . the patterns we find for one particular time will be present in another'.[63]

Migration motives

Studies of migration motives have relied principally upon questionnaires asking people why they moved. Normally the compilers of these surveys have interviewed migrants living in the largest cities rather than attempting the more difficult task of questioning potential migrants.[64] There is some danger, therefore, that *post-hoc* rational-

Table 19: The Motives for Migration (percentages)

Motive	*Lima*	*Arequipa*	*Chimbote*	*El Carmen Bogotá*	*Bogotá*	*Barranquilla*	*Monterrey*	*Santiago*
Economic	61	60	73	47	34	62	70	59
Family/social	23	25	20	17	51	21	17	12
Study & education	9	7	1	4	6	3	7	10
Health	3	4	3	4	0	3		
Rural violence				13	1	0		
Housing	1	1	1		0	7		
Boredom/dissatisfaction				4				
Military service	4	2	0	4	1	0		
Others	1	1	3	7	7	4	6	19
Sample size	22,461	1,797	1,230	106	121	150	810	1,080
Author	Matos Mar (1968)			Flinn and Cartano (1970)	Reyes (1964)	Havens and Usandizaga (1966)	Browning and Feindt (1970)	Elizaga (1966)

izations have been included in many of the replies. Nevertheless one cannot help but be impressed by their overwhelming homogeneity.

As can be seen in Table 19 the major motivation behind migration is economic. Of the eight sets of analyses in this table only two found more than 41 per cent of their sample who had moved for non-economic reasons. Despite this high degree of homogeneity, care should be taken in interpreting these results, since the 'economic' rationale is likely to contain a variety of different motives. In addition, although the economic factor may be the final and definitive motivation, migrants might not have moved had other motives been unsatisfied. The desire for work may be the main factor influencing a migrant, but without the presence of relations in the city he may not be prepared to risk moving. The presence of relations allows him temporary accommodation, contacts and information, and, while it may be a secondary factor, it may well ease his response to the primary motivation. Similarly, the availability of health and education facilities in the urban areas, although a secondary motive for most migrants, is still likely to influence his decision to move.

The migrant in the city

(I) OCCUPATION AND EMPLOYMENT

One less well-documented aspect of the migration process concerns the nature of job opportunities open to migrants in the cities. The popular view of migrant employment suggests that the majority work in marginal services and trades. However, it should be quite apparent from the above discussion that many migrants are relatively well qualified and are therefore eligible for non-manual and even management jobs. The popular view is also incorrect in as far as it suggests that the opportunities open to migrants are inevitably inferior to those open to residents.

In this latter context, it is interesting to consider the schema of Balan,[65] who has suggested that two paired sets of variables can explain the major variations in migrant experience (Table 20). Ac-

Table 20: Ability of Migrants to Obtain Employment in Urban Areas (After Balan)

Classification of communities of origin

	Rural	*Urban*
Stagnant	Large pool of low status, poorly educated migrants	Relatively large numbers of qualified personnel
Developing	Few, qualified migrants	Large numbers of highly qualified personnel

Classification of communities of destination

		Credentialism	
		Low	*High*
Rate of creation of jobs in sectors of high productivity	*Low*	Indeterminate – original differences between migrants and natives remain	Maximum differential between migrants and opportunities for migrants
	High	Many opportunities for migrants – few differences between natives and migrants	Fewer opportunities for migrants, employment differentials between natives and migrants

cording to the first set of variables the probability of obtaining employment depends greatly upon the kind of environment from which migrants come. Migrants from developing urban areas are more likely to be educated than those from a stagnant rural area, and stand a higher chance of obtaining better jobs.

The likelihood of obtaining jobs, however, does not depend only upon their relative skills and education. Balan suggests that it depends also upon the formal entry requirements which are built into the employment structure; he calls the latter 'credentialism'. 'This variable is of strategic importance in the present context, since migrants more often than natives lack the proper credentials. They may know how to read and write, but they lack the primary-school certificate. They may be hard workers, but they lack a letter testifying to this fact. They may be skilled in their jobs, but they find it difficult to become members of the union that controls the jobs. Therefore, the more important credentials become, the more handicapped migrants tend to be.'[66] In addition, migrant employment opportunities will depend upon the rate of job creation in higher-productivity sectors in urban areas. According to this paired set, therefore, migrants are more likely to obtain employment and employment commensurate with their ability in those cities where there is a high rate of job creation and a low level of 'credentialism'.

Taking the two sets of variables together the worst situation for migrants is one where 'a larger proportion of them come from rural areas, their lack of credentials handicaps them in occupational structures that place a high value on credentials, and a fast rate of population growth is not matched by an equally fast rate of creation of desirable jobs'.[67]

There can be little doubt that this schema does characterize some of the situations found in different Latin American cities. In Santiago, for example, there is a high level of urban–urban migration and reasonable opportunities for the rural populace to attend schools. This situation is reflected in the relatively similar employment structure of migrants and natives in the city (Table 21). One interesting aspect of this table is that migrants occupy more of the highest-status jobs and more of the lowest. A similar occupational distribution is found in Guatemala City, where there were no obvious differences between the education levels of migrants and natives and no serious restraints posed by credentialism. In Mexico City, too, there was no major difference in the occupational structure, despite the fact that the educational level of most migrants was inferior. In contrast, it appears that in São Paulo, despite the high standard of migrants and the rapid rate of industrial growth, difficulties were encountered by migrants owing to demands for formal qualifications.

These analyses of migrant adjustment to the urban milieu say little about one factor which may be of major importance in certain cities – ethnic differentiation. As suggested earlier, racial prejudice does exist in Latin America and does affect labour recruitment. This

Table 21: Employment Structure of Natives and Migrants in Selected Cities

	Santiago		Mexico City		San Salvador		Guatemala City	
	Native	*Migrant*	*Native* (30–44 years)	*Migrant* (30–44 years)	*Native*	*Migrant*	*Native*	*Migrant*
Professionals & technicians	8·0	10·3	7·2	6·7	11·4	10·6	7·8	7·8
Owners and managers	9·3	14·5			1·5	2·0	5·7	5·3
Office workers	11·4	11·6	18·1	15·9	11·9	13·0	8·3	8·6
Salesmen	12·1	9·7	15·8	15·9	6·7	12·0	7·6	7·3
Drivers and deliverymen	7·5	5·0	5·8	10·1	8·7	13·3	7·9	10·1
Farmers and miners	1·3	2·1	48·8	43·4	1·7	2·9	5·0	5·9
Artisans and operatives	35·1	29·5			49·3	35·5	46·2	33·2
Unskilled manual	4·6	4·8					5·5	8·4
Personal service	7·9	11·3	6·1	7·9	6·7	8·4	1·9	10·7
Unclassified	1·6	0·9			2·2	2·4	4·2	2·6
Seeking work for first time	1·2	0·3						

Source: Morse, R. (1971).

is very noticeable where racial differences are combined with differences of language, as is the case in most of the countries with an Indian population. Whether this prejudice is directed against migrants more than the resident population will depend on the racial balance of the migrants *vis-à-vis* the local population. For, if the racial mixture is the same in both, then it is unlikely to be important compared to the factors discussed above. This is certainly the case in the southern nations, where racial differences are in any case very small. It is less likely to be true in countries such as Peru and Bolivia, where there are important racial differences between the rural and the urban groups. As yet, no definitive statement can be made on the role of racial differentiation, for the simple reason that so few migration studies have considered this question.

(II) THE HOUSING AND DISTRIBUTION OF MIGRANTS

Having moved to a major city, the migrant is faced with the problem of finding a home. Limited income is likely to preclude the poorer migrant from purchasing accommodation and so his choice rests between renting a room or constructing his own dwelling. Many writers have suggested that the latter is the inevitable reaction and that the migrant builds his shack on a vacant patch of land in a peripheral shanty-town. It is becoming increasingly clear, however, that this is not the normal pattern. A variety of studies have shown that most shanty-towns are occupied not by recent migrants but by people born in the city and by migrants with several years' experience in the city. In a study of three *barrios* in Barranquilla, for example, it was found that only 30 out of 169 people interviewed had not lived previously in another part of the city.[68] All of the others had made one move or more, with the majority, 93, having made two moves or more. In the case of the Caracas *ranchos*, 'close to 100 per cent came from *barrios* within the city, not from the countryside' and in the case of one Lima *barriada* 'the average time of residence in Lima for heads of families was nine years, and practically none of them had been in Lima less than three years'.[69] A similar pattern was found by studies in Santo Domingo, Mexico City, Guatemala City, Bogotá, Montevideo, Santiago and Rio de Janeiro.

If the newly arrived migrants do not move directly to the shanty-towns, where do they go? One answer seems to be that they move to rented accommodation close to the city centre. Such accommodation, while inadequate for long-term occupation, does provide an initial base from which to search for a job. Through multi-family occupation it also has the advantage of low outlays; individual families often occupy single rooms in large houses originally designed for higher-income families who have moved to other parts of the city. And, through their proximity to the city-centre, the costs and inconvenience of travel are often minimized. As anything more than short-term accommodation, however, these *conventillos, vecinidades, corticos*, etc. are entirely unsuitable. They are rarely provided with adequate services – especially those in the older-style housing arranged around a central patio. They are normally over-crowded, pose a constant drain on limited incomes and do not provide their inhabitants with any security. Unfortunately, some families are forced to remain in these places; especially large families and those without a male income-earner. It is here that the worst conditions are found in Latin American cities.

In comparison with these inner-core slums the squatter settlements sometimes represent a major improvement. While the inner-core slums can only deteriorate until they are eliminated, the *barriadas* are seen increasingly as a partial solution to the housing problems of the cities. One reason why the image of squatter settlements has changed is that more detailed studies have shown that their inhabitants succeed in improving the settlements over time.[70] In particular, such studies have shown that those who live in them are highly organized, are seldom drawn from one social class and make considerable investments in their humble abodes.

The degree of organization in the settlements is frequently very impressive – often owing to the manner in which they were established. Many squatter settlements, in fact, have been formed through an organized process of invasion whereby a group of settlers have built their houses illegally on land belonging to other people or public institutions. Often the planning behind these invasions has been meticulous; the land has been sub-divided ahead of the actual invasion, and occupation has taken place overnight or on a holiday when the authorities have been least able to prevent it. Not all squatter settlements, however, have been formed in such a way. In many cases the settlers have purchased the land from private owners – often at a high price per hectare – and have constructed their houses on this land although they have rarely applied for planning permission. In some cities most housing is of this kind; in Bogotá it accounts for 50 per cent of all housing.

Whichever form of occupation has been followed, however, the level of *barrio* organization has normally been high. This is because every squatter area needs to approach government agencies to acquire public services such as water and light. Even if they do not succeed in obtaining such help many organizations serve to assist in the provision of the squatter's own communal services. And it is only when the squatter settlements become increasingly absorbed into the city, or as political and personal rivalries grow, that the organizations finally tend to dissolve. Usually by this time the squatter settlement is well on its way to becoming an ordinary working-class suburb of the city. The do-it-yourself housing may take many years to complete, but it does represent a sizeable investment for many of the inhabitants and a hedge against inflation. The houses, too, although giving the impression of being slums to visitors from developed nations, will sometimes be filled with consumer durables such as television sets and radios.

The stereotyped view about migrants and squatter settlements, therefore, is quite wrong. Squatter settlements are not filled mainly with recent migrants but with people who have been in the city for some period of time and who have been able to participate in some invasion or squatter organization.* The settlements suffer very severe problems, but they are not areas of extreme deprivation, starvation and disease. If such areas exist, they are nearer the centre of the cities,

*Even this pattern is beginning to change. For, as public authorities and commercial developers change the face of the city-centres, less rented accommodation becomes available. At the same time, the inhabitants of older-established shanty-towns begin to rent out rooms in their own houses. Increasingly, therefore, the migrants are moving not to the central-city cores but to older shanty-towns which have now become ordinary working-class districts of the city.

where families occupy limited rented accommodation and do not own houses, as do most squatters. The squatter settlements themselves seem to be areas of gradual improvement, of organization and of mixed employment structure.

Another preconceived idea about the squatter settlements relates to their location within the city; most studies suggest that they are situated on the edge of the city or on less desirable sites such as steep hillsides. To an extent this is true, but changes do occur in this pattern as the city grows. Settlements established on the edge of the city may ten years later find themselves relatively close to the city centre owing to the expansion of new building beyond them. Such a process has occurred in Caracas, where a variety of squatter settlements are very near to the major employment centres, while the higher-class residential areas are strung out along the motorway system up to ten miles from the old city core.[71]

The impression should not be given, however, that Latin American cities consist entirely of slum and squatter settlements, nor that the respective national governments have done nothing to provide housing. In some cases new cities like Brasília and Ciudad Guayana consist largely of public housing. In general, however, public action has not been directed at solving the problem of slum and squatter settlements, because it is quite obvious that the problem is too large to be easily or quickly resolved. Instead most national and urban authorities have concentrated upon providing housing for low-paid groups in regular employment. For example, large-scale public schemes can be visited in virtually every large city which house government and industrial workers.

In certain cases direct action has been taken on slum and squatter settlements. The actions of the Brazilian government in the past few years has led to the construction of large numbers of new houses for squatter settlers. But many doubts have been expressed about this particular programme, especially over the policy of deliberately destroying settlements near the city centres and rehousing the population in new areas distant from the city.

An increasingly common policy has been to construct areas with basic services such as water, drainage and electricity, but to leave house construction to the squatters. This represents a cheap method of housing, one more suited to the funds available, and to the needs of the squatters.

Effects on the areas of out-migration

To generalize about the impact of out-migration upon an area involves weighing a complex set of factors, including the nature of the migrant flows, the nature of the out-migration area, the propensity of migrants to send back part of their income and the impact of the early migrants' example on the resident population. Nevertheless, evidence is accumulating to suggest that many areas of out-migration are suffering from the process.

In the first place, we have already seen that it is the younger element who leave for the city areas. As a result a deterioration in the age structure of the resident population occurs which may affect the labour force of the area. This is the situation in one of two Peruvian villages studied by Preston. Mito, the first village, has experienced considerable migration while the other, Carcas, has remained largely isolated from such a movement. The result has been that Mito has 'a lower proportion than Carcas in the age groups 20–34 for men and 20–29 for women as well as a much higher population aged over 55'.[72] This departure of the younger element in the work-force is bound to have a negative effect on production except in those circumstances where there is high, whole-year unemployment.

Secondly, the evidence on migrants' characteristics shows that it is the more educated members of the community who tend to leave. This selective migration may harm the rural areas, especially in so far as it reduces opportunities for economic expansion. Some commentators, however, would say that this exodus is not necessarily harmful, because they are critical of the education system in most Latin American countries. The system, they argue, is in large measure irrelevant to the needs of the community, and the educated people who leave are of no real help to the community. Other writers suggest that the education system actually accelerates out-migration, since it serves 'as a means of socialization for future out-migrants'.[73] A similar interpretation of the role of the education system in Peru has been posited by Lowder. 'Here, however little he may learn, one can be sure that he receives a vivid image that Lima is the "best" place to be in Peru. This is partly because of the nature of the state-school programme, and partly because the majority of teachers have urban origins and pass on their personal dissatisfactions with the "outback" to their pupils.'[74] Obviously if Margulis is right in suggesting that the education system 'does not correspond to the economic needs of the region of origin', then little may be lost. However, this still leaves the problem that, if the selection system operated by the school is at all effective, then it will be the most talented people who will leave the community.

Thirdly, there may be a detrimental effect upon the agricultural labour supply. Obviously the loss of a higher proportion of migrants from the labour force will affect the supply of labour in conditions of full employment. Many economists, however, have claimed that because of the inequitable land-tenure system and the low levels of training, the marginal productivity of many labourers is extremely low. Their departure from the land will lead to no real fall in production and may lead to higher levels of *per capita* income. Other writers have shown that marginal productivity rarely approaches zero, even when labour is redundant most of the year, because it is frequently in short supply at times of harvest or sowing.[75] In such circumstances, the departure of further migrants exacerbates the problem.

Naturally, certain areas do gain from out-migration. First of all the departure of labour may raise agricultural productivity and wages, especially when investment capital is made available to the area. Secondly, many migrants return for fiestas or family reasons and bring with them products, techniques and other innovations from the urban areas. Although it naturally depends upon the particular innovation the net result of out-migration in the community may be beneficial. Lastly, there are many regions where migrants to the city send funds home to the rural areas. Despite these advantages, however, a number of recent studies suggest that most rural communities do suffer a net loss from the process of out-migration.

Rapid urbanization is taking place in Latin America and is likely to continue for some years to come. Unfortunately, it seems as if it is largely divorced from industrial growth and is being fed mainly by high fertility rates in the cities themselves. Consequently this expansion is leading to the growth of tertiary activities and to the expansion of unemployment. This does not necessarily mean, of course, that urban growth should be reduced, for even in Cuba, where agricultural and rural development are being encouraged, city growth is continuing. It does mean, though, that serious attention should be given to providing employment for these people.

One aspect of urbanization which may be undesirable is its form. If the vast majority of the urban population become concentrated into giant metropolitan centres, it is possible that the development process will be distorted. This generalization is hedged by a reservation about the social structure and the objectives of development. If a nation's social structure is rigid and the objectives of development exclude the attainment of a more equitable distribution of income, primacy is unlikely to have any effect upon the future path of change. However, if one of the objectives of development is equality, it is probable that the form of urbanization will affect the society's chances of success. It is for this reason that Castro's Cuba instituted a definite policy to restrain the growth of Havana.

It is obvious, though, that any attempt to alter the distribution of cities will be fraught with difficulties. The major attempts so far made to establish new cities such as Brasília and Ciudad Guayana have been expensive (see Chapter Eight), while less spectacular attempts have not been notable successes. One reason for this has been the unwillingness of industries and private companies to establish themselves outside the major primate centres. Another is, of course, the fact that an increasing part of urban growth seems to be caused by natural increase within the cities. Lastly, there still remains the question of migration and how to dissuade rural and urban dwellers from moving to the primate centres.

Whatever problems or opportunities may be related to the form of urbanization there can be little doubt that urbanization *per se* is not detrimental to the total growth of the economy. In the first place it seems as if the shanty-towns and other lower-class residential areas in the city do contribute to saving, investment and production. Secondly, it seems as if there is some social and political adjustment to the new environment which may accelerate not only economic growth but more widely based developmental change. Certainly, too, it is clear that the city-bound migrants make rational decisions founded upon previous visits to the city and on family information about city conditions. The only real losses are those felt in the rural areas, which are often deprived of their most educated and talented youth and are neglected by governments eager to develop the urban areas.

5: The Rural Sector

While the inability of industry and commerce to provide sufficient employment for urban dwellers has led to enormous problems for the cities, the rural areas have been faced by still greater difficulties. In general the process of economic growth has by-passed them, and the development of industry, electric power, roads, housing and so on has centred on the cities. In many cases, development policies have not only neglected the rural areas, but have actually harmed them.

An appreciation of this situation can be gained by comparing *per capita* incomes and labour productivity in the two kinds of area. As may be seen from Table 22, average urban incomes in the early sixties were often twice as high as those in the rural areas. In addition, the proportion of low-income groups found in the latter was normally far higher than that in the cities. In terms of labour productivity, agriculture has performed very poorly compared with most urban activities. Rural productivity has also grown very slowly; between 1952 and 1964 there were at least three countries, Colombia, Chile and Peru, where agricultural production grew more slowly than the population.[1] (See Table 23.)

Limited productivity and material poverty are symptoms of a number of problems presently facing the rural sector. Among the more important of these problems are the land-tenure system, the pattern of change in agricultural practices, technology, and marketing systems and the distribution of social services.[2]

Table 22: Rural and Urban Incomes in the Income Structure in Selected Countries (percentage shares)

Country and sector	*Average income (rural income = 100)*	*Share of all income units*	*Lowest 20%*	*Income groups 30% below the median*	*Top 5%*
Venezuela					
Rural	100	40·8	72·9	48·6	12·2
Urban*	250	59·2	27·1	51·4	87·8
Mexico					
Rural	100	44·2	68·7	54·7	10·7
Urban†	231	55·8	31·3	45·3	89·3
Mexico					
Agricultural	100	43·7	68·2	56·3	20·7
Non-agricultural	198	56·3	31·8	43·7	79·3
Brazil					
Agricultural	100	45·4	62·2	65·1	12·1
Non-agricultural	273	54·6	37·8	34·9	87·9
Costa Rica					
Agricultural	100	50·0	76·4	80·3	19·6
Non-agricultural	184	50·0	23·6	19·7	80·4
El Salvador					
Agricultural	100	60·2	100·0	87·9	18·8
Non-agricultural	229	39·8	—	12·1	81·2
Argentina					
Agricultural	100	14·8	21·9	20·0	14·9
Non-agricultural	115	85·2	78·1	80·0	85·1

*All settlements with more than 5,000 inhabitants.
†All settlements with more than 2,500 inhabitants.

Source: ECLA, *Economic Survey of Latin America*, 1969, 402.

Table 23: Growth of Agricultural Production and Population in Selected Countries, 1952–64 (percentage annual growth rates)

	Agricultural production	*Population*
Argentina	1·8	1·8
Brazil	3·2	3·0
Chile	1·8	2·5
Colombia	2·4	2·8
Mexico	6·7	3·2
Peru	2·3	2·6
Venezuela	5·3	3·8

Source: Furtado, C. (ed.) (1970); ECLA, *Economic Survey of Latin America*, 1966.

Problems of the rural areas

(I) THE LAND-TENURE SYSTEM

Since the time of independence a number of changes have occurred in the land-tenure system in Latin America. The massive colonizations which took place in southern Brazil, in Argentina and in western Colombia led to the emergence of many small-scale family farmers. More dramatically, the revolutions which took place in Mexico, Bolivia and Cuba brought about large-scale land reforms. Despite these and other modifications, however, the ownership system in several parts of Latin America still shows many similarities with the pattern that had developed during the colonial period. This has been made clear by a series of studies carried out by the Inter-American Committee for Agricultural Development (ICAD) during the 1960s.[3] These studies, made in seven countries which had not experienced major land redistributions, showed that ownership patterns and tenancy arrangements were highly reminiscent of the past in the control they gave a few land-owning families. They found, for example, that the level of land concentration was very high in comparison with most other areas of the world. Compared with the United States, where only 1 per cent of the country's cultivated land was in farms large enough to provide employment for more than twelve labourers, 65 per cent of Chile's cultivated land and 20 per cent of Argentina's were enclosed in holdings of this size.[4]

The ICAD studies also showed the degree of inequality contained in the land-ownership structure. In Guatemala and Ecuador, more than 85 per cent of the total farm units occupied less than 20 per cent of the land.[5] In Peru the situation was still more extreme, with some 88 per cent of the holdings occupying 8 per cent of the land, while

Fig. 10a

many families had no access to land at all. In the ICAD sample the category of landless labourers commonly represented a high proportion of the total agricultural families – varying from 23 per cent in Colombia (1960) to 60 per cent in Brazil (1950).

The concentration of land guarantees that there are large numbers of *minifundistas* and landless labourers prepared to work on a seasonal basis.* In many plantation areas many of the landless remain idle most of the year hoping for 3–4 months' employment on the sugar or cotton harvest. In plantation areas in Guatemala, highland Peru and Bolivia and north-west Argentina *minifundistas* provide the casual labour force. Unfortunately their very numbers

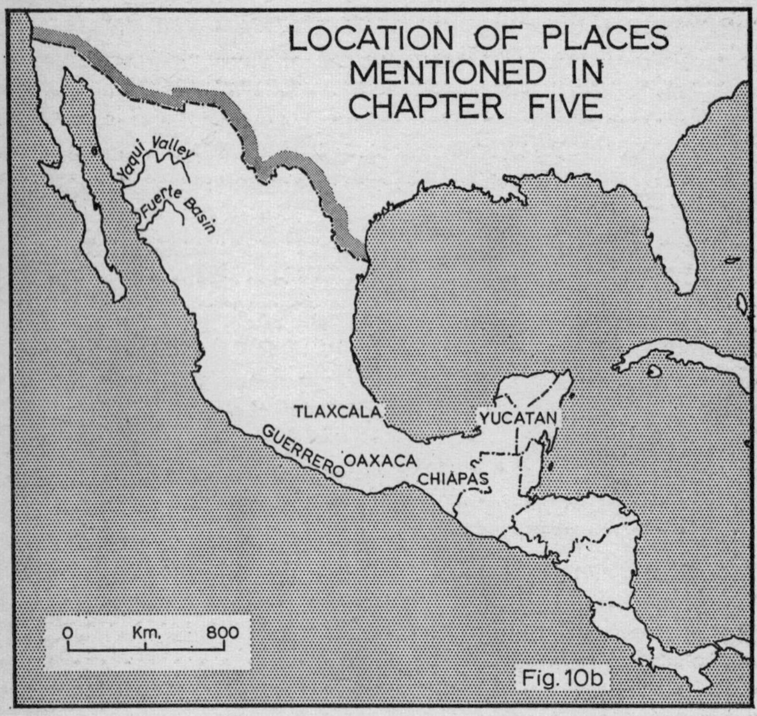

*The occupiers of minute plots of land which are too small to support a family and which frequently belong to the large estates (*latifundios*) owned by *latifundistas*.

guarantee that wage rates remain very low. In many cases these rates remain well below the minimum laid down by law; one study in Brazil, for example, found that the wages of cane cutters were as much as 40 per cent below the legal minimum.[6]

A fundamental problem, therefore, is that there is a close association between land concentration and low incomes. Such an association is not fortuitous, for many claim that it has been deliberately fostered by the landowners. Since control over the land limits the emergence of prosperous small-scale farmers it thereby assures the landowners of a cheap labour supply. As Barraclough and Domike have written 'these land-tenure institutions are a product of the power structure. Plainly speaking, ownership or control of land is power in the sense of real or potential ability to make another person do one's will. Power over rural labour is reflected in tenure institutions which bind workers to the land while conceding them little income and few continuing rights.'[7]

While the land-tenure situation is a principal cause of rural difficulties, the position of the rural poor has hardly been helped by the rapid increase in their numbers. As was mentioned in Chapter Two, the twentieth century has brought about the elimination of many contagious diseases and a marked reduction in infant mortality. As a partial consequence, the average rate of population growth in the continent is today nearly 3 per cent per annum. Much of this increase is occurring in the rural areas and is one of the principal causes of the impoverished situation of *campesinos* in many countries.* This situation is only partially mitigated by the rapid outflow of people to the urban areas, for, although the rural population is growing less quickly than that of the cities, absolute numbers are increasing in most rural areas. In Colombia, the population living in urban areas (*cabeceras*†) more than doubled between 1951 and 1964 largely owing to migration.[8] At the same time the population living outside those centres grew from almost 7 to more than 8 millions. It has been predicted that the rural population in every nation except Argentina and Uruguay will increase between 1950 and 1980, and that in Para-

**campesino* = country dweller, farmer or agricultural worker.

†The *cabecera* is the administrative centre of the *municipio*. Frequently it is only a small village.

guay and certain Central American countries it will double.[9] Despite the fact that the percentage of urban dwellers in the continent is likely to rise from 39 per cent in 1950 to 71 per cent in 1980, an increase in the rural populace from 95 to 143 millions is probable! In circumstances where the rapid growth of population has already led to the constant sub-division of property into smaller and smaller holdings, this represents a fundamental crisis. This crisis is particularly acute in the Andean countries and in Central America. 'In the highlands of Guatemala, for example, where population is increasing by nearly 3 per cent per year, one study shows average arable land per small farm to be 1·1 hectares, most of which is on steep hillsides. This is land enough to occupy only one-fifth of the available family labour even at the low levels of technology used.'[10]

The social consequences of the land-tenure system are bad enough, but there is growing evidence to suggest that the acute concentration of land slows down the adoption of agricultural improvements, restricts the total level of production and induces a deterioration in every nation's balance of payments.[11] Despite the fact that it permits the survival of a large number of efficient commercial producers, it encourages inefficiency in the use of land, labour and capital throughout the rest of the agricultural sector. Such evidence contradicts the conventional view that large holdings are automatically beneficial to economic growth, because they are intrinsically more efficient than the smaller units and because they encourage a higher rate of capital creation through savings.

As regards efficiency, a superficial analysis shows that there is a strong relationship between farm size and labour productivity. Table 24 shows, for the ICAD countries, that labour productivity on the large multi-family farms in Colombia is nearly ten times as high as that on sub-family farms, in Brazil nearly seven times higher and in Argentina more than six times higher. However, this measure of efficiency does not take into account the other factors of production nor what is happening in the small-farm sector. It neglects the fact that the large-scale farmer uses the land far less intensively than the small farmer. It neglects, too, the fact that large quantities of machinery and capital are needed; capital-output ratios in the large coastal estates of Peru in the sixties were as high as 6·0 compared to

*Table 24: Relationships between the Value of Agricultural Production, Agricultural Land, Cultivated Land and the Agricultural Work-Force by Farm-Size-Class in Selected ICAD Study Countries**

Country and size groups	*Per cent of total in each country*			*Relative value of production as per cent of that of sub-family farms*		
	Agricultural land	*Agricultural work-force*	*Value of production*	*Per Ha. of agricultural land*	*Per Ha. of cultivated land*	*Per agricultural worker*
Argentina (1960)						
Sub-family	3	30	12	100	100	100
Family	46	49	47	30	51	251
Multi-family Medium	15	15	26	51	62	471
Multi-family Large	36	6	15	12	49	622
Total	100	100	100	30	57	261
Brazil (1950)						
Sub-family	0†	11	3	100	100	100
Family	6	26	13	59	80	291
Multi-family Medium	34	42	43	24	53	422
Multi-family Large	60	21	36	11	42	688
Total	100	100	100	19	52	408

Table 24 (contd.)

Country and size groups	*Per cent of total in each country*			*Relative value of production as per cent of that of sub-family farms*		
	Agricultural land	*Agricultural work-force*	*Value of production*	*Per Ha. of agricultural land*	*Per Ha. of cultivated land*	*Per agricultural worker*
Colombia (1960)						
Sub-family	5	58	21	100	100	100
Family	25	31	45	47	90	418
Multi-family Medium	25	7	19	19	84	753
Multi-family Large	45	4	15	7	80	995
Total	100	100	100	23	90	281
Chile (1955)						
Sub-family	0†	13	4	100	100	100
Family	3	28	16	14	47	165
Multi-family Medium	13	21	23	12	39	309
Multi-family Large	79	38	57	5	30	437
Total	100	100	100	7	35	293

Ecuador (1954)						
Sub-family	20	‡	26	100	100	‡
Family	19	‡	33	130	179	‡
Multi-family Medium	19	‡	22	87	153	‡
Multi-family Large	42	‡	19	35	126	‡
Total	100	‡	100	77	135	‡
Guatemala (1950)						
Sub-family	15	68	30	100	100	100
Family	13	13	13	56	80	220
Multi-family Medium	32	12	36	54	122	670
Multi-family Large	40	7	21	25	83	706
Total	100	100	100	48	99	224

Sub-family farms: Farms large enough to provide employment for less than 2 people with the typical incomes, markets and levels of technology and capital now prevailing in each region.

Family farms: Farms large enough to provide employment for 2 to 3·9 people on the assumption that most of the farm work is being carried out by members of the family.

Multi-family medium: Farms large enough to provide employment for 4 to 12 people.

Multi-family large: Farms large enough to provide employment for more than 12 people.

* Gross value of agricultural production in all countries except Argentina, where the estimates are of added value. Comparable data are not available for Peru.

† Less than 2 per cent.

‡ No information available.

only 2·5 in the United States.[12] Since both land and capital are scarce in most Latin American economies such efficiency may be achieved at no little cost to the nation as a whole.

The fact that there are many inefficient large-scale producers in Latin America means that agricultural productivity often fails to increase in direct proportion to farm size. In Brazil, Cline has shown that on 1,000 sample farms, located in seven states of Brazil, the returns to scale were constant in fourteen out of seventeen state/product sectors.[13] Naturally the situation varies with the type of enterprise – commercial estates certainly do produce with increasing returns to scale – but for large estates in general this is not true.

One reason why most large estates are less productive than their resources permit is because of the failure of landowners to dedicate themselves fully to the task of farm management. Barraclough and Domike cite cases where little effort is made to increase productivity even though only marginal improvements are required. The causes rest in the practice of absentee landlordism and in the lack of social prestige to be gained from efficient farming. While it is prestigious to own land, a career in agriculture earns less respect than many urban activities. Consequently owners are more likely to work hard on their urban careers than on agricultural development. This situation can only be changed by altering the land-tenure system and the ruling social ethos.

While low labour productivity on many large estates owes much to social factors, on the small farms it is a response to the land-tenure system and the lack of credit facilities. In many ways, however, the small farms perform well, given their limited inputs: yield per hectare and productivity with respect to capital are normally quite high. This paradox arises from the fact that labour is the only factor of production readily available to the small farmer. In the absence of sufficient land or credit he is forced to put in as much effort as possible on his limited plot or remain idle. The overall result is that the farmer receives a low income while the land is over-cropped and rapidly loses its fertility. Were more land available the small farmer would be able to increase labour productivity.

The structure of land-holding in many parts of the continent, therefore, results in the factors of production being inefficiently employed. By permitting the large-scale producer cheap land and labour, high profits can be obtained without recourse to diligent farming. Meanwhile the shortage of land available to the *minifundista* leads to a severe waste of human manpower. In addition, the land-tenure situation fails to encourage the creation of capital. The extremely low incomes of the landless and the *minifundistas* leave no surplus for investment. There is also evidence that many large landowners save little and spend a high proportion of their incomes on luxury goods.[14]

An inequitable land-tenure situation, therefore, has a pronounced effect upon the nature of consumption. The high proportion of income in the hands of large-estate owners has the effect of increasing demand for the production or importation of luxury products. When luxuries are imported into a country a further strain is placed on the balance of payments. When the goods are produced at home it drains scarce capital and entrepreneurial skills into their manufacture that could more usefully, but less profitably, be employed elsewhere. Most important of all, the distribution of income means that the majority of the population lack the money for necessary manufactured goods such as clothing; in turn this forces the textile industry to work at less than full capacity. Not surprisingly several studies have recently appeared which have attributed limited industrial development to the inequitable land-tenure systems existing in some Latin American countries.[15]

(II) AGRICULTURAL PRACTICES AND TECHNOLOGY

To a certain extent, the backwardness of Latin American agriculture is due to the limited use made of modern techniques: tractors, fertilizers and high-yield seed are used only in a small percentage of the continent's farms. Where they are employed most intensively, as in Argentina and Uruguay, average yields per labourer are far higher than those in neighbouring countries. Changes are occurring throughout the continent, however, and there are large numbers of commercial enterprises in most countries producing for urban markets, industry and for export. Examples can be seen in the highly efficient sugar estates of Colombia and Peru, in the irrigated farm areas of north-west Mexico and in the intensive market-gardening operations that surround some of the major cities such as São Paulo and Mexico City. Meanwhile other new forms of technology are being diffused to the rural areas, and the introduction of radios, bicycles and new tools is reaching many of the poorer farmers.

Unfortunately, the peculiar structure of the Latin American rural sector means that many of these changes are creating further problems for many rural communities. As Pearse has said, 'the values, organizational norms, ideologies, economic practices, money and technical means of the larger cities impinge upon the rural sector in such a way as to upset rural routines and structures throughout the continent. This does not mean that there have not been changes and upsets before, but previously the process through which equilibriums were upset, regained or transformed were local. Today conditions of modern life have set in motion a total attack on the traditional system.'[16]

An example of this process has been illustrated by Browning for El Salvador, where the construction of the Littoral Highway, in the early sixties, induced a major expansion in commercial cotton production and in many ways accelerated economic growth.[17] This expansion increased the nation's export production and transformed many of the *latifundios* of the coastal zone. Unfortunately, it also exacerbated the conflict between subsistence and commercial producers over land. The changing practices on the cotton estates resulted in tenants and share-croppers being pushed off the estates to become landless labourers and squatters. This process, together with rising numbers, led to a situation where the landless began to invade any unutilized or undefended land. The result was to increase the conflict between the interests of the landowner in preserving private property and those of the squatter searching for land on which to cultivate his maize. It also led to the creation of a seasonal employment pattern whereby a large number of labourers were employed for sowing and harvesting but laid off during the rest of the year.

A similar but less widespread process has been observed in Ecuador. 'On a fifteen-thousand-hectare hacienda . . . owned by Swedish interests, half of the resident population were sent away when the farm was transformed into one of the most "efficient" in the country.'[18] Such a process is in many ways a sign of progress in the rural areas. At the same time, the shortage of non-agricultural employment opportunities and the absence of land for subsistence plots create major difficulties for the majority of the rural populace.

The adoption of new techniques is not confined to the large estates. In many small ways *minifundistas* are accepting new agricultural methods, imbibing new values and using new social facilities. In many cases, this permits a higher standard of living. Just as common, however, is the situation where synchronous changes reduce standards of living. Such a process has been noted by Pearse in a rural community which was reached by road transport thirty years earlier. 'Adoptions include the following: the universal adoption of fodder grass as property boundary, of quality breeds of cows, pigs, and fowls, of factory-made clothes bought in place of homespuns, and of hand-mills for corn . . . the situation today at the end of the period of adoption is that the peasant is poorer than he was before the road came. His soils are worse and are producing less; he has come to rely on money to purchase his necessities and the price of consumer goods rises steadily while the selling price of his products fails to keep pace.'[19]

In discussing these problems neither the need for new technology and practices nor the need to accelerate their rate of adoption is being opposed. It is rather that the socio-economic structure of the communities may have to change before the new technology can be successful. It is necessary to provide small farmers with sufficient land and credit before new methods are introduced. At present it seems that large numbers of the rural populace are not benefiting from the introduction of new technology and industrial products. Unless new opportunities are created for the population or the effects of the changes are cushioned, the benefits of this diffusion process for the rural masses will continue to constitute one of the 'seven myths of Latin American Development'.[20]

At least part of the difficulties experienced by small agriculturalists is caused by their inability to sell products at a fair price. In many cases it is here that the real exploitation of the *campesinos* takes place. Lack of storage or transport facilities and ignorance of ruling market prices mean that the producer is frequently defenceless against the shrewd middleman. At times this exploitation takes on a physical form and producers are forced to sell at low prices. This kind of exploitation is particularly common in areas where there is a racial distinction between producer and buyer – as in parts of Mexico, Central America and the Andean states.[21] Certainly any attempt to improve the lot of the *campesino* will founder unless the marketing structure is altered.

(III) SOCIAL INFRASTRUCTURE AND SERVICES

Limited social infrastructure and services are also a feature of rural backwardness. For, while there are local variations, most rural areas receive only a fraction of the facilities that are granted the urban areas. In turn the low level of facility provision reduces levels of productivity and welfare.

The extent of service deprivation in rural areas is easy to demonstrate whichever social variable is selected. In Colombia rural areas containing 63·6 per cent of the population are served by only 4·5 per cent of the country's nurses.[22] In Mexico, urban and rural school drop-out rates show a similar imbalance. In urban areas 10 per cent of pupils are in the last year of primary school but in rural areas less than 3 per cent. In Brazil, the same picture is reflected in the provision of piped water: while 72·2 per cent of the inhabitants of cities with more than 100,000 inhabitants were provided with water, only 1·1 per cent of people living in settlements with less than 2,000 people were supplied.[23] A similar picture could be painted for practically every country in the continent of virtually every kind of social infrastructure – housing, roads, lighting, water, health, sanitation and education. Naturally the situation does vary – rural Cuba, Costa Rica and Puerto Rico are far less neglected, but the tendency is apparent even there. Similarly the processes which cause this situation are fairly general throughout the continent. With the sole exception of Cuba it can be claimed that there are three principal causes: firstly, the poor quality and low-income-generating power of local authorities in rural areas; secondly, the failure of national or second-tier authorities to dispense facilities outside the urban areas; and, thirdly, the unwillingness of trained manpower to work outside the main urban centres.[24]

The failure of the local (*municipio*) authorities in most parts of

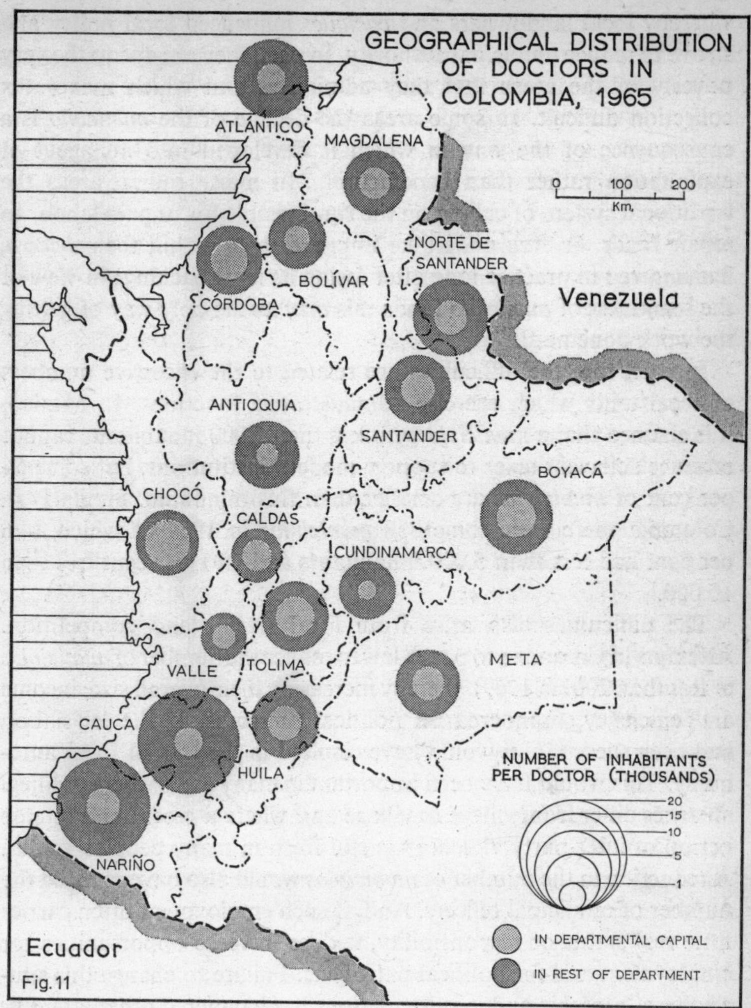

Fig. 11

Latin America is well known and has been mentioned in Chapter Two. Today this failure is manifest in the low quality of their manpower, their inability to generate adequate funds and the limited functions they perform.[25]

Many of these difficulties have emerged from the colonial tradition whereby local landowners and *caciques* influenced local policy and strove to reduce municipal authority. In part, they are due to the very poverty of the areas that they administer and which makes tax collection difficult. In some areas the decline of the *municipio* is a consequence of the way in which it developed into an agent of exploitation rather than benefaction. 'In many Indian areas the traditional system of calling on the rural people for unpaid labour to repair roads, or even undertake improvements within the *cabecera*, has lingered in practice long after losing its legal backing; in view of the scantiness of *municipio* funds this may be the only way of getting the work done at all.'[26]

In part, too, the difficulties are related to the excessive numbers of local units which exercise administrative functions. In Mexico, it is claimed that a *municipio* with less than 5,000 inhabitants cannot produce sufficient taxes to support modern institutions, but some 54 per cent of *municipios* are smaller than this minimum. Similarly in Colombia there were some 838 *municipios* in 1964 of which 14·6 per cent had less than 5,000 inhabitants and 49·1 per cent less than 10,000.

The difficulties also arise from local rivalry and competition. Attempts in Colombia to pass a law to reduce the number of *municipios* to less than 200 (in 1969), thereby increasing their overall size, income and efficiency, foundered on political pressures. If the legislation had been successful it would have resulted in the loss of local autonomy. This would have been important in many areas where political alliances differ from village to village and where a recent and intense period of inter-party violence* is still fresh in many peoples' minds. A reduction in the number of *municipios* would also have reduced the number of municipal officers. And, if such employment often carries little real status or responsibility, it does increase opportunities for employment and for political patronage. Failure to change this situation in Colombia and in other nations has hampered other attempts to improve *municipio* efficiency.

The inability to improve the efficiency and status of *municipios*

*The *violencia* lasted from 1948 to 1953. It involved large sections of the Colombian population and the two principal parties, the Conservatives and the Liberals.[27]

has resulted in their gaining low-quality personnel and even in their loss of existing responsibility. 'The *municipios* in many instances have been deprived of educational, public health, policing and other functions with which they were entrusted, as national standards for these services rose, and municipal ineffectiveness became more notorious.'[28] It has also meant that the large number of new functions which governments have acquired during the last twenty years have not been entrusted to the *municipio*. Rather there has been a strong tendency for the central government to retain authority over these new functions or to delegate them to the second-tier authorities – the departments, states or provinces – or to new decentralized institutes. Only in the larger cities has the *municipio* been granted control over services such as water, sewerage, schooling and health.

There can be little doubt that this tendency towards centralization has resulted in the creation of a large number of efficient and technically competent organizations in many countries of the continent. At the same time, relatively few of the benefits of this newly found competence are reaching the rural areas. This is true whether the functions are administered by the national ministries, the decentralized institutes or the second-tier authorities. Each kind of authority neglects the rural areas.

One reason for this neglect arises from the manner in which taxes are generated in Latin American countries at the departmental level. The principal sources of revenue tend to be taxes on land, industry and commerce and duties on sales of tobacco, alcohol and other products. As a result there is an obvious bias in the tax-generating process in favour of urban authorities, in whose area the majority of commercial transactions take place, and also the departments which contain prosperous urban centres. Such a situation is frequently made worse by the fact that some central governments contribute to the revenues of departments in partial proportion to the income they generate. Thus while the proportion of funds given to the poorer departments may exceed their share of revenues, the absolute aid given to each favours the more prosperous. The total result of this system is that the urban departments receive a higher *per capita* budget than the rural.

To a certain extent this system should favour the rural areas situated in departments with prosperous urban centres. In general, though, there is remarkably little difference between *per capita* expenditures in rural areas in different departments.[29] The expenditure of each is heavily biased towards urban areas and upon projects which favour the urban areas, such as road development or electricity generation. In general, this bias explains the neglect of the rural areas as much as the differential in tax incomes.

Urban bias in government expenditure is also implicit in the majority of central government budgets. The Colombian health plan, for example, recommended that 5·6 hospital beds per 1,000 people should be provided in urban areas with more than 500,000 inhabitants, but only 0·8 beds per 1,000 in rural areas.[30] Central government ministries and institutes, like the departments themselves, allocate more funds to urban than to rural areas.

Frequently the reasons for this tendency are related to the overall policy of the national government. Funds dedicated to industry or to developing infrastructure to support that industry will naturally be concentrated in urban areas. At other times the concentration of resources may be due to the attempts of the central institutes to spend money that will benefit the largest number of people possible. Such a justification is made by the Colombian Ministry of Health to explain the seven-to-one discrepancy between the hospital beds planned in large urban and in rural areas. The rationale behind this claim is that the utilization of beds in urban areas is higher than in rural ones, largely because more doctors are available in the former to recommend patients to the hospitals.

While efficiency in the allocation of funds in Latin America is always to be encouraged, it does lead to certain difficulties over time. The principal problem is that by allocating facilities to particular areas a pressure group is created which will be able to demand better facilities in the future. Thus by appointing most doctors to posts in the cities a group is created which is committed to the improvement of health facilities in those centres. In the absence of a competing group in rural areas this is likely to result in further neglect. This tendency will be particularly marked when there is a professional reluctance to work outside the urban areas (see below).

Efficiency criteria, therefore, can lead to highly concentrated patterns of resource distribution. Frequently, however, such concentration owes more to political than to economic considerations. In the first place, the demand for services in urban areas is likely to be more vociferous because of the higher concentration of middle-class and trade-union groupings in the cities. Again the relative absence of a similar pressure group in the rural areas will lead to rural neglect. This will be particularly true when the urban groups have access to strong political power. Such a process will naturally affect the departmental administration directly, especially when political power is concentrated in the administrative centre. However, it is also likely to affect the national agencies, for as Wolfe has pointed out 'the local officers of national social services and programmes, even if administratively responsible to a central agency, as is most often the case, cannot remain detached from the local-power structure. Their ability to maintain good relations with a locally dominant clique or cacique with connections in the capital may determine their chances of promotion, or even their chances of avoiding dismissal. This circumstance naturally helps to confirm the concentration of services in the cabecera, and makes it likely that their local meaning will be quite different from the policies promulgated at the national level.'[31]

Another factor which also reduces the level of rural facilities is the attitude of professional groups. In general professional people do not wish to work in the rural areas. Many feel that they can earn less money outside the urban areas, while others simply do not wish to live there. In large part the problem arises because most workers of this kind originate from the urban areas. However, it is also a consequence of the lack of facilities in the rural areas. A doctor may be most reluctant to go to an area where his family will not have access to normal urban facilities such as pure water, electricity, cinemas or schools. In many ways, this reaction is understandable. At the same time it is guaranteed to harm the rural areas still further.[32]

Lastly, there is the important point that many infrastructural services in Latin America are administered by institutions outside the public sector. This situation is particularly marked in the case of health and education. In Colombia, 54 per cent of secondary-school pupils attended private schools in 1968 and 47 per cent of the qualified doctors worked predominantly or exclusively outside the public-health sector. This would not matter were it not for the fact that private facilities are still more highly concentrated in the urban areas than are public services. While 61 per cent of Colombian public primary-school teachers are working in urban areas (where approximately 55 per cent of the population live) 93 per cent of private primary-school teachers work in the same areas. The principal reason is that the majority of the higher-income groups of the society are concentrated in the urban areas, and any service that is based on fees will tend to concentrate in the higher-income areas.

The factors mentioned here represent only a few of the reasons why social infrastructure and services in rural areas tend to be neglected. In general they could be resolved if more money were available to national governments or if greater stress were placed on developing these areas. In Argentina, Puerto Rico or Chile, where higher tax revenues accrue to the national government, the rural problems are less severe than in the poorer countries of the continent. On the other hand, the nation where the rural areas are best endowed *vis-à-vis* urban areas is Cuba. In that case a deliberate policy decision was taken to favour the rural areas.

The general statement that more government funds should be spent in rural areas is subject to the important reservation that such expenditures need to focus on projects which will truly benefit the rural population. In the past investment in social infrastructure has often failed to do this. In the education sector, for example, wholly inappropriate forms of education have frequently been provided. A notorious example of this has been when schools employing only Spanish-speaking teachers have been established in Indian areas.[33] Another, more common, situation has been the provision of wholly academic forms of schooling to groups requiring more practical forms of education. And, even when some attempt has been made to introduce a special system of education, it has often had the unfortunate result of establishing a dual system whereby rural children have been unable to proceed to institutions of higher learning in the urban areas. In part problems of this kind have arisen because education has been offered as a single, often politically motivated, palliative to more deep-seated rural problems. Another reason has been that education authorities have not fully understood nor been interested in the rural communities which they have controlled. If future investments in social infrastructure are to be made therefore, the past experience in education shows that more understanding as well as more funds will be required.

Future directions and possibilities for change

(I) AGRARIAN REFORM AND LAND REDISTRIBUTION

While the causes of rural neglect are manifold, one of the principal problems is the distribution and ownership of land. Not only does this pose social problems, but it also slows the rate of economic and political change. Not surprisingly, therefore, the literature on development grants a high place to agrarian reform, whatever the nationality or the academic discipline of the writer. The present discussion is intended to serve merely as a brief introduction to the problems involved and to the past experience of the few countries where extensive reforms have taken place.

(a) *The Mexican agrarian reform.* The Mexican revolution heralded the beginning of the first important land reform in Latin America. It occurred in Mexico partly as a result of the extreme inequality which had developed during the preceding half-century. Since the middle of the nineteenth century, when expropriation of the Church's estates had begun, the distribution of land-holding had become more and more concentrated. In particular, the selling of this land on the free market had hastened the growth of the *hacienda*, foreign ownership and commercial agriculture. In some ways this brought positive improvements, as foreign owners introduced new techniques and methods into farming, but the negative consequences of this process were serious and widespread. In particular, *hacendados* brought increasing pressure on the communal lands – pressure that was increased when it became clear that a landless labouring class was being created which would serve as a cheap source of labour. The local outcome of this pressure varied according to the amount of labour available and the type of production. In the cattle-raising capitalist estates of the north, share-cropping and tenant labourers were most common, while in the south forced labour was more important, the sisal workers of Yucatán and the coffee workers of Chiapas being recruited in this way. In every part of the country, however, the process increased the dependence of *campesinos* on the large estate.

This annexation of communal lands meant that Mexico acquired one of the least-equitable land-tenure situations in Latin America. It is commonly claimed that in 1910 some 1 per cent of the population owned 97 per cent of the land and 96 per cent of the population, 1 per cent of the land.[34] The land was distributed among *haciendas* which made up some 54 per cent of the national territory (200 million hectares), small-holdings making up 20 per cent, state lands 10 per cent, communal land 6 per cent and the rest waste. In terms of employment 88·4 per cent of the agricultural labour force were landless labourers, 11·6 per cent farmers (small and medium owners, leaseholders, share-croppers, communal owners, free workers) and 0·02 per cent estate owners.

This situation need not have generated rural unrest. It might merely have channelled the displaced agricultural population into the cities or into the virgin agricultural areas. The fact that it did cause unrest was probably due to the manner in which the displaced populace remained in the rural areas in united communities.[35] In turn, the creation of these discontented but united rural groups was a principal factor leading to the Mexican revolution, and the espousal of agrarian-reform policies.

While land redistribution was an undoubted outcome of the revolution, it was hardly an immediate one. In some ways reform was not fully instituted until the middle thirties, and even today 40 million hectares are still available for land redistribution.[36] The most important statutes on land reform, however, were enacted during the revolution, principally in the 1917 constitution. These statutes laid down three basic aspects of the reform. Firstly, that it genuinely aimed to distribute land to the peasants. Secondly, that a great deal of land was to be distributed as small-holdings. And thirdly, that the remaining land was to be granted to communities as *ejidos* on which individual members of the community were to be given the right to cultivate the land.

By no stretch of the imagination, however, can the Mexican land reform be seen, either originally or as it has developed through time, as an attack on the principle of private property. This is clearly seen by the way in which the original *hacendados* were permitted to retain the care of their estates. The amount of land that they were permitted to keep varied but it generally amounted to some 200–300 hectares of ordinary land, or 100 hectares of irrigated land. The same philosophy dictated the policy of allocating land to small-holders. Perhaps all land would have been redistributed in this fashion had it not been that there was simply insufficient to give to all the landless labourers. The solution to this problem, the *ejido*, represented a novel attempt to employ the community concept and to provide a means by which labour could be kept on the land. Under this system land was granted to a community as an inalienable right. The community was to control it and individuals were granted the right to use individual plots but not to buy or rent them. The actual amount allotted to each *ejidatario* varied but was normally quite small; the 1934 Agrarian Code specified only 4 hectares of irrigated land or its equivalent. As we shall see below even this specification frequently could not be met. Even within the *ejido* system few of these units developed into community projects and the majority are now a distinct but definite form of *minifundio*.

The early period of reform tended to neglect the *ejidos* and relatively few were created. Between 1911 and 1934, for example, only 10·0 million hectares of land was transformed into *ejidos* as compared to 17·6 millions during the period of the Cárdenas administration (1934–40). Equally, the facilities provided for the *ejidos* were neglected and it was only under Cárdenas that credit facilities were created through the auspices of the National Ejido Credit Bank. After Cárdenas the growth of ejidal land again slowed, as may be seen from Table 25.

After 1940 far greater attention was paid to the private sector. While its share of land did not increase, the number of private proprietors certainly did – by 91 per cent between 1940 and 1950. As a corollary of this emphasis the absolute number of landless labourers increased – less rapidly than the total agricultural labour force between 1940 and 1950 but almost twice as rapidly during the 1950s.

Table 25: Growth of Ejidal Land in Mexico, 1930–60 (per cent)

Kind of land	*1930*	*1940*	*1950*	*1960*
Non-ejidal land greater than 5 hectares	93	77	72	73
Non-ejidal land less than 5 hectares	1	1	1	1
Ejidal land	6	23	27	26

Source: 1930–50: González Navarro, M. (1965); 1960: Stavenhagen, R. (1970b), 241.

The growth of the landless labour force is one of the problems of Mexican agriculture which could not have been circumvented even if the aims of the land reform had been completely fulfilled. It should not therefore be seen as a fundamental criticism of the land reform, which did succeed in reducing the degree of land concentration and in raising the morale of the peasantry.

Despite this obvious social advantage, two other aspects of the reform have been less successful. The first is that large estates remain and many more are being formed. The second is that although the *peonage* system and the political dominance of the *latifundio* were removed, the social structure supported by them was not. Examples of extreme inequalities of land ownership are still numerous. 'For example, in the Yaqui valley 85 proprietors control 116,800 hectares of the best irrigated land, which are registered under 1,191 names. In other words, each landowner holds an average 1,400 hectares.'[37] In 1960, in fact, 73 per cent of the land was concentrated into 16 per cent of the total properties. While circumvention of the statutes is, as in the Yaqui valley, one means of creating new *latifundios*, it is really a natural result of the market system condoned by the revolution. The principal problem is that the owner of a large estate is in a position to purchase or rent other land even from *ejidatarios*. This means that new *latifundios* are formed every week, while the land-reform administration is unable to act sufficiently quickly to reduce their number.

The decision to leave the existing social structure, by permitting the old *hacendados* to maintain the care of their estates, was made to encourage the development of commercial agriculture. Such a move ensured that the foreign-exchange situation would not deteriorate, owing to the need to import food, and also guaranteed agricultural surpluses with which to supply the urban areas. Without the maintenance of these small estates there is no doubt that productivity would have declined much more rapidly than it did.

While the social classes were in many ways left intact, the land reform did remove the landless and the *minifundistas* from the worst excesses of the *latifundio* system, such as share-cropping and debt peonage. But, owing to the pressure of people on the land, it did not remove the tiny *minifundio* unit. In 1960 there were some 900,000 units with less than 5 hectares of land. Since these units covered 1,300,000 hectares of land, the average size was 1·4 hectares. Such a situation has affected not only the private owner but also the *ejido* system. In some areas where land pressure is high, the individual ejidal plots are well below the official minimum of 10 hectares of irrigated land. Land shortage in Tlaxcala, for example, has resulted in *ejidatarios* receiving no more than 1 hectare apiece. In other *ejido* areas grants have been more generous but have included practically valueless land.

At the same time the average *ejidatario* and what Furtado calls the *microfundista* are both subjected to similar exploitation from third parties. Both are short of credit and land. Both suffer from the lack of infrastructure and new techniques because they are neglected by the central government. In some ways the *minifundista* is the less well off because he is dependent upon what Stavenhagen terms the rural bourgeoisie – 'a new regional upper class whose pre-eminence comes not from property or land but rather from the monopolistic control of commerce, the distribution of goods and services, and regional political power. The *minifundistas* usually face a monopolistic market and a retail structure which lies entirely out of their control, and the kind of subordination they suffer is as harsh and exploitive as was the erstwhile *latifundista*'s control over his peons.'[38] While the medium-sized proprietor is relatively well off, the small-scale owner is very poor. The situation of the *ejidatario* by contrast tends to vary with his location. In the prosperous *ejidos*, on irrigated land in the north-west, for example, he is likely to be relatively well off; the credit facilities and services offered him by the National

Ejido Credit Bank will be good. On the other hand, one quarter of the *ejidos* do not receive credit from the Bank because they are very poor. This is particularly true of the *ejidos* in areas with large Indian populations (Guerrero, Oaxaca and Chiapas), where land shortage is superimposed upon social subordination. 'The exploitation of the peasant populations as a social class is here reinforced by its exploitation as an Indian group, that is, as a colonized people and an oppressed minority.'[39] This situation is, however, typical of the *ejido* which normally suffers much more from the bureaucracy and inefficiency of the centralized state organization of which they form the bottom rung. However, 'In spite of its economic rigidity and its administrative corruption, the *ejido* remains the best protection for the weaker and most neglected peasant groups, which in a pure capitalist economy would have perished long ago.'[40]

But while the *ejido* serves an undoubted social purpose, there has been considerable criticism of its economic role. Flores, for example, has shown that ejidal lands tend to be less productive on a crop-for-crop basis than private land.[41] There are, however, many reasons for this, notably that the average quality of ejidal lands is poorer. According to Stavenhagen 'the idea of the inefficient *ejido* is one of those myths which are propagated without any scientific basis. There is no serious study of Mexican agriculture which does not show that, given equal conditions, the *ejidatario* and the private owner can make the soil produce with equal efficiency.'[42]

But whatever the truth of the *ejido*'s productivity *vis-à-vis* the private sector, the post-reform performance of Mexican agriculture has been better than that in most other Latin American agricultural sectors. Agricultural production trebled in the twenty years up to 1965. 'Maize, wheat, beans, and rice, the basic elements of the national diet, are now produced in adequate quantities and efficiently distributed through national organizations, which guarantee adequate remuneration for the growers while ensuring low prices for the consumers.'[43] Such a situation has been assisted by many factors, and especially by the irrigation policy under which 2½ million hectares were irrigated between 1928 and 1960. Agriculture has taken advantage of these opportunities, and as Furtado has said 'its capacity to raise technical standards and to increase and diversify output constitutes a unique case in Latin America, a phenomenon difficult to explain without the agrarian reform'.[44]

(b) *The Bolivian agrarian reform.* Before the agrarian reform of 1952 the Bolivian agricultural sector represented one of the least efficient and egalitarian systems in Latin America. Land was concentrated in a few hands, agricultural wage labour was the rare exception in an environment of share-cropping and peonage, and a tiny fraction of the total land was used for agricultural production. The extent of land concentration can be demonstrated by the following figures. In 1950 units of over 10,000 hectares made up 49·6 per cent of the agricultural land, but less than 0·7 per cent of the total units. At the other end of the scale, units of less than 5 hectares occupied a mere 0·23 per cent of the land but constituted 59·3 per cent of the total units.[45] This system of land tenure, which had evolved during colonial times and which had become even more concentrated after independence, was the foundation of a semi-feudal social structure. In this system the larger part of the agricultural population was forced to work under a share-cropping or peonage system, and relatively few were in receipt of wage payments. The political role of the agricultural regions was reflected in the way that presidents at that time were elected by 30,000 or so voters out of a population of two and a half millions.[46] Lastly, there were few parts of the agricultural sector that could be described as efficient. Many products had to be imported and a general indication of the level of efficiency is that the agricultural crop land of Bolivia represented only 0·3 per cent of the country's total area – the lowest proportion in Latin America.[47]

Under such circumstances it is not surprising that the reform required a genuine social revolution to implement it. That such a revolution in fact occurred is made plain by the first actions of the National Revolutionary Movement (MNR) on gaining power in 1952: they immediately nationalized the tin mines and introduced a major urban reform, as well as instituting the agrarian-reform programme.[48]

The basic tenets of the agrarian-reform law represented a strong attack on the *latifundio* as an institution. Article 12 of the 1953 law stated quite clearly that 'the State does not recognize the *latifundium*, the large rural holding which is minimally exploited by antiquated labour-intensive methods, and which perpetuates a system of feudal oppression in the altiplano'. Such *latifundios* were to be 'completely abolished', 'expropriated in full' and divided among those who tilled the soil. On the other hand, the law had no intention of destroying the few commercial (agricultural) enterprises which did exist, providing that 'unsalaried tenancy is combined with wage labour, modern techniques are employed, and at least twice the initial capital is invested'. On these enterprises land was to be given to unsalaried tenants by dividing up all land over the maximum permitted by law, or if the farm did not reach this size by dividing up as much as 33 per cent of the total land. Nor was there any attempt to destroy the small or medium-sized properties that existed. While it strove to maintain efficiency the law also made an effort to preserve the Indian communities. It did this by establishing 'indigenous communities', under which Indian communities were given 'all the rights and obligations of private and co-operative landowners'. Like the *ejido* in Mexico these communal lands could be farmed collectively or apportioned among families according to custom.

The law was to be implemented by the National Society for Agrarian Reform (SNRA), which possessed a body of technical advisers and employed judges to decide on expropriations and the apportionment of land. In addition, a form of peasant mobilization was instituted by the establishment of syndicates which were seen as 'a means of defending member's rights and conserving social conquests'. They should also 'intervene in the execution of the Agrarian Reform'. Other progressive institutions were also envisaged by the law, notably co-operatives and committees to establish rural schools.

The agrarian-reform law represented, therefore, a major legislative attempt to improve the position of the rural areas. And in evaluating its success most commentators would seem to recognize that its implementation did improve the lot of the average rural inhabitant. At the very least they agree that it broke the worst social and political characteristics of the *latifundio* system and gave plots of land to large numbers of families. García, for example, while highly critical of the extent and speed of the reform, has agreed that 'the agrarian structure based on the manorial hacienda *will never be able to exist again*. This is the irreversible nature of the revolution.'[49] The officials of the SNRA claim that 'the first stage of the reform' is complete in large areas of the country. Heath has shown that between 1955 and 1967 nearly 200,000 *campesino* families received land from the 7,906,283 hectares distributed. And, lastly, Furtado has argued that the reform had two marked results: 'it altered the income distribution pattern in favour of the rural masses and it enabled the communities, formerly "imprisoned" by the large estates, to recover their independence on the social plane.'[50]

Despite this general approval, however, every commentator is highly critical of the manner in which the reform was carried out. With respect to the law's principal aim, the breaking-up of *latifundios* and the redistribution of land, most agree that its implementation has been excessively slow, bureaucratic, political and corrupt. In large part this problem has arisen from the nature of the law itself. For, 'considering the complexity of the process and the extreme centralization of authority, it is little wonder that the simplest claim for confirmation requires at least two years, and that some cases have dragged on over a decade'.[51] Such complexity has the immediate disadvantage of permitting landowners ample grounds for delay. It has also resulted in some efficient enterprises being expropriated, while backward estates have been able to protect themselves for long periods. Delays in implementing this complex legislation were hardly helped by the poverty and lack of facilities provided for the main land-reform institutions, nor by successful attempts to reduce the salaries of judges administering the reform.[52]

While the reform did redistribute land these difficulties certainly slowed the process. García has pointed out that by 1963 'land reform beneficiaries probably represent[ed] no more than one tenth of the agricultural labour force' and complained that only 16 per cent of the redistributed land was in fact cultivable.[53] The regional impact of the reform also varied, with some areas benefiting much more than others. In the departments of Chuquisaca and Cochabamba, for example, more than 20 per cent of the total land was affected by redistribution measures against less than 3 per cent of that in Santa Cruz.

Another fundamental criticism is that the reform did little more than redistribute land. Little was done to develop new forms of farm enterprise or to place the efficient commercial units under communal ownership. Particularly disappointing were the cooperatives, which failed because of inadequate organization and technical advice. By 1964 there were only 317 in existence, with only 24,782 members.[54] Nor was much done to raise the standards of living of the peasants beyond redistributing land. In this respect little credit was provided, nor was any real attempt made to regroup land parcels or to encourage resettling away from densely populated areas through colonization schemes. Perhaps in a nation such as Bolivia, which was among the poorest of Latin America, all this was inevitable, but it was still disappointing. Possibly the only real success in follow-up efforts was in the education field: between 1951 and 1961 the percentage of children between seven and fourteen years who entered rural schools increased from 27 to 50 per cent, and the school drop-out rate during the same period declined from 92 to 70 per cent.

It may have been a consequence of this neglect that production has failed to increase as rapidly as had been hoped. While it is generally accepted that an initial drop in production was soon recovered, relatively few major improvements have taken place. As Heath has said, 'in cold economic terms . . . the reform is a mixed bag of a few dramatic successes and several dismal failures, with very little information at all on far too many crucial subjects'.[55]

Perhaps therefore the Bolivian reform is best seen as a major social improvement which was achieved at relatively little cost and which has provided an opportunity, still shamefully neglected, for further rapid development. It has certainly improved the social position of the rural populace by abolishing the feudal tenancy arrangements so common before 1953. And, while it is difficult to substantiate Heath's view that 'most campesinos are *relatively* much more affluent now than a decade ago' or that they 'are generally pleased with the 1952 revolution', there is no definitive evidence to the contrary.[56]

(c) *The Cuban agrarian reforms.* In comparison with the reforms that had taken place before 1959, the Cuban experience was distinguished by its speed, the new institutions it created and its ideological basis. In many respects these differences were due to the fact that

Cuba was principally an agricultural economy with a very limited non-agricultural sector; not only did the rural sector give employment to the greater part of the population but it was also the primary source of exports. Agrarian reform was thus a vital plank in Castro's revolution, a fact which he recognized when announcing the first agrarian reform from the mountains of the Oriente in October 1958. After he had assumed power, the policy was implemented by new laws and decrees and by the founding of the National Institute for Agrarian Reform – the most powerful single organization in the country.

It is quite clear that the reform was necessary. Like most other nations in the continent the land-tenure system was inequitable. At the time of the 1946 land census, farm units which held more than 500 hectares represented only 1·5 per cent of the total farms but occupied 47·0 per cent of the land.[57] While this situation was less acute than that in Bolivia or Mexico, the fact that Cuba was a small island made the situation worse (it had only 9,077,100 hectares of agricultural land). In addition ,many of the *latifundios* were in foreign and especially North American hands. One other difference between Cuba and other Latin American nations, and indeed a difference that was to prove vital in the success of the reform, was that there were few *minifundios* and larger numbers of wage-earning labourers.

Despite its ideological importance in the revolution, it has been argued that the reform would have been less radical had there been fewer political difficulties.[58] Without the conflicts with the United States, for example, it is probable that the expropriation of foreign-owned land would have been slower. Similarly had it not been for opposition from medium-sized landowners, manifest most acutely in the slaughter of animals and the burning of sugar cane, the reform might have been confined to the larger farms. This point has been demonstrated by Gutelman, who has noted that of the 4,448,879 hectares of land expropriated by May 1961 only 27 per cent was taken under the auspices of the 1959 reform law.

Certain elements of the agrarian reform were very different from what had occurred in Bolivia and Mexico. No attempt was made to divide up the large cattle or the sugar farms. Rather they were left as production units and operated by cooperatives, in the case of the sugar and agricultural estates, and directly by INRA, in the case of the cattle farms. There was from the start a high measure of centralism in the Cuban system. Later it became still more centralized when 'people's farms' were abolished. It was not until 1963, when the 'people's farms', the 'sugar cooperatives' and the directly administered farms were all made into 'state farms' and regrouped into fifty-eight regional *agrupaciones*, that some measure of decentralization was reintroduced.[59]

As in Bolivia and Mexico the original treatment of the private farm was motivated more by a wish to preserve efficient units than to destroy private enterprise *per se*. Commercial enterprises with less than 402·6 hectares were not expropriated, and if productivity was 50 per cent higher than the national average this maximum could be raised to 1,342 hectares. These limits did not apply to rented land, however, which was expropriated irrespective of the size of holdings. Tenants who were farming land were entitled to claim 27 hectares, even if they had been farming less than this area; by this single act 101,000 peasants received ownership of 2,725,000 hectares. By 1963, attitudes towards the medium-sized holdings had altered and the maximum permissible private holding was lowered to 67 hectares. This action was instrumental in transferring another 1,800,000 hectares to the state while expropriating only 9,825 owners. Nevertheless, the fact that more private farmers were created than had existed before shows that the Cuban revolution was not hostile to private ownership.

The most distinctive feature of the Cuban agrarian reform was the way in which the rural population was more fully integrated into the life of the nation. This was achieved less through popular participation – for the system of control is still highly centralized – than by improving the social infrastructure and services of the rural areas.[60] Schooling, health, communications and sanitation were all improved and state shops established to replace exploitative stores. The lot of the average rural inhabitant of Cuba has undoubtedly improved as a result.

(d) *Agrarian reform in other parts of the continent*. While these reform experiences have been disappointing in some respects, few would argue that redistribution did not benefit the majority of rural dwellers. In some ways, therefore, it is surprising that so little redistribution occurred in other parts of the continent.

This lack of progress was certainly not expected at the beginning of the sixties. The example of the Cuban revolution had inspired or frightened a number of national governments and international groups into taking some action. The Alliance for Progress in particular had placed agrarian reform high on its list of priorities; and Objective 6 of Title 1 of the Charter of Punta del Este, signed by all of the continent's nations except Cuba, required 'the effective transformation of unjust structures and systems of land tenure and use with a view to replacing latifundia and dwarf holdings by an equitable system of land tenure'.[61] In support of this and similar notions, a number of countries did indeed set up land-reform agencies – notably Colombia (1961), Venezuela (1960), Brazil (1963), Peru (1964) and Chile (1962). The establishment of these institutes was greeted by many observers as a basis for future optimism.[62]

Unfortunately, the action that followed this legislation was very limited. In Colombia only 598,871 hectares of land had been received by INCORA, the nation's land-reform agency, by the end of 1970 – a mere 2·0 per cent of the nation's total agricultural land. Of this, only 280,466 hectares had actually been purchased or expropriated; the rest had been ceded to the Institute and was in many cases of very low quality.[63] In terms of the rate of land distribution progress was even slower: by November 1970 only 212,852 hectares had been distributed to families. The total effect of eleven years' redistribution was to benefit 13,854, or 1·8 per cent, of the nation's poorest families.[64]

In neighbouring Venezuela, somewhat more families benefited from the agrarian-reform programme; IAN, the National Agrarian Institute, claims that 118,737 families benefited from its programmes between 1959 and 1965. Even so, land redistribution was in many ways less important in the reform programme of this country than had been hoped. Instead of expropriating land the IAN tended to use colonization schemes as the main method for providing the poorer families with land. While this did bring some improvements it did not directly help the large number of small cultivators whose farms were too small to provide them with an adequate income. In making an overall assessment, Heaton has commented that 'existing information on the operation of the agrarian reform programme indicates that it has contributed very little to increasing the amount of land available to family-type farmers of Venezuela'.[65]

Even less successful was the agrarian reform in Brazil, where, Cline has commented: 'In sum, despite the existence since 1964 of legislation providing for expropriation and redistribution of large farms, virtually no land redistribution has occurred to date (1970).'[66] Redistribution had not even been implemented in the region with the greatest problems: the north-east. This was true despite a plan to 'restructure' the sugar-cane industry of the region in a manner which would mechanize the estates while the owners would sell or donate land to workers displaced by the mechanization. Each displaced worker would be provided with 15 hectares on which to establish his own family farm. By the end of 1969, however, only one sugar plantation had been modernized.

In Central America little action was taken during the sixties, even though there were a number of areas where the land problem had become acute. In most countries respective governments made pronouncements in favour of agrarian reform but did little to redistribute land. The only real exception was in Guatemala where between 1952 and 1954 the Arbenz Government redistributed nearly 500,000 hectares of land to some 55,734 heads of families. Unfortunately, this significant reform was largely reversed by the succeeding government; an action which had a retarding influence on reform movements in other parts of Latin America.[67] More typical of the experience of Central America as a whole was that of El Salvador where, despite statements of support for reform from successive national governments after 1932, little change had taken place by the sixties.[68] And, even if a favourable view is taken of the limited changes which did occur in that country, it is clear that the present government 'has abdicated its previous commitment to institute basic reforms'.[69] A similar abdication of previous commitment and lack of fervour for reform typifies the actions of other Central American governments.

Similarly in Chile and Peru, the passing of land-reform legislation during the sixties did not lead to large-scale redistribution, in spite of strong government commitment to redistribution. This was partly due to the complexity of the legislation and the consequent difficulties in applying it.[70] While the two experiences up to the end of the decade were in some respects similar, the Chilean land-reform programme did make greater progress. During the period of the Frei administration the proportion of land owned by the top 5 per cent of landowners declined from 87 to 77 per cent.[71] This programme also gave land to about 25,000 new proprietors, encouraged more than 100,000 *campesinos* to become members of unions and affected, in some way, 16·3 per cent of the nation's irrigated land.[72] By comparison with the effect of other reforms during the sixties the Chilean experience was relatively successful. Measured against its own targets and the expectations that the *campesinos* had of it, however, it was considered to be a failure.

There were of course numerous reasons why so many of these agrarian laws and institutes were unsuccessful. Some were fortuitous, but on the whole it is impossible to escape the feeling that many were quite deliberately erected. Feder, in fact, has argued that the agrarian-reform experience of the sixties should be called 'counter-reform' – since its demise was brought about by the united power of landowners, foreign enterprise and conservative politicians.[73] Many of the factors that obstructed the implementation of the programmes were the result of deliberate opposition from these groups – and many were deliberately built into the agrarian-reform machinery. One technique was to produce legislation which was too complex to implement quickly and effectively. Such was the case with the Peruvian and Chilean land-reform legislation; the former consists of some 250 articles and fills a small booklet of eighty pages. Another common technique was to place difficulties in the way of the agency in charge of land redistribution. Frequent changes of director, selection of men who could be manipulated, restrictions in funds, demands for the submission of detailed plans on priority areas and methods of implementation were all employed in different countries. A third difficulty was that the position of the United States government, which had strongly supported the programmes, was highly equivocal. Feder suggests that such a situation was inevitable in as far as 'United States investors and businessmen with real-estate, commercial or industrial interests in Latin America cannot be expected to relinquish their holdings any more than Latin American estate owners and will fight to the bitter finish to preserve them'.[74]

By the late sixties, therefore, an air of pessimism pervaded the agrarian-reform lobby throughout the continent. All reference to land redistribution was dropped from propaganda messages, such as the 1967 Declaration of the Presidents of America. Within individual countries little was being done and land agencies were concentrating more on colonization than upon redistribution. In most countries this is true to this day. However, the situation in two countries, Peru and Chile, has recently altered radically as a consequence of a change of government. The usurpation of power by General Velasco Alvarado in Peru in 1968 and the election of Salvador Allende in Chile two years later changed the whole attitude to reform throughout the continent.

Within six months of taking power the Velasco government had implemented existing legislation and expropriated the cattle and agricultural estates of the United States Cerro de Pasco Corporation. A few months later, on 24 June 1969, a new law was passed with the joint objects of expropriating large estates and of reducing foreign control over the country's agricultural exports. The day after the law was passed eight sugar estates in the departments of Lambayeque, La Libertad and Lima were expropriated – an action which placed 90 per cent of sugar-cane production in the state's hands.[75]

Having taken over the estates, the government decided to maintain them as single production units and organized them into cooperatives. As in Cuba, however, the term cooperative was in many ways a misnomer, since administration was placed in the hands of technocrats appointed by the military government. It was only after strikes over the partial suppression of trade unions and the lack of worker participation that two workers' delegates were appointed to the management team.

The action taken on the sugar estates suggests that while the law was nationalistic it was neither socialistic nor opposed to foreign capital. Certainly there were a number of novel aspects to the reforms, which were designed to maintain harmonious relations with both national and foreign private enterprise. The first was that the government was at pains to demonstrate that the expropriation of foreign assets was confined to the agricultural sector. This was made clear by the way it returned the industrial installations of Grace and Company the day after those installations and the company's sugar estates had been expropriated. The manner in which compensation for expropriated land was paid also reflected the government's interest in redirecting foreign capital into other sectors of the economy. Although a certain amount of cash compensation was paid, most was tied up in two forms of bonds, the first repayable over a period of twenty years, the second transferable for shares in any of the state's industrial enterprises. Most interesting, however, was the fact that these bonds could be cashed at their face value if an equal sum was invested in new industrial plant in the private sector.

While the reform was not anti-capitalist it did aim to redistribute land. Medium and small independent owners were permitted to keep their land, but maximum limits were laid down. The permitted level of land-holding was quite generous and varied according to the region and the kind of enterprise, but it will force a number of large estates to be redistributed. At the other end of the spectrum, *minifundios* benefited by a stipulation that no farm should be less than 3 hectares. In addition, the landless may gain some benefits under the article which established 'peasant communities' along the lines of the Bolivian reform. The ultimate aim, it appears, is to create cooperatives from mere peasant communities.

Overall, therefore, the land redistribution is likely to benefit the rural population, especially as it is also intended to improve the physical infrastructure in the rural areas. At the same time, it is likely to benefit certain groups more than others. Those peasants with small-holdings as well as the workers on the great estates are likely to gain considerably. However, 'in contrast, the growing mass of rural wage-earners who do not own land and who are not tenants on the "traditional haciendas" will probably see a worsening of their present status in the countryside and will therefore swell the ranks of those migrating to the cities'.[76] Whether the total impact on the rural sector will be favourable will depend on the future priorities of the government.

In the case of Chile there is still too little information to be clear about the implications and changes that are taking place. Certainly the land redistribution has been accelerated and all farms over a basic maximum of 80 hectares of irrigated land have been taken over from their owners, with some measure of compensation. The total effect of this land redistribution, some of which has taken place illegally, is difficult to assess from the reports that are presently emerging from the country. This can only be gauged over the next few years as propagandist tracts from both sides are replaced by more detailed studies.

(e) *General implications of agrarian reform.* In those countries where land redistribution has been implemented, relatively little impact has been made on the pattern of agricultural production. In Cuba, for example, the island is still fundamentally an area of sugar and cattle production; to alter the nature of production would have been to attempt to defy physical constraints. In addition, little change occurred in the pattern of farm-size; the large sugar plantations and the cattle *hacienda* remained, normally as a deliberate decision of government to maintain production levels. Similarly, in Bolivia attempts to maintain production levels preserved the medium-sized estates and brought little change in the nature of production. In some parts of Bolivia and Mexico, however, the large estates survived less by design than through the inefficiency of the land-reform legislation. Long legal battles over complex legislation allowed large estates to survive and in many cases new ones emerge. What all the reforms did achieve, of course, was the abolition of the worst *latifundios* and the creation of a large number of viable family-sized farms. Unfortunately, despite attempts to lay down minimum land-holding units, the *minifundio* and the minute plot of land have not disappeared. In many cases, particularly in the Bolivian altiplano and in many parts of Mexico, this has been less the fault of the land reform than a consequence of population growth and pressure on the land.

Population pressure has also been a limitation on governments' ability to give land to the landless. In many cases it has forced governments to give land only to those families who had been tenant farmers. This was the situation in Cuba, and appears to be the case in Chile as well. In Mexico, Bolivia and Peru on the other hand an attempt was made to give land to the landless through the creation of *ejidos*, indigenous and peasant communities. The problems which were thereby created are numerous, but the underlying difficulty of too many people on too little land was insuperable in terms of land redistribution alone. In every country this difficulty will remain and will continue to ferment cityward migration unless complementary policies such as colonization or the socialization of agriculture are effectively implemented. The last policy has of course been followed in Cuba, where it is now claimed that there is a shortage of rural labour at certain times.

If the reforms did not change the land-use pattern, destroy all the large estates or solve the problem of the *minifundios* and the landless, they did change social relationships within the society. The virtual elimination of feudal forms of bondage such as *inquilinaje* and *huasipunguaje* has had vast political, social and economic ramifications in Bolivia and Mexico and is having a similar effect in Chile and Peru. It has increased the demand for education and encouraged communities to work together to build schools. In Bolivia it has helped to change the social position of the majority, signified by the change in term of address from '*indio*' to '*campesino*'. In Cuba, it has provided the landless labourer with regular rather than seasonal employment. In some cases it has created new institutional forms which have given greater dignity to the rural dweller. The creation of syndicates in Bolivia, *ejidos* in Mexico and 'cooperatives' in Cuba, Peru and Chile may frequently have had little economic success but have brought great social advantages. This success might have been greater had more support been given to communal attempts at production. Had more Mexican governments supported the communal *ejidos*, or Bolivian governments helped to develop an understanding of the idea of cooperativism, greater progress might have been made. As it is, few governments have really granted the peasants freedom to make their own decisions; even in Cuba and Peru the cooperatives are closely controlled by government administrators. It remains to be seen if the Chilean attempts will be less centralized.

But while land reform has succeeded in changing several aspects of the relationship between the land's tiller and its owner, it has failed to remove all forms of dependency. In particular, the new landowners are frequently exploited by wholesalers and traders, particularly where there is a racial difference between the two, as in parts of Mexico, in the Peruvian *sierra* and on the Bolivian *altiplano*. Such a situation has become very marked in Mexico, where the landowner has been replaced by a new rural bourgeoisie which lives in the local towns and prospers through trade. These countries demonstrate the consequences of partial reform – the basis of ownership is changed but not the marketing or credit structure. Such a mistake was not made in Cuba. There the direct intervention of the state in the distribution of agricultural production and its establishment of state-operated shops was deliberately intended to remove this difficulty. While it placed the rural inhabitant firmly in the hands of the state, for most *campesinos* this constituted a relatively benevolent pair of hands; as Dumont has said, 'if the USSR exploits its peasants, Cuba spoils them too much'.[77]

Only in Cuba was land reform associated with any reduction in the dependency relationship between urban and rural areas; the rural areas were deliberately favoured after the revolution and the growth of Havana deliberately retarded. In some other areas, notably in Mexico, land reform was seen as a means of increasing the importance of the urban and non-agricultural sector. Having granted land to the peasants, most Mexican governments then forgot the sector outside areas where irrigation programmes were being instituted. The rural populace having been given their principal demand, other priority areas could receive most attention.[78]

In sum, therefore, land redistribution should not be interpreted as a panacea for rural neglect. It should be seen mainly as a means by which other forms of rural improvement can be effectively introduced. While land reallocation *per se* does bring some benefits – Lehmann calculates that the real incomes of rural families in Chile doubled where land reform occurred – it cannot be relied upon to bring automatic, large-scale improvements in welfare, productivity or social integration.[79] For these changes a number of secondary improvements are needed, notably the creation of non-agricultural employment opportunities, increased water, sewerage, health and education facilities, road development, credit advancement and better marketing systems. Changes such as these are needed in all regions.

(II) LAND COLONIZATION

A major difficulty facing agrarian reform in many parts of Latin America is that there are simply too many people farming too little land. This problem would exist even if substantial land redistribution took place. This is demonstrated by the Mexican experience, where the shortage of land available for redistribution forced the government to use the *ejido* as a means of absorbing surplus rural labour. Similarly in Bolivia the 'indigenous communities' were set up partly to deal with this problem. In both countries, recent population growth has led to an increase in the numbers of landless labourers and *minifundistas*. Such a predicament is also faced in extensive areas of Central America, Colombia, Ecuador, Peru and north-east Brazil where land redistribution has not occurred.

At the same time, most of the nations containing areas of land pressure also possess large tracts of under-utilized and sparsely settled territory. All of the Andean countries except Chile have extensive areas of potentially productive land lying to the east of the Andes. This paradox has led many writers to recommend colonization as a possible solution to land pressure and indeed to low agricultural productivity in general.[80] If governments would encourage colonization, large numbers of peasant farmers with insufficient land could be resettled in the new areas of expansion. At the same time the application of credit and new techniques in both the old and the newly settled areas would provide a major boost for agricultural production.

Such a view is especially attractive in Latin America, where many countries have experienced large-scale colonizations. During the nineteenth and early twentieth century the growth of Argentina, southern Brazil, eastern Colombia and southern Chile was closely associated with the movement of settlers into sparsely settled or Indian lands. In Argentina, the past movements represented a major element in the spatial integration and development of the nation.[81] Colonization involved the movement of millions of people into the interior of the country, many of whom were European immigrants. It also involved the state in frontier battles with Indian tribes in the Chaco, the Pampas and Patagonia. Most fundamental of all was the role it played in turning Argentina into one of the world's main suppliers of meat, wool and cereals and in developing Buenos Aires into a major metropolitan city.

In Brazil colonization movements also played an important role in integrating and opening up the nation.[82] These movements had started with the arrival of the Portuguese, but they assumed renewed drive and importance during the nineteenth century as a result of the growing world demand for coffee. During the middle nineteenth century coffee plantations were quickly established in the Paraíba valley. Later the abolition of slavery and exploitative methods of land use destroyed this area as a principal coffee producer and the frontier moved on into the state of São Paulo. In turn this led to coffee becoming Brazil's principal export commodity, to the investment of profits in commercial and industrial activities and to the explosive growth of the city of São Paulo.[83] Having exhausted the available land in São Paulo, however, the frontier did not pause. Rather, under the pressure of land shortage and the exhaustion of soils, it moved into the neighbouring states of Minas Gerais and Paraná.[84]

Similarly in Colombia, the southward movement of the Antioqueño people into the old Caldas region helped to create the country's principal coffee region and three of its principal cities, Manizales, Pereira and Armenia.[85]

Despite the profound impact of these particular movements not all colonization efforts were successful. In many ways the 'hollow-frontier' development in the Paraíba valley was a failure; it exhausted the soil and left the population engaged in subsistence agriculture. Another failure was the rubber boom which made Manaus and Belém into booming cities but which collapsed as rubber plantations developed in South-east Asia.[86] Equally, the large numbers of small projects in other countries which were never successful should not be forgotten. Even so the surprising factor about colonization in the nineteenth and early twentieth centuries was that so many frontiers were created and effectively settled.

Since 1940 these great colonization movements have been matched only in two countries: in Brazil and to a lesser extent in Mexico. Between 1940 and 1960 'some three million largely rural-to-rural migrants moved into Paraná, Goiâs and the Minas triangle, and

Mato Grosso' in Brazil.[87] More recently the creation of Brasília and the construction of the Belém–Brasília Highway has led to the population living near the road increasing from less than 100,000 to around 2 million. These same developments have also led to significant increases in the production of maize, beans, rice, cotton and other crops and to a growth in the cattle herd from almost nothing to about 5 million head.[88] This rapid movement of settlers is likely to continue in the future. The construction of the trans-Amazonian road network plays a fundamental part in the government's commitment to opening up the Amazon region. To encourage settlement, road construction sites are being built on a semi-permanent basis to act as market and service centres, and strips of land 10 kilometres wide are being reserved for colonists on each side of the new roads.

In a very different manner the Mexican government has increased the amount of land under agriculture by means of irrigation schemes. Since 1926 the amount of irrigated land increased from about 1 million hectares to something between 3·6 and 5 million hectares. 2·7 million hectares of the newly irrigated land was financed by the government and of this area 1·5 million hectares had previously not been cultivated. In Mexico, however, unlike Brazil, there are signs that progress is beginning to slow down owing to the expense of irrigating more difficult areas. Fox has calculated that the amount of irrigated land added between 1955 and 1964 was only one half that added in the preceding ten years.[89]

In comparison with that of Brazil and Mexico, recent colonization in other countries has been limited. Even so, substantial numbers of settlers have moved into the many colonization areas. In Bolivia a number of projects have been under way since the early 1950s which have attracted many colonists. The opening of the Santa Cruz–Cochabamba road in 1954, for example, led to a major expansion in the Santa Cruz region.[90] In the areas to the north-east of Cochabamba, along the River Chapari, 10,000 new families had settled by 1962. And, in the Alto Beni region near La Paz nearly 1,500 colonists had settled in the ten years up to 1968.[91]

Similarly in Peru there have been a number of colonization schemes. Many of these, like those in Bolivia, have been associated with ambitious road-building projects and intended primarily to resettle families from more overcrowded regions. In particular, small but relatively successful population movements have been taking place in the Pucallpa and Tingo María regions.[92] Along the Peruvian coast a number of irrigation projects have also been started near Chimbote and Arequipa.[93]

Further north colonization has been taking place on both sides of the Andes in Ecuador and Colombia. In Ecuador many farmers have settled east of the mountains around Puyo and in the Zamora valley, as well as on the Pacific side in the region of Santo Domingo de los Colorados.[94] Similarly in Colombia settlement has occurred in several parts of the Llanos to the east of the mountains as well as in the Montería region to the north-west.

Even in Central America there have been substantial colonization movements. In Costa Rica and Guatemala large numbers of settlers moved into the Pacific lowlands. In addition large numbers of settlers moved from El Salvador to neighbouring Honduras until war broke out between the two countries.

While colonization is taking place in a number of areas there are many problems involved in the process. Perhaps the principal problem facing national governments is to decide how far they wish to be involved in the administration of the movement and to decide how much infrastructure should be provided for the settlers. These are questions which have been extensively considered in the literature, principally in the debate about the relative advantages of planned versus spontaneous migration.

There would appear to be many disadvantages attached to spontaneous colonization. In contrast to the planned schemes, no official selection procedure is involved, no credit facilities are provided and infrastructure is usually lacking. In addition the settler's lack of credit, poor communications with the nearest market and poorly developed marketing systems mean that he often gets low prices for his commercial production. Further problems are likely to be caused by insecure land titles. In many cases settlers have cleared land and then legal proceedings have resulted in their ejection. Such a process has been observed recently in several parts of Colombia, but it seems also to have been a problem to nineteenth-century settlers.[95] Unaccustomed physical and climatic conditions may also be a problem for the spontaneous colonist. This is especially likely in the Andean countries, where most settlers originate in temperate mountain regions but settle in sub-tropical lowland areas. There may also be longer-term difficulties, such as soil erosion and shifts in the demand for the settlers' products. While many of these problems face all kinds of settler, colonists on planned schemes should be more adequately protected.

In practice, however, the advantages of planned colonization are less clear-cut. Firstly, there is a major difference between planning and good planning, and many public and private schemes have failed for lack of the latter. In particular, bad land surveys, inadequate support services, poorly selected settlers and corrupt management have been common factors leading to failure. Secondly, it has been shown that spontaneous settlers are often more enterprising, innovative and enthusiastic than those on planned projects. Dozier argues that this arises because planned schemes eliminate what he calls 'natural selection'. 'Spontaneous indicates that the colonization has been completely willed, that the initiative has been taken by the individual colonist, without encouragement or concession, to "pioneer" for himself in a strange environment. Few persons without genuine need, agricultural experience, and incentive to endure hardships would freely choose such a life.'[96] Examples of this kind of spirit have been documented for a number of colonization areas, an instance of which is the movement of Indians in Peru from the highlands to the sub-tropical Pucallpa valley.[97]

That the individual settler on a planned scheme does have a higher chance of success is certain. This does not mean, however, that planned schemes are normally more popular with governments. For while spontaneous colonization is full of difficulties for the settler, there is no risk involved for most governments. Spontaneous settlement involves the government in road construction and perhaps some credit provision; the planned scheme involves it in major administrative and infrastructural expense and in the possibility of failure as well. Even where planned schemes have been adopted and have been successful, the average cost of establishing each settler has been high. The relatively cheap Alto Beni project still cost about 1,350 dollars per family.[98] In choosing between the two kinds of scheme, therefore, the critical issue for governments is usually cost. The advantages of the planned scheme have to be weighed against giving partial support for a larger number of spontaneous colonists or spending money on other rural projects.

It is on this last point that several writers have criticized large expenditures on colonization projects. They have basically argued that the advantages of colonization have been exaggerated and that it has sometimes been used to screen inaction on more important rural projects. In particular it has been argued that direct help to farmers in overcrowded areas would be more effective than colonization. By offering improved qualities of seed, by giving technical advice about crop rotation or contour ploughing, or by establishing more efficient and less exploitative market systems, average incomes in these areas would increase. Another argument is that large sums of money should not be spent on major colonization schemes, because the quality of land now generally available in Latin America is quite poor. As Dozier has said, 'the continent has been well explored – if not well exploited – and there are no agricultural El Dorados waiting to be discovered. The leftovers are mainly subhumid areas which would require irrigation and tropical forest lands which must be cleared.'[99] While this rather overstates the case, since good-quality land has been found on recent schemes, it does underline the importance of only encouraging settlers to move to areas with development potential.*

Perhaps the most critical view of colonization has come from writers who see it as a diversionary tactic used by those who are hostile to the fundamental issue of land redistribution. Such a view has been put forward by Feder. 'Emphasis on colonization, in theory and in practice, achieved what it intended: divert attention from land reform and confuse it with it. Today land-reform institutes and other government agencies are engaged in a few such schemes, with or without foreign financial assistance, and since most of the colonization schemes end in failure, a great deal of public money is squandered without criticism. Colonization schemes are the tranquillizers

*Kleinpenning mentions that good-quality land has been colonized along the 600-km. stretch of the trans-Amazonian road between Altamira and Itaituba.[100]

of the landed élite and counter-reformists in the Americas. In contrast, expropriations of *latifundios* for real land reform are about as scarce as skeletons of the Neanderthal period.'[101]

These and other criticisms of colonization are important to balance excessive optimism. There can be little doubt that colonization can contribute greatly to more rapid and equitable rural development, but it should not be considered an easy route. There are many difficulties involved, especially in large-scale schemes.

(III) INFRASTRUCTURE AND OTHER IMPROVEMENTS

The emphasis that has been laid in this chapter on land redistribution and colonization should not be interpreted as meaning that other changes are not both necessary and desirable, for it has been assumed that synchronous changes in the provision of infrastructure and social services will accompany these major changes. New roads are necessary to increase rural mobility so that *campesinos* may choose where to sell and thereby improve the price they obtain for their products. Similarly where an exploitative market system exists it may be appropriate for governments to establish controlled markets, as in India,[102] or government shops, as in Cuba.[103] In addition, rural conditions cannot be improved without further efforts in health provision. In many areas major epidemic diseases have been removed by means of vaccination campaigns, but endemic debilitating diseases remain. These should be eradicated by measures such as providing fresh piped water, if not to every house at least to each village. Education is also required to improve rural productivity and social conditions, but it must be an education which is adapted to the needs of the poor areas. Instruction at the primary level in personal hygiene, in basic literacy and in mathematics is more relevant than the traditional school curricula. Naturally all this costs money and cannot be done immediately. However, there are ways of reducing costs, as is presently being discovered by the Colombian government. Various ministries are collaborating on the idea of 'rural concentrations', where a number of educational, medical and agricultural services will be grouped together.[104] Equally there are economic benefits from this kind of investment, as has been demonstrated by various education studies.[105]

In sum, therefore, the rural areas present major difficulties for most Latin American countries. They normally contain the larger proportion of the poorest and most neglected people. They are often exploited by urban groups and neglected by governments. While some of these problems will be overcome by out-migration, much has to be done to help them directly. Unless it is, wide rural–urban disparities will remain and larger numbers of rural inhabitants will be subjected to continued poverty.

6: Transport Development

The poor state of the transport system in many parts of Latin America is one of the first features to attract the attention of the foreign visitor. Although he will normally have arrived by international jet and have been cosseted into the city centre in the comfort of a Ford or a Chevrolet, the unmade state of many of the roads will soon have made their presence felt. The main shock, however, will have come had he decided to visit the less prosperous suburbs or the rural areas surrounding the city. Such a visit will have made him aware of two things. Firstly, that poor countries have limited amounts of money to spend on roads and railways. And, secondly, that, even if these funds are sometimes spent on *autopistas* and inter-city jets, the larger and poorer parts of the nation gain few benefits from these investments.

Perhaps it is this initial shock which has convinced so many social scientists and politicians that one mark of a 'modern' nation is the condition of its transport network. In addition they will cite a variety of empirical studies which have demonstrated that there is a strong level of association between measures of transport growth and different indices of economic development. A well-known example of this kind of study is the work of Kansky, which showed that for a cross-section of twenty-five nations, at different stages of development, there was a close statistical relationship between various measures of economic and transport development.[1] Similarly, other authors working at a national or sub-national scale have found an identical relationship. Working in Ghana, for example, Gould found that the spatial patterns of transport and economic development were closely associated; in Kenya, Soja recorded the relationship between road and rail development and the spread of 'modernization'; and in south-east Brazil, Gauthier demonstrated the effect of road development on the expansion of São Paulo.[2] Such a relationship is clearly valid throughout Latin America, one aspect of which is demonstrated in Table 26.

Table 26: Passenger Vehicle Registration and Gross National Product, 1967

	Number of passenger vehicles per 1,000 inhabitants, 1967	*Gross national product per capita at market prices, 1967*
Argentina	47·5 (3)	672 (2)
Bolivia	3·0 (17)	158 (18)
Brazil	17·9 (7)	329 (9)
Chile	12·6 (9)	592 (4)
Colombia	7·2 (12)	319 (10)
Costa Rica	18·7 (6)	426 (7)
Dominican Republic	7·4 (11)	279 (13)
Ecuador	3·6 (16)	231 (16)
El Salvador	9·6 (10)	279 (13)
Guatemala	7·1 (14)	302 (11)
Honduras	4·8 (15)	247 (15)
Mexico	20·1 (5)	528 (6)
Nicaragua	7·2 (12)	368 (8)
Panama	26·3 (4)	581 (5)
Paraguay	3·0 (17)	224 (17)
Peru	15·8 (8)	284 (12)
Uruguay	51·7 (1)	640 (3)
Venezuela	48·1 (2)	911 (1)

Source: Ruddle, K., and Hamour, M. (eds.) (1970), Tables 4, 100, 106.

While such a relationship does not mean that individual transport investments will induce economic growth, it does indicate that transport improvements are an important dimension in the total development process. Most Latin American governments have accepted this conclusion and have committed themselves to the improvement of their transport networks. While this effort has been continuing over the past century or more, progress has been particularly marked during the past twenty years. During that time, roads have been built connecting previously isolated areas, the length of paved roads has expanded rapidly, airports have been built in most of the larger cities and sea ports have been modernized. An impression of this progress can be gained from Tables 27 and 28. In terms of road improvements the length of the network has more than doubled in most parts of the continent, and in the last fifteen years the number of cars, lorries and buses has increased by more than five times in several countries. In terms of air transport, the traffic on scheduled airlines has often doubled in less than ten years, and many new areas have been linked into the scheduled routes for the first time.

The development of land transport

The important role to be played by transport in accelerating economic change was the main rationale behind the early development of

Table 27: Expansion in Numbers of Road Vehicles, 1953–69 (thousands)

	Passenger vehicles		*Commercial vehicles*	
	1953	*1969*	*1953*	*1969*
Argentina	329	1,304	254	715
Bolivia	4*	19†	—	25†
Brazil	338	2,003	338	656
Chile	48	151†	43	136
Colombia	50	151	43	135
Costa Rica	7	35	5	20
Dominican Republic	6	33	4	18
Ecuador	5	25	12	31
El Salvador	10	34	5	16
Guatemala	10	40	7	23
Honduras	2	14	3	17
Mexico	248	1,133	196	537
Nicaragua	3	24	2	9
Panama	11	42	4	13
Paraguay	2	14	2	13†
Peru	49	220	40	109
Uruguay	48	130	42	90†
Venezuela	113	522	82	230†
United States	46,258	86,710	9,272	17,155

*1950
†estimated

Source: Ruddle, K., and Hamour, M. (eds.) (1970), Table 100.
Ruddle, K., and Odermann, D. (eds.) (1972), Tables 166, 167.

*Table 28: Civil Aviation Scheduled Services: Estimated Passenger Kilometres, 1960–68 (millions)**

	1960	*1968*
Argentina	989·6	1,775·0
Bolivia	47·3	61·4
Brazil	2,679·0	3,648·7
Chile	413·7	601·5
Colombia	777·4	1,561·7
Costa Rica	54·7	112·5
Dominican Republic	10·6	28·7
Ecuador	42·2	225·6
El Salvador	55·4	138·7
Guatemala	30·2	77·4
Honduras	44·0	109·2
Mexico	1,309·0	2,131·4
Nicaragua	11·8	59·4
Panama	49·9	51·8
Paraguay	10·1	30·6
Peru	123·7	569·2
Uruguay	82·8	76·9
Venezuela	386·4	955·8
United States	62,542·2	183,393·1

* Domestic and international flights

Source: Ruddle, K., and Hamour, M. (eds.) (1970), Table 97.

transport in the continent, the construction of railways. From the middle 1850s until 1930, in fact, railway development was one of the chief symbols and hopes for accelerated growth throughout Latin America. During this period, when most of the continent's railways were constructed, the association between economic expansion and railway development was very close. Wherever there was a prospect of rapid economic expansion railway investment was forthcoming. And, in the areas where economic growth occurred fastest, notably in Argentina, Uruguay, Chile and southern Brazil, extensive rail networks developed. Only in countries such as Colombia, Ecuador and Paraguay, where economic expansion was less rapid, did rail development take place more slowly.

While the rate of railway development differed greatly between areas, the basic motivation behind construction was very similar. Principally, this was to provide routes for primary export products

Table 29: Development of Shipping, 1960–70

	Number of vessels		*Gross registered tonnage (000s)*		
	1960	*1968*	*1960*	*1968*	*1970*
Argentina	151	141	1,042	994	1,266
Brazil	227	227	1,055	1,231	1,722
Chile	48	47	246	263	308
Colombia	24	29	91	163	235
Costa Rica	21	0	71	0	0
Cuba	28	44	89	248	333
Dominican Republic	5	4	13	10	0
Ecuador	8	7	24	39	0
Guatemala	2	2	4	4	0
Honduras	27	13	154	51	60
Mexico	30	46	179	369	381
Nicaragua	6	5	18	14	0
Panama*	495	623	4,236	5,165	5,646
Peru	26	31	120	184	378
Uruguay	15	17	67	112	141
Venezuela	42	35	349	315	393
United States	3,272	2,290	24,837	20,401	18,463

*The majority of this fleet is operated under the Panamanian flag of convenience.

Source: Ruddle, K., and Hamour, M. (eds.) (1970).
Ruddle, K., and Odermann, D. (eds.) (1972).

and imported manufactures. In Argentina and Uruguay railway construction was designed to ease the shipment of meat and wool to Britain, and in Chile, Bolivia and Peru to carry copper, lead and tin to the ports of the Pacific.

While this aim was often sufficient to encourage extensive railway construction, it was rarely enough to lead to the evolution of a network linking all parts of the national territory. Even in countries experiencing rapid growth, areas where export production was insignificant or where there was little demand for imports remained isolated and dependent upon more traditional forms of transport. Occasionally efforts were made to integrate these areas, for example, in Mexico between 1876 and 1911 and in the development of Chile's Northern Railway. In general, however, the length and the orientation of the networks throughout the continent were geared to a pattern of economic growth based on export production; social factors rarely entered into this question.

This pattern and orientation of rail development, moreover, seems to have characterized other less-developed areas. This, at least, is the conclusion to be drawn from a comparison of the Latin American experience with a model of transport development based on Ghanaian and Nigerian experience.[3] In this model, the spatial evolution of land transport networks is seen to fit into four stages. (See diagram below.) The first stage describes the manner in which early colonial conquest

SPATIAL MODEL OF NETWORK DEVELOPMENT IN A LESS DEVELOPED COUNTRY

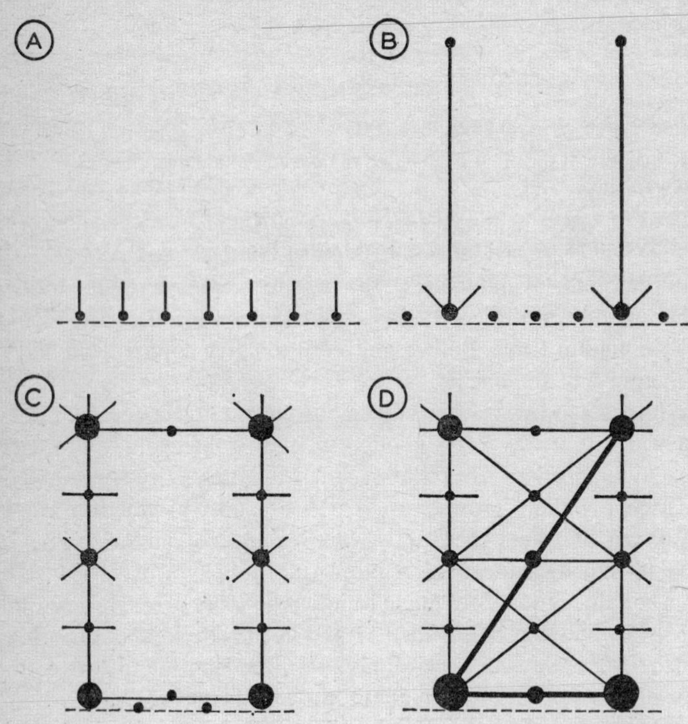

Source: Taaffe, Morrill and Gould (1963), 504

creates a system of settlements and berthing points along the coast wherever adequate sites are available. Slowly a second stage evolves as penetration routes are constructed which link the best-located of these ports to the mining and population centres inland. This stage is linked with the development of an efficient administrative system and especially with the evolution of export production. Gradually, the process of export-based growth stimulates growth in the interior and a number of intermediate centres evolve along the principal access routes. This process in turn gives rise to the third stage of transport evolution, the growth of feeder routes and links from the inland centres. Finally, as the economy becomes more integrated and standards of living rise, the transport system continues to evolve and a further stage is reached where all the principal economic and population centres are interconnected.

While the historical experience of Latin America has in many ways been different from that of West Africa, especially in as far as it obtained independence much earlier, the development of the rail network in several parts of the continent conforms closely with the first three of these hypothesized stages. Haggett has shown that the rail network of south-east Brazil evolved in this manner; his maps show that there was a tendency for the first routes to be built inland into the export-producing regions and for a gradual infilling of the system to occur which matched the third stage of the model[4] (see Fig. 12). In Ecuador, the earliest and principal railway was built from the main port of Guayaquil inland to the capital Quito and to the

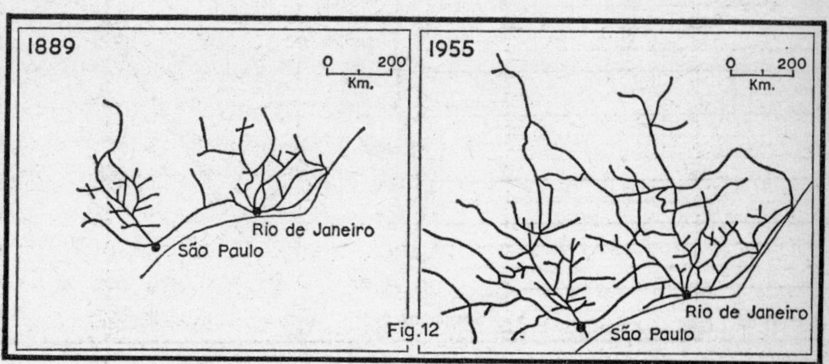

THE DEVELOPMENT OF THE RAILWAY SYSTEM IN SOUTH-EAST BRAZIL (After Haggett)

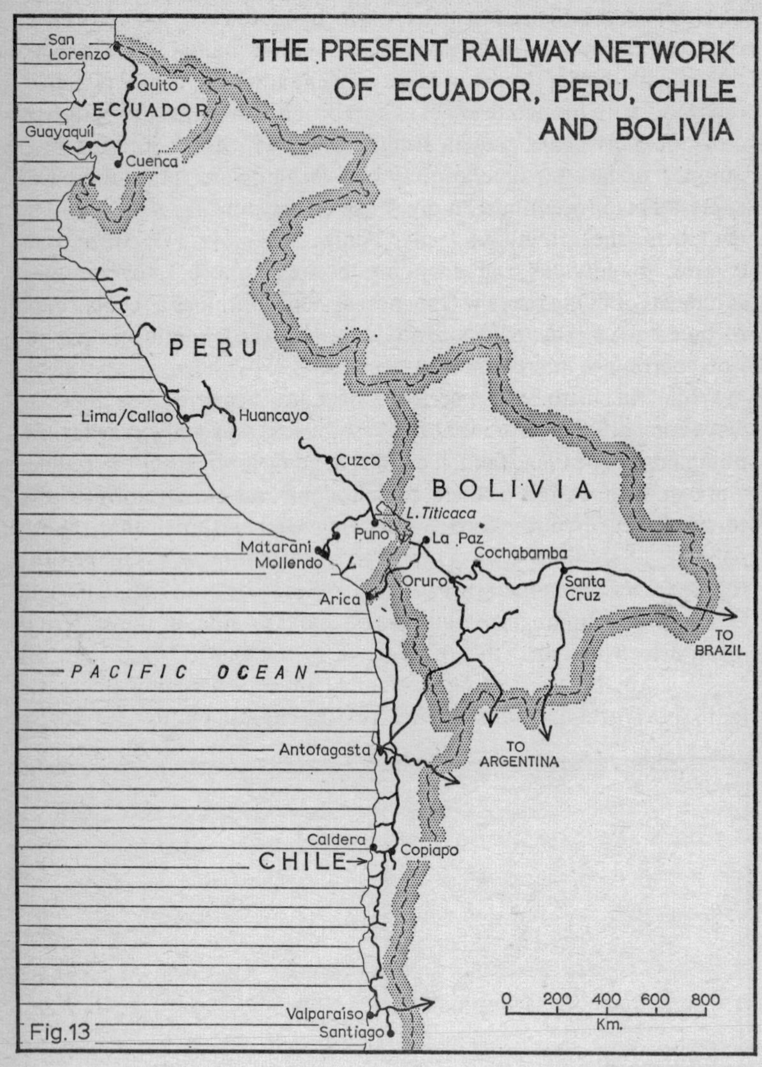
THE PRESENT RAILWAY NETWORK
OF ECUADOR, PERU, CHILE
AND BOLIVIA
San
Lorenzo
Quito
ECUADOR
Guayaquil
Cuenca
PERU
Lima/Callao
Huancayo
Cuzco
BOLIVIA
L. Titicaca
Puno
La Paz
Cochabamba
Matarani
Mollendo
Oruro
Santa
Cruz
Arica
TO
BRAZIL
PACIFIC OCEAN
TO
ARGENTINA
Antofagasta
Caldera
Copiapo
CHILE
0 200 400 600 800
Km.
Valparaiso
Santiago
Fig.13

country's third city, Cuenca (see Map 13). In Peru, the Southern and Central railways were constructed from the ports of Mollendo and Callao, stretching inland to the mining centres of the *sierra* and, in the former case, to Lake Titicaca and Bolivia. In Chile the earliest railways like the Caldera–Copiapó, Valparaiso–Santiago, and Antofagasta railways linked the ports with major cities and mining centres inland. However, the limited development of Bolivia, Ecuador and Peru meant that railway development did not extend beyond the second stage of the model, as it did in Brazil.

In other parts of the continent this pattern of development was modified by special geographical and political conditions. In Argentina and Uruguay, for example, railway construction centred on one port rather than several, with the progressive concentration of routes upon one city. In Argentina, the development of the meat industry, the locational advantages of Buenos Aires and the monopoly position Rosas established for the port during the nineteenth century led to terminals for the majority of railways being established there (see Fig. 14).[5] As a result the third stage of route development was marked not by the gradual interconnection of provincial cities,

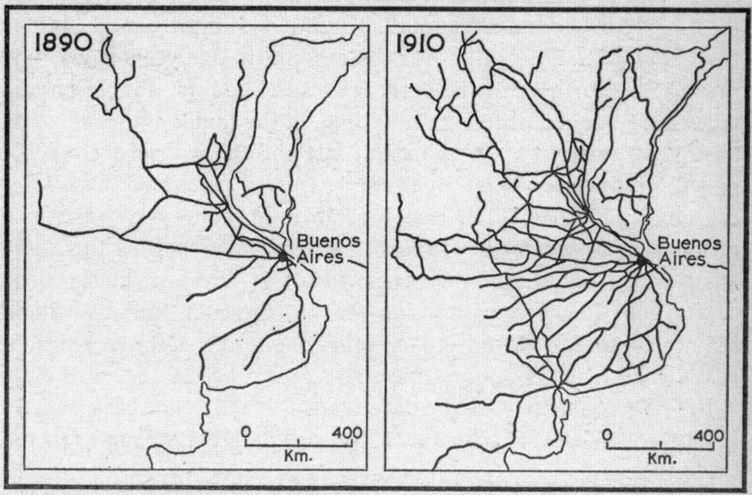

THE DEVELOPMENT OF THE ARGENTINIAN RAILWAY SYSTEM (After Scobie)
Fig.14

but by their integration with Buenos Aires. Another pattern occurred in Colombia, where the difficulties posed by the mountainous terrain induced a pattern of railway development which linked the major cities to the Magdalena river. Only the banana line from Fundación to Santa Marta, the Barranquilla–Puerto Colombia railway* and the Cali–Buenaventura line provided direct links to the coast.

In virtually every country the pattern of rail development was one which was oriented towards export production and international trade.[6] With the gradual emergence of a philosophy of development based upon import substitution, however, these transport networks were found to be inadequate. For industrial development to be successful a larger market was required which could be achieved only if the major population centres were linked together by an efficient transport network. If a balanced form of development were to emerge, the third and fourth stages of transport development had to be encouraged. Consequently the 1930s and 1940s saw a number of national governments paying more attention to the needs of the transport network. But, unlike the earlier period of transport growth, this stage of development was based primarily on road extension. In Colombia, for example, Santos's 'Revolution on the March' which took place between 1934 and 1938 stimulated improvements in the road network.[7] Gradually over the next thirty-five years it was improved still further; in the early forties the country's three largest cities were connected for the first time, in the middle fifties the first road links between the Caribbean coast and the interior were completed, and in the sixties great emphasis was placed on improving the quality of these links (see Fig. 15).[8] In Venezuela petroleum revenues financed major transport investments, such as the *autopistas* which link Maracay, Valencia and other cities with the national capital, and the motorway system which operates in Caracas.[9] Similarly in south-east Brazil, in Argentina, Chile and Mexico extensive paved road networks began to evolve.

In many countries, too, the development of roads has been used to satisfy certain social criteria. In Mexico different administrations

*Puerto Colombia lay to the west of the mouth of the Magdalena river about seventeen miles from Barranquilla. The railway connecting the two was completed about 1888 but no longer exists.

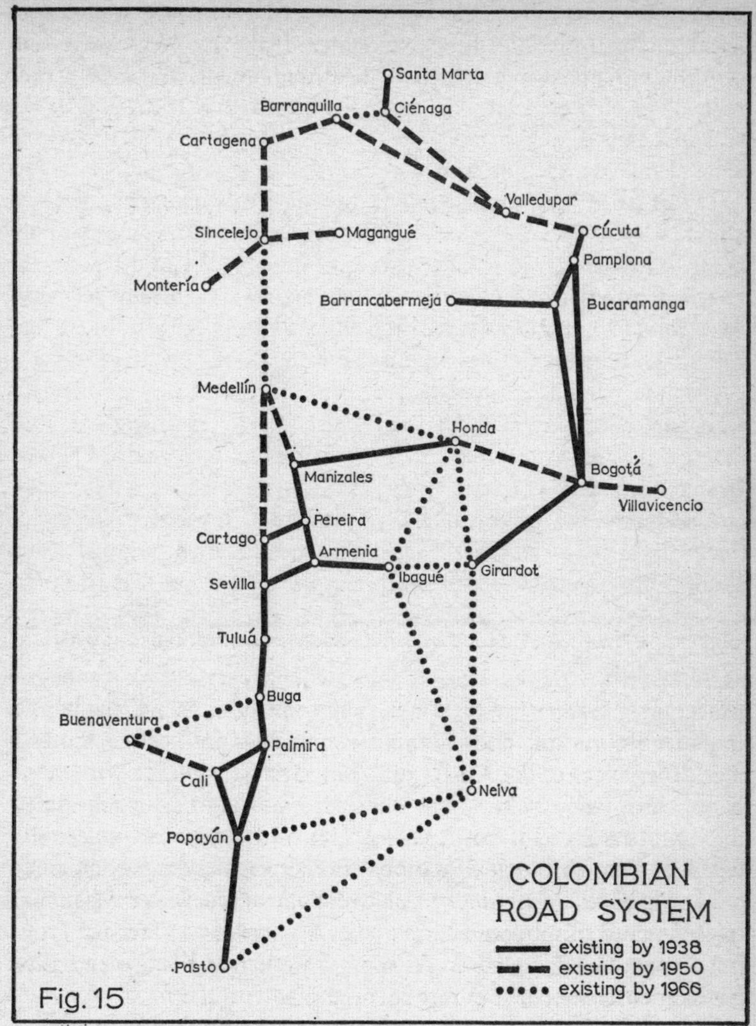

Fig. 15

have instituted a programme of 'social roads' and in Cuba road development has been seen as an important means by which the rural areas can be provided with adequate social services.[10]

Unfortunately these general road improvements have meant

major problems for the railway systems. In most cases where direct road competition has been encountered, the railways have been forced into operating deficits. This situation has frequently been

Table 30: Development of the South American Railway Network (km.)

	1945	*1955*	*1960*	*1964–9*
Argentina	42,578	43,930	43,923	40,180[2]
Bolivia	2,343	3,302	3,470	3,524[5]
Brazil	35,280	37,092	38,339	32,054[5]
Chile	8,188	8,366	8,685	10,136[4]
Colombia	3,064	2,834	3,562	3,435[3]
Ecuador	1,124	1,152	1,152	1,154[1]
Paraguay	499	499	499	441[6]
Peru	2,875	2,726	2,934	2,620[3]
Uruguay	3,005	2,991	474	2,762[3]
Venezuela	997	997		484[3]

1. 1964
2. 1965
3. 1966
4. 1967
5. 1968
6. 1969

Sources: UN ECLA (1965); Ruddle, K., and Hamour, M. (eds.) (1970), Table 96.

exacerbated by the way in which many rail systems are plagued by undercapitalization, poor administration and political pressures.[11] The experiences of the Argentinian railways are well-known. Undercapitalized owing to the difficulties of importing new stock during and after the Second World War, their position was further complicated by Perón's threat to nationalize the privately run companies. When the government finally took over control, the whole system was badly in need of modernization and in no position to face the growing competition from road transport. In a period of rapid inflation running costs soared, but fare increases, cuts in the number of railway employees and even closure of the least-profitable lines were politically inexpedient. With the roads taking the highest-yielding traffic, the only solution was to run at a deficit, something that the Argentinian railways have been doing for a number of years.[12]

If the Argentinian case is the most exaggerated, it does demonstrate many of the difficulties that have faced every South American railway at one time or another. All the continent's railways, whether private or state-run, operate at a deficit and there is little sign that there will be any short-term improvement. In these circumstances further railway construction would not be expected. But for a number of reasons several countries have built new lines. In 1961 the Chihuahua–Pacific line was opened in Mexico and the Ferrocarril del Atlántico in Colombia (see pp. 202–6). In the fifties railways were built in Bolivia linking the Santa Cruz region with Yacuíba in Argentina (1957) and with Corumba in Brazil (1955) and, in Ecuador, the Guayaquíl–Quito line was extended to Otavalo and San Lorenzo (1957). In Brazil several stretches of line are now being constructed, notably a shorter connection between Pôrto Alegre, São Paulo and Brasília.

A number of factors influenced the decision to build more lines. The need to export mineral products from inland sites was the main motive behind the Chihuahua–Pacific line, the Corumba–Santa Cruz railway was built as a result of the Brazilian government's wish to import petroleum from Bolivia, and the desire to link Brasília more firmly into the space-economy motivated construction of the Pôrto Alegre–São Paulo–Brasília link. While the motives differed, each decision represented a major transport investment with important spatial effects. We will consider some of these effects in the context of one new railway development below.

Air transport

Air travel was adopted quickly throughout Latin America because of the long distances, the difficult terrain facing land transport and the lack of alternative traffic modes. Scheduled air services were operating as early as 1919 in Colombia, and by 1925 the Compañía Mexicana de Aviación and Lloyd Aéreo Boliviano had been founded. Since this time the network of air routes has gradually expanded and today most cities are served by scheduled services.

The air system which has developed in the continent serves two principal functions, firstly as a major passenger transporter between the larger cities and, secondly, as a general carrier serving isolated rural areas. Inter-city travel has become particularly important in recent years as services have improved and today dominates the air traffic pattern in most countries of the continent. In Brazil, for example, large numbers of services cater for business travel between the major cities of São Paulo, Brasília and Rio. In Ecuador 55 per cent of all scheduled passenger journeys in 1966 were between the cities of Quito and Guayaquíl and another 12 per cent were made up by traffic from Cuenca to Guayaquíl.

Quantitatively less important but vital to the communities involved is the role of air transport in linking areas which are poorly served by other transport modes. Indeed a vast network of small landing strips has developed all over the more isolated regions of the continent by which passengers and cargo traffic are carried to the city areas. The importance of these links is reflected not only by the number of small air companies which operate in these regions, but also by the way the military frequently supplements these services.

In terms of resources, however, the majority of public funds are directed towards improvements in inter-city and international services. Large sums of money have been spent in building modern airports to accommodate the rising number of flights. In addition, most Latin American countries also operate their own international airlines; a practice which has been relatively successful in a number of cases but which has on occasion proved very expensive, as for example with the recent scandals concerning Aerolineas Peruanas S A.

Water transport

The coastal location of most Latin American nations and their dependence upon trade with Europe, the United States and Japan has made them rely heavily on sea transport. (As Fox points out, Mexico is something of an exception to this rule because it is so well linked by road with its principal trading partner, the United States.[13]) At the same time, a number of factors connected with port and shipping services in the continent have caused them considerable problems.

After Cole, J.P. (1966)

The first is that the majority of Latin American trade is carried by foreign shippers, a service which imposes a further drain on each nation's balance of payments and limits trading flexibility.[14] In Peru, for example, 82 per cent of the country's imports were carried by foreign-owned carriers in 1970. Not surprisingly, perhaps, many countries have long been attempting to develop their own shipping companies and to ensure that a percentage of all their trade is carried by these services. Thanks to these efforts the registered tonnages of the merchant marine of Brazil, Colombia, Cuba, Mexico, Peru and Uruguay have increased in recent years. Even so, it is quite apparent from Table 29 that these fleets are still tiny beside that of the United States.

The second major difficulty facing the continent is that port facilities in many areas are still inadequate. This is particularly the case with general-purpose ports where old-fashioned administrative procedures, slow handling speeds and a shortage of storage facilities frequently cause considerable delays and congestion. In some places limited berthing facilities cause shipping delays and result in the imposition of surcharges by the major carriers. Such a situation existed in the ports of Arica, Antofagasta and Matarani in 1968. Another common problem facing many general cargo ports is pilferage, which in some cases, especially in lighterage ports, has caused traffic to be diverted to competing ports.

By comparison with the general-purpose ports, those harbours which handle mainly bulk minerals or petroleum have relatively few difficulties. Many of them are operated directly by mining companies and can afford expensive handling equipment. Such is the case with the Tubarão terminal at Vitória, which handled some 18 million tons of Brazilian iron ore in 1969, and with the port of San Juan in Peru, which handled more than 10 million tons of iron ore in 1970. Similarly well equipped are those terminals which handle petroleum traffic, particularly those concerned with Venezuelan exports.

Apart from these few modern bulk-mineral ports, Latin American ports are generally poorly equipped and inadequately linked to their hinterlands. Such problems are fairly common throughout the continent, but undoubtedly the worst problems are faced by those nations without direct access to the sea. Bolivia, for example, has until recently faced a particularly severe situation, since both the ports and the rail routes which its traffic uses have been poorly equipped.[15] To use the rail route through Peru, traffic had to be loaded on to steamers at Guaqui in order to cross Lake Titicaca, before being transferred to the railway and continuing to Matarani. Even this tortuous route, however, has in the past been preferable to the alternatives through Chile. The shortest route from La Paz, through Arica, involved a notoriously slow rail journey and the use of lighters in the port itself. The longer route via Antofagasta was normally more efficient, but for La Paz traffic involved a journey of 1,170 kilometres compared to the 484 kilometres to Arica. Fortunately for Bolivia the past five years have seen a number of major improvements in this situation. Diesel working on the Arica–Viacha line has removed the need to use a rack system over a stretch with a 7 per cent gradient, and the construction of a new five-berth port at Arica has made direct loading possible. On the Peruvian route, a new mineral loader has been built at Matarani and new train ferries introduced on Lake Titicaca.

These improvements affecting Bolivia, Chile and Peru reflect the general tendency throughout the continent towards improving port facilities and the communications to them. In many ways there has been a revolution in port services as national governments have invested large sums of money in modernization programmes. The Colombian government introduced a major port-improvement programme in 1968, and since 1964 the Mexican government has built five new deep-water ports including two major ones at Mánzanillo (Calima) and Puerto Vallarta (Jalisco). Similarly in Brazil and Argentina many new ports have been built and in Peru major new berthing facilities have been constructed at Salaverry, Paita, Pisco and Ilo. Naturally there is still much to be done, but in this area at least Latin America shows genuine signs of making rapid progress.

One other aspect of water transportation in Latin America should also be mentioned – the use of rivers in certain lowland areas. Most of the major rivers of the continent, the Amazon, Orinoco, Plate and Magdalena, have traditionally been used as major transport routes, and on the Amazon sea-going vessels of up to 4,000 tons can reach Iquitos in Peru. While some of these routes have recently been suffering from competition from other modes of transport, they still carry large quantities of bulk products such as oil and cement. In addition in areas like Amazonia, where other transport links are limited, the river still represents the principal method of transport.

Examples of transport improvements

In recent years most Latin American governments have committed considerable sums of money to transport improvements. In the process they have revolutionized their port, rail, air and road facilities, which have produced many benefits for all sections of society. At the same time they have been faced by major doubts whether money spent on roads should have been spent elsewhere in the transport sector or even on investments outside the sector. Naturally enough, some governments have made incorrect decisions and have been severely criticized for choosing one investment rather than another. At the present time, for example, criticism is being levelled at major plans to improve international airports to accommodate the jumbo jet, at projects to build underground railways and urban motorways and at the Brazilian programmes to build roads across the Amazon basin.

In the next few pages attention will be paid to two such objects of criticism – the transcontinental roads and the Ferrocarril del Atlántico in Colombia. In considering these two sets of projects several points should be remembered. The first is that the different modes of transport pose very different problems of evaluation. The building of an oil pipeline, for example, involves few social changes and it can be evaluated on strictly commercial grounds. On the other hand, the construction of roads into rural areas has all kinds of social effects which makes any simple method of evaluation redundant. This means that any form of transport investment is more than simply a technical calculation – it is a political decision which involves the weighing of conflicting economic, social and political factors. Secondly, even the few technical criteria which are available to planners are subject to complications. Cost–benefit analysis, which is the most commonly employed technique, is probably more difficult to apply in less-developed countries than elsewhere. (See Appendix Two.)

Consequently, the reader should be reminded that there can be no simple answer to the question whether the decisions have been correct or not. Any criticisms are based more on differences in political values and philosophy than on matters subject to purely technical evaluation.

(I) THE TRANSCONTINENTAL ROADS

One idea which has long fired the imagination of many Latin Americans has been that of linking all parts of the continent into a single transport network. As long ago as the 1880s, the idea of a Pan-American Railroad was being actively canvassed, and a Pan-American

Fig. 17

Highway was first approved at a conference of American states in 1923.[16] It was the rapid construction of roads after 1940, however, that gave substance to the ideas of transcontinental links, and such roads have formed an important part of transport thinking ever since. In particular three sets of schemes have dominated such thinking: the Pan-American Highway (PAH), the Carretera Marginal de la Selva (CMS) and the trans-Brazilian projects (see Fig. 17).

The most advanced of these projects is the Pan-American Highway. Today the road extends some 45,648 kilometres from Cíudad Juárez in northern Mexico to Brazil and Chile. The road is complete with the exception of one stretch of 830 kilometres between Panama and Colombia, although long sections do not conform to the standard of an international highway. Of the total network in existence in 1963, in fact, only some 61 per cent was paved, and several sections near the borders of Bolivia, Peru, Colombia and Ecuador are in very poor condition. By the general standard of roads in many Latin American countries, however, it constitutes a relatively well-developed system.

By comparison the CMS is still very much an aspiration. The project was initially proposed during the sixties and was intended to run along the eastern flanks of the Andes from the Colombian–Venezuelan border, through Colombia, Ecuador, Peru and Bolivia to Paraguay. Of the 5,500 kilometres that required construction, less than 1,000 have actually been built; most of this is in Bolivia, where the Cochabamba to Santa Cruz road forms part of the route.

Much greater progress has been made with several of the trans-Brazilian roads. The idea of these roads was integrally connected with the Brasília project, and since completion of the federal capital two of the roads have grown apace. The Belém–Brasília road was finished during the fifties, and since 1970 the federal government has invested large sums in the Transamazónica. This latter project is intended to run 3,500 kilometres from Recife in the Brazilian north-east, through Itaituba, to Humaitá. There it will link with an existing road through Pôrto Velho and Rio Branco to the Bolivian frontier and will eventually provide a through route to La Paz and Lima. The Brazilian section is expected to be completed by 1974. Attention will then be directed to completing two other major projects, the

Cuiabá–Santarém road, which is planned to link the Transamazónica with the existing Pôrto Velho–Cuiabá–Brasília road, and the Brasília–Manaus–Bogotá road.

The extent, imagination and especially the expense of these three sets of projects I believe justifies considerable attention. If they are successful they will radically change the geography of the continent. Even if they are not, discussion of their objectives will shed considerable light upon some of the major ambitions of Latin American governments, particularly with regard to international economic integration, land colonization and regional development.

(a) *The objectives behind the projects.* Perhaps the principal aim of the PAH and of considerable importance to the other projects is the idea of accelerating international economic integration. Such an aim, of course, has been especially important since the creation of LAFTA and CACM. For, without an improvement in communications, even the most pronounced tariff reductions would have had only a limited impact on trade generation, especially since other forms of communication between Latin American countries such as coastal shipping have been sadly neglected.

Naturally, the development of such roads would have only a limited effect on trade generation in the case of the most widely separated nations. The 14,200 kilometres between Mexicali in north-west Mexico and Concepción in Chile, for example, is likely to preclude most direct cargo movement.[17] However, the main value of such roads is to integrate nations which are close geographically and where alternative transport links are not well developed. An important factor here is the nature of the regions linked by the road. In this respect it is interesting to compare the PAH and the CMS projects. The former passes through neighbouring areas of relatively high population density, which are likely to take advantage of improved road links and the reduction of trade tariffs. The CMS, however, is planned to link sparsely settled areas with low production. Here, the generation of traffic depends not only upon the comparative advantage of each area but upon the actual colonization of those areas. The result is likely to be much less productive than that of a road passing through an already colonized region.

A second motive, which has been particularly important in the case of the CMS and the trans-Brazilian projects, is to increase the rate of land colonization.[18] We saw in the last chapter that such an aim has formed an important part of the objectives of many agrarian-reform programmes. Certainly in Brazil, the construction of roads has been seen as a means of accelerating this process and thereby attracting large numbers of settlers from areas of land pressure in the north-east. Similarly with the CMS the idea of resettlement has been important in as far as all of the countries through which the road will pass have major land-distribution problems.

Related to this question of land colonization is the additional desire of many governments to use road development as a means of discovering and exploiting the resources of the nation. The possibility of developing large mineral deposits has played an important part in justifying the Brazilian projects, especially as it is known that there are extensive deposits of iron ore awaiting development.

Whether land colonization and mineral development are best achieved by means of such ambitious projects is another question. A case could be made that land colonization would be more successfully advanced by building short stretches of road between fertile land and the existing road network and by spending greater sums of money on supporting infrastructure. Perhaps the main reason why such an approach has not been adopted is the existence of a third motive – the underlying appeal of large-scale projects to national status and pride. An international or transcontinental road has much of the same appeal and glamour as that gained from building a steel works, establishing a national airline or launching a satellite – the project may gain publicity and bring domestic and international acclaim for the government. Such a motive has undoubtedly been important in several of these projects. Kubitschek's justification for building the Belém–Brasília road was based on such thinking, as was the support given to the CMS by ex-president Belaúnde of Peru. Similarly the present Brazilian government is strongly influenced by the effect such projects may have on national identification. This attitude has been conveyed in a recent pronouncement by the Minister of Transport: 'We have to conquer Brazil completely, and this will do it. The Transamazónica will be the dorsal spine of Brazil.'[19]

(b) *The realization and effects of the projects.* The extent to which these different projects have been implemented, and the basic objectives which motivated their construction, have obviously varied. Consequently any general evaluation of their impact is difficult and the following comments should only be seen as a tentative and preliminary judgement.

In the case of the PAH the principal objective of the road has been partially achieved. Trade between the different countries has increased during the past decade, in part owing to the formation of LAFTA and CACM but also because of the road. This effect would have been greater had less trenchant difficulties been encountered by the two main trading groups, but some of the potential advantages may be reaped now that the Andean Pact has been formed.

Certainly in comparison with the other projects the scheme has achieved some of its objectives at little real cost. This is because most of the route forms part of the individual nations' main road networks and would eventually have been improved as part of national transport planning. Only marginal additional costs have been involved in making these sections into parts of an international highway. Some improvements in quality have been made and some extensions near the frontier, but little more. This is made clear by the way that the best sections of the road run between areas with strong commercial connections and the worst sections are characteristically on the frontiers and in the more peripheral and backward regions. The best sections of the highway in Peru, for example, run along the coast linking the major cities and best farming areas, while the worst section runs up to the poorer *sierra* region and Bolivia. In Colombia, the sections between the largest three cities have all been paved, while the section south from Popayán through the poorer departments of Nariño and Cauca has not.

In one sense, of course, this situation demonstrates the project's lack of success and the low regard held for international agreements throughout the continent. At the same time, however, it is probably correct to say that the designation of national roads as part of an international road has encouraged construction in certain areas where it might otherwise have been delayed. It has been achieved through a certain amount of international pressure on particular national governments and by easing the task of transport ministries in obtaining national loans. It is also important to point out that those sections which have been most neglected have normally been the subject of some domestic political dispute. In the unbuilt section between Panama and Colombia, a whole series of arguments about the best route have delayed construction on the Colombian side; while one route passes through the city of Medellín, the second by-passes it. Consequently there is a great deal of political pressure being exerted on the national government to route the road one way rather than the other. Similarly, along the section between Arequipa and La Paz, political factors have delayed construction. In this case the main problem has been that a large part of the route runs parallel to the Southern Railway of Peru and to the La Paz–Guaqui railway in Bolivia. Any improvement to the road would seriously affect the competitive position of the railway, particularly since the latter is faced with the problem of shipping Bolivian traffic across Lake Titicaca in steamers. Consequently the Peruvian Corporation, which ran the railway until April 1971, campaigned actively against any improvements to the road and against permits being issued to lorries operating from Bolivia to the port of Matarani.

The PAH, therefore, has suffered from political difficulties concerning both its construction and the economic integration which was its principal rationale. The designation of long sections of national highways as an international road, however, has placed a premium on road construction and may have accelerated road improvements in certain areas, by creating an aura of prestige around the projects. Since this aura has required that few additional resources be diverted from priority projects in other sectors, few criticisms of the project can be made.

Quite the contrary, of course, has been true of the Brazilian projects, for these have posed a considerable burden on the exchequer and have caused funds to be diverted from other programmes. On the other hand, the completed projects have partially achieved some of the claims made for them. In particular, land colonization has led to rapid population growth in the area around the Belém–Brasília road. To some degree this has provided a safety valve for the country's major problem area, the north-east. Construction of these roads has provided employment for a large number of north-easterners, many of whom have been persuaded to remain in the area as colonists.[20] At the same time, however, doubts must be expressed about the wisdom of spending more money on road construction than on aid for farming families, if the principal aim of the projects is to encourage colonization. A less-ambitious road programme would have allowed the provision of more infrastructure and the granting of loans to settlers. This would seem to be of major importance in the light of comments which have recently been made that private road contractors are cutting the few services they are providing for settlers in an attempt to reduce costs and obtain contracts from the government.[21]

In sum, therefore, the Brazilian efforts have obviously had and will continue to have a major impact on the pattern of development in large areas of the nation. On most counts, however, the whole programme would seem to be over-ambitious and to have been achieved at the cost of more valuable projects. Fewer advantages will be gained by the north-east, for example, than if the funds had been invested in land reform or in infrastructure in the region itself. Similarly the discovery of new mineral resources could probably have been achieved more cheaply by encouraging foreign mining companies to pay part of the cost of road construction. Lastly, if colonization is in fact the principal goal, more attention should have been paid to the kind of area through which the road passes and to the facilities being provided for settlers. As it is, ease of road construction seems to have been the main factor orienting the direction of the road and little has been done for the settlers. The overall impression of the programme is that it is motivated as much by a reluctance to undertake radical reform programmes in other parts of the country as by the specific virtues of the roads themselves. Also influential has been the fact that the whole project has been endowed with an aura of progress which fits in well with what some Brazilians have suggested is the country's escapist psychology. It is just unfortunate that such feelings should be expressed at such a high financial cost to the society at large, and at a still higher price to the Indian societies which find themselves in the way of this 'progress'.

In many ways support for the CMS project reflects a similar escapist attitude. The difference is of course that this has not been sufficiently strong to get the road built, largely because the nations through which it would pass have insufficient funds to finance it. This is made clear by the figures in Table 31, which clearly show that

Table 31: Cost of the Carretera Marginal de la Selva Relative to National Road-Investment Budgets

	Construction cost of CMS (US $ millions)	*Cost of CMS as a % of total funds available for road investment*
Colombia	74·3	11·0 (1965–74)
Ecuador	53·5	15·6 (1964–73)
Peru	174·7	44·0 (1964–76)
Bolivia	50·8	47·3 (1965–79)

Source: Stokes, C. J. (1970), 134–8.

the road could not be built without drawing considerable resources away from other priority projects.

Certain sections have been completed, however, notably the stretch between Cochabamba and Santa Cruz in Bolivia. For this section at least, it has been calculated that 'it appears to have been a worthwhile investment from the economic point of view'.[22] It is interesting to note, though, that this conclusion was reached despite omitting the benefits to be derived from colonization. Rather, the principal benefits from the project accrued from savings on existing traffic costs and from the advantages gained by linking a major town and agricultural region to the rest of the country. While this explains why this stretch of road should be successful, it does not bode well for any other sections of the CMS, where the major benefits would be derived from colonization alone.

(II) THE FERROCARRIL DEL ATLÁNTICO

The Ferrocarril del Atlántico (see Fig. 18) was opened in 1961 and extends from La Dorada, a port on the River Magdalena, to the Caribbean port of Santa Marta. At La Dorada, the railway linked with the existing tracks from Bogotá and Ibagué, met the line from Medellín at Puerto Berrío, and the Bucaramanga railway near Puerto Wilches. The total length of the new line was some 700 kilometres.[23]

In deciding to build the railway the Colombian government had two main objectives in mind. The first was to provide a cheap and efficient transport link between the inland cities and the Caribbean

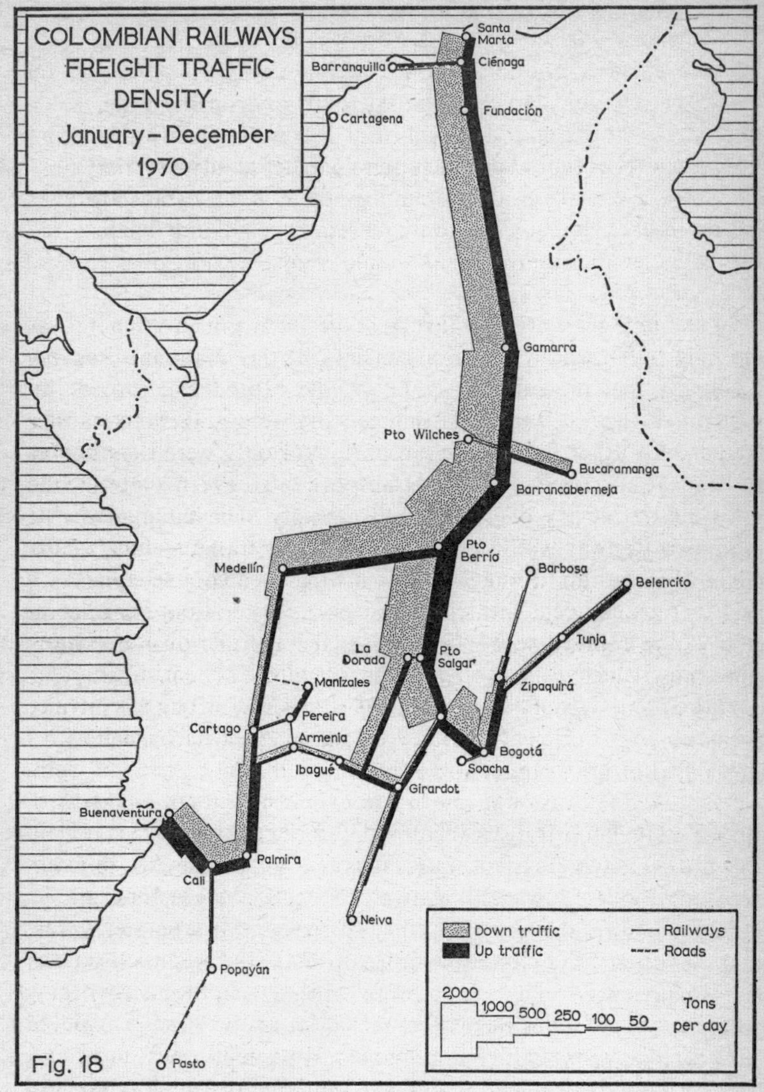

COLOMBIAN RAILWAYS
FREIGHT TRAFFIC
DENSITY
January – December
1970
Santa Marta
Barranquilla
Ciénaga
Cartagena
Fundación
Gamarra
Pto Wilches
Bucaramanga
Barrancabermeja
Pto Berrío
Medellín
Barbosa
Belencito
Tunja
La Dorada
Pto Salgar
Zipaquirá
Manizales
Pereira
Cartago
Armenia
Ibagué
Bogotá
Soacha
Girardot
Buenaventura
Palmira
Cali
Neiva
Popayán
Pasto
Down traffic
Up traffic
Railways
Roads
2,000
1,000
500
250
100
50
Tons per day

Fig. 18

coast, while the second was to integrate the various isolated branches of the existing network into a single system.

At the time the decision was made there was no adequate route between the coast and the interior. International traffic depended on two circuitous and largely unpaved roads and on the water route offered by the River Magdalena. For a country highly dependent upon imports of capital products and upon her ability to export competitively priced coffee, a major improvement in these transport links had a high priority. The only question remaining unanswered was whether the improvement should take the form of a railway or a paved road.

In making the decision in favour of a railway the government was strongly influenced by the argument of the National Railway Company that the railways could not be expected to provide an efficient service when their existing network obliged them to transfer traffic onto other modes of transport. Not only were they unable to compete effectively with lorry transport, but they could not use the individual stretches of line to full capacity. The building of the Atlántico Railway would allow them to carry traffic to both coasts (the line from Cali to Buenaventura having been completed in 1915) and thereby compete with road transport. In addition, the integration of the railway network would increase traffic on the existing lines thus reducing the average total cost of the system.

Although the second argument was sufficiently strong to convince the national government and the World Bank, the decision met with a great deal of criticism. It was argued, for instance, that the inefficiency of the railways was due less to the deficiencies of the network than to maladministration. In addition, some critics suggested that an integrated railway system was unnecessary because the different transport modes functioned relatively efficiently. Stokes, for example, commented that the air, road, rail and river transport systems were complementary and 'the expenditure to build the Atlántico railway was unnecessary'.[24] The counter-argument was that the inter-working of the different modes was in fact inefficient and links were achieved only at the expense of a certain number of wasteful trans-shipments.

A further criticism, and in my opinion the most telling, concerned not whether the railway should have been built, but about where it should have terminated. The decision to build it only as far as Santa Marta was extremely controversial, since it meant that the two largest Caribbean ports were not linked into the system. As Barranquilla and Cartagena are also the largest industrial cities in the area, by-passing them has had a detrimental effect on the total volume of traffic using the new line. Admittedly, considerable engineering difficulties would have been involved in crossing the swamps that line the lower Magdalena, but the advantages to be gained from linking the cities into the network would have been considerable. Moreover, at the time the railway was built Santa Marta did not possess adequate harbour facilities: so by failing to extend the railway the government became committed to a major port-expansion programme.

Whatever the criticisms, however, the decision to build the railway had a very important effect on the national transport system. The opening of the line brought about changes in the port traffic along the coast, affected the volume of shipping along the River Magdalena and meant that the roads to the coast were not paved. The effect on Santa Marta was by far the most dramatic. The total volume of imports increased from 28,271 tons in 1961 to 341,496 tons in 1969, and the fact that exports did not increase at a similar rate was due more to the decline in banana production in the Santa Marta area than to any failure of the railway.[25] The impact on the two main ports of the coast differed, however, for while Cartagena's traffic showed a marked decline, the total tonnage through Barranquilla actually increased. But there is no doubt that, had it not been for the railway, traffic through Barranquilla would have grown much more rapidly; it is probably only the city's commercial and industrial importance that has enabled it to maintain its share of the traffic.

The effect of the railway upon the total tonnages using the River Magdalena is also interesting, since traffic has actually increased despite the added competition. To a large extent this situation has arisen from factors unassociated with the railway's operation, and specifically because of increases in petroleum production from the oilfields around Barrancabermeja. In 1960, the volume of traffic dispatched from the town was 608,115 tons, 33 per cent of total river traffic. By 1967, that volume had risen to 1,053,428 tons, which represented 44 per cent of the total tonnage on the river. Of this increased volume originating in Barrancabermeja nearly 70 per cent was destined for the port of Cartagena, which of course the railway does not serve. The opening of the railway did affect traffic to some places, however, for the tonnages reaching Barranquilla declined from 237,616 tons in 1961 to 65,446 tons in 1969.

A further important effect of the railway was the manner in which it improved the efficiency of the railway system as a whole. It did this by helping to bring about a 53 per cent increase in freight ton/kilometres and a rise in the average length of haul from 141 to 420 kilometres. On the Atlántico railway itself, the average haul, for the Magdalena section, rose from 49 kilometres in 1960 to 810 kilometres in 1970.[26] Since the total tonnage carried by Colombian railways declined by more than 50 per cent during the same period, the building of the line and the consequent improvement in efficiency was particularly important.

The total effect on traffic density, however, was not as great as had been hoped. In 1960 the average density over the whole national network was 215 ton/kilometres, a figure which had risen to only 341 ton/kilometres by 1970. But the major disappointment for the railways was how little traffic from Barranquilla used the line. Even given the need to tranship in Ciénaga, the 1970 traffic was very small. In comparison with the 478,000 tons which passed through Santa Marta in that year, only 73,000 tons was destined for, or originated in, Barranquilla. The only comment to be made on this is that it was an inevitable result of the failure to extend the railways to Barranquilla. Indeed, this is so clear that plans were announced at the end of 1970 to extend the line from Santa Marta to Barranquilla and perhaps even to Cartagena as well.

Considerable improvements have been made in Latin America's transport system during the past twenty years: road networks have been extended and many new routes have been paved, air-systems have embraced new national and international services, and port capacities have been expanded through investment in new berths, handling equipment and storage facilities. In turn, these improvements have stimulated changes in different aspects of economic life. Paving and extending the domestic road system has encouraged interregional trade, widened the market for manufactured products, improved the marketing opportunities open to many farmers, and generally increased mobility in the rural areas. Improvements in air networks have cut travel times between major cities in Latin America and provided better links with developed countries. Extensions of sea-ports have reduced the cost of both imports and exports, thereby encouraging international trade.

It is clear that most of these improvements have brought widely distributed benefits. Extensions in the road network, for example, have accelerated the rate of national integration. This positive view would seem to be supported by the fact that both Cuba and Brazil have implemented major road programmes despite their widely different developmental objectives. Similarly, the development of international roads would seem justified in as far as they have encouraged Latin American economic integration. On the other hand, a number of projects have been less clearly beneficial to Latin American development. These projects may be classified under two headings: (1) those schemes which have tended to improve links between Latin America and the developed world, and (2) those which, by their sheer size, have raised questions relating to their cost, their specific purpose and their effect on less-privileged economic groups.

The first set of projects includes those which have tended to accentuate the traditional pattern of network orientation in the Third World. The construction of major railway lines has linked the continent's main export and consumption centres more firmly to the economies of Europe, Japan and North America. Similarly, the construction of new international harbours and airports has encouraged the development of trade not only between Latin American countries but between Latin America and the developed world. The improvement of these links may accelerate economic development; it is clear, however, that many Latin American intellectuals would disagree with this conclusion. They would argue that strengthening the connections with the developed nations can only accentuate the dependency relationship which is the basic cause of Latin American underdevelopment.

The second set of projects includes the construction of underground railways and the trans-Brazilian roads, and the establishment of international airlines. These projects would seem to demand answers to a number of critical questions. Could the enormous funds which have been devoted to them have been more effectively spent on other transport improvements? Should the Atlántico railway have been built, for example, or would the funds have been better spent on local road improvements? How many countries have established inefficient national airlines and merchant shipping fleets and in how many cases were the decisions to found them based on arguments of national prestige rather than on economic viability? Would the development of a Latin American fleet or airline have been a more profitable investment as well as a more-effective means of developing international co-operation? How far could major projects, such as the trans-Brazilian roads, have been carried through with less blatant disregard for powerless groups in the way of such projects?

None of these questions can be answered easily. Nevertheless, they do constitute issues which should be examined carefully by future students of transport development and considered by governments when they evaluate the benefits which will accrue from further transport improvements.

7: Regional Differences in Income and Welfare

The previous chapters have examined the spatial incidence of industrialization, urban development, rural change and transport improvements. So far, however, no real attempt has been made to assess the combined impact of these phenomena on spatial differentials. This chapter attempts to remedy that position by considering one facet of that problem: the pattern of inter-regional income and welfare disparities in different Latin American countries.

In undertaking such an analysis, it will be useful to consider certain empirical and theoretical studies made of this question in different parts of the world. Only by considering the Latin American experience in the light of these studies are we likely to understand the future directions of change.

Theoretical and empirical studies

In theory relative and absolute disparities in *per capita* income or welfare may follow a number of directions through time. They may increase or decrease, they may remain steady or they may follow a gradual parabolic or inverted parabolic course. The specific course followed depends upon the particular economic, social and political changes that take place within different societies and upon the overall economic growth performance.

A number of empirical studies, however, have suggested that there may be a universal pattern underlying regional disparities. In particular, they have suggested that there is a relationship between the growth of national income and the decline in relative regional-income disparities. While this convergence may take a number of years and may be preceded by a period of divergence, it will eventually occur in most countries.[1] The particular studies on which this conventional wisdom is based have two sources. The first consists of a number of studies of the North American experience, where there are bountiful data over a period of seventy years.[2] The second source is a single study of the differing experiences of a number of countries from all parts of the world.[3]

The evidence from the United States suggests that between 1880 and 1950 there was a pattern of gradual convergence. Easterlin, for example, found that the differences between *per capita* incomes in the eight economic regions of the country had declined throughout the period with the exception of 1920–30. Such a trend, he claimed, was the result of a gradual decentralization in industrial activity, of changes in the composition of final demand, and of the migration of labour from poorer to richer areas.

The study of different countries offered a slight variation on this pattern. In the first part of this study, Williamson analysed the regional-income differentials in twenty-four countries in relation to their national incomes, and found that the nations with the largest differentials were drawn from a group in an intermediate range of incomes. On the other hand, those nations with relatively high and those with relatively low *per capita* incomes had much smaller regional differences. In order to substantiate this finding he gathered time-series data on differentials in seven countries. From this second study he concluded that 'what little information we have on nineteenth- and twentieth-century Italian, Brazilian, US, Canadian, German, Swedish and French experience suggests that increasing regional inequality is generated during the early development stages, while mature growth has produced regional convergence or a reduction in differentials'.[4] From the two sets of evidence, he suggested that the ideal-typical sequence of change is one where as *per capita* income increases in a nation, relative regional differentials first widen, then level off and finally decline. He did comment, however, that the cross-section results offered stronger evidence in support of convergence than for early divergence. If this is the case, then they are more compatible with the United States evidence, which suggests gradual but persistent convergence.

While these results suggest that most countries may expect convergence, there must be reservations about applying them to areas such as Latin America. Firstly, there are a number of problems concerning the statistical data used which may weaken their validity. Secondly, there are several reasons why the experiences of the developed nations, which were the main source of information, should not be representative of what may happen in Latin America. In particular, the fact that most of these countries developed on an industrial base at a time when few competing areas existed suggests that industrial-based growth may not offer a similar panacea for Latin American underdevelopment. Thirdly, there is the problem that most of the evidence was drawn from studies of 'mixed economies'. In as far as many Latin American nations reflect a similar mixture of private and public enterprise, this evidence may be directly relevant. However, it is highly likely that the experiences of Latin American societies will vary more widely, owing to differences in government policy towards the goal of equality. There is little reason, for example, to believe that regional inequalities will follow the same path in socialist Cuba as in Colombia or Venezuela. And, since it is obvious that regional convergence in the developed countries has normally occupied more than half a century, there is every reason why certain Latin American governments may attempt to accelerate this tendency and why others may try to retard it. Lastly, while the evidence supports the view that relative differentials may decline, it says little about absolute differentials. There is a strong possibility that in some countries the narrowing of relative differentials may be accompanied by the widening of absolute differences in income. In general, therefore, this empirical evidence provides certain support for the idea of eventual regional-income convergence, without guaranteeing that absolute differences in *per capita* incomes will become more equal in the different regions of the continent.

A still more equivocal view emerges from an analysis of the theoretical literature on this problem, where a wide spectrum of views exists, ranging from certain neo-classical economic theorists who argue that convergence is inevitable, to certain Marxist writers who argue that increasing divergence is unavoidable within a capitalist system.

(I) NEO-CLASSICAL ECONOMIC THEORIES

According to a number of studies carried out by neo-classical theorists, convergence is likely to occur within a free market system.[5] The basis of this argument is that the factors of production in different regions (labour, land and capital) are employed in combinations which equalize the return on each factor in every region. Although these production inputs may be combined initially in a way which does not produce equal returns to each factor in the different regions, under perfect competition the mobility of factors will soon produce equilibrium. Thus, if wages paid in one region are higher than those in another, labour will move from the lower- to the higher-paid area, and thereby lead to an adjustment in the relative wage rates. Similarly, since the return on capital is higher in the low-wage region, capital will move from the capital-rich to the capital-scarce region. The mechanism in a free-market economy is likely to be self-adjusting and automatic.

The difficulty with this body of theory is that it is based on a number of strict assumptions, many of which are inappropriate in less-developed nations. In particular, the assumption of perfect competition, including perfect mobility of factors and full employment, is hardly characteristic of such societies. Consequently, the theory is incapable of explaining the pattern of regional differentials in wage rates and income in most less-developed countries.[6]

(II) ECONOMIC, SOCIAL AND TECHNOLOGICAL DUALISM

An alternative, but related, explanation of regional differentials is contained in the 'dualist' model. The principal idea behind this is that less-developed economies are characterized by two distinct but fully developed kinds of society. The first of these societies is backward, traditional and static in economic, social and technological terms. Its techniques of production are unsophisticated and labour-intensive, its values traditional and its commercial relationships with other parts of the nation are limited. On the other hand, parallel to this traditional society is a modern sector which is characterized by a dynamic growth-oriented economy. Within this economy, modern techniques of production and management, large injections of capital and the specialization of labour are characteristic.

There is general agreement that the dualist model fits most Latin American countries and that it is a highly undesirable feature of those societies. There are, however, fundamental differences between writers about the solutions required to change this situation. In part, these differences depend upon the ideology and the discipline of the observer. Writers who adopt a sociological or institutional approach to less-developed nations tend to emphasize the fundamentally different values in the two kinds of societies. Frequently, they conclude that this fundamental difference is due to the 'clashing of an imported social system with an indigenous social system of another style. Most frequently the imported social system is high capitalism.'[7] Any solution to underdevelopment therefore has to adopt two conclusions about policy: 'First, that as a rule one policy for the whole country is not possible, and second that what is beneficial for one section of society may be harmful for the other.'[8]

In opposition to this view, however, are a number of writers who believe that there are not fundamental social differences between the two kinds of society. Rather the differences are technological and the term 'technological dualism' is more appropriate than 'social dualism'.[9] In support of this case various economists have produced studies which show that the economic reactions of many backward societies are similar to those of more advanced societies. Bauer, for example, has demonstrated how the Yoruba tribes of Western Nigeria adopted cash cropping in response to market opportunities.[10] Higgins, in a critique of the idea of social dualism, has summed up many of these views as follows: 'Such institutional factors are indeed obstacles to economic development. They must be taken into account in any complete analysis, and still more in any recommendations for policy. But they are not immutable; the recent experience of Japan, and some recent anthropological studies of primitive cultures subjected to the 'shock' of occupation by American armed forces and similar cases, suggest that cultures can change with astonishing rapidity, and apparently with little pain, if the right formula is found.'[11]

Having accepted that institutional and social factors can be altered, many economists have developed models by which the modernization of such societies can be accelerated.[12] The basis of most of these ideas has been to absorb increasing numbers of workers into the advanced sector and to accelerate the diffusion of innovations and technology into the backward one. This kind of integration would accelerate development throughout both societies through a number of social, economic and political processes. Industrial activity in the urban centres, for example, would generate a demand for raw materials that could be produced in the backward areas. In time the movement of factories from the early industrial centres would take place, as managers began to seek lower labour costs and land rents. In addition, the characteristic ideas and innovations of the cities would gradually diffuse to the smaller towns and rural areas. This trickling down of technology would enable agriculture and commerce to become more efficient, thereby raising labour productivity and incomes in the poorer areas. If the whole process were actively encouraged by national governments the desired stage of 'take-off' would eventually be reached.[13]

A number of economists, however, have foreseen difficulties. Eckaus has noted that factor-market imperfections in less-developed societies might limit employment opportunities in the advanced sectors and slow down economic growth.[14] Several others have argued that problems might be encountered if the advanced sector formed an isolated economic and social enclave. Such an enclave, of which plantations and mines were typical examples, might export the economic surplus produced from cheap labour supplies and thereby fail to invest it in a way that would benefit the backward sector. Despite these difficulties, however, large numbers of writers have been optimistic about the chances of removing dualism by increasing integration between the advanced and the backward sectors. If such integration could be achieved, elimination of the associated income differentials would be an inevitable result.

(III) THE WORK OF HIRSCHMAN, MYRDAL AND FRIEDMANN

While the writing on 'dualism' is directly relevant to the problem of regional differentiation, it has not been written specifically in a spatial context. Two theories which emerged during the late fifties, however, did take regional interaction more directly into account. Both these theories tended to build upon the doubts of writers such as Eckaus, and suggested that regional interaction tended to perpetuate or increase the disparities between rich and poor areas. In these theories, Myrdal and Hirschman both accepted that, although backward regions gained many benefits from interaction, their relationship with more dynamic areas also activated strong negative effects.[15] On the one hand the benefits from the diffusion of ideas and economic activities tended to equalize incomes; on the other the polarization forces tended to perpetuate and increase these income differentials. The main problem was that, in a developing economy operating under a capitalist system, the differential-generating forces tended to outweigh the equalizing forces.

The main difference between their ideas and many of the dualist theories, therefore, revolved around the question of disparity-generating forces. In many cases they felt the dynamic sector's effect upon the backward areas was not beneficial but detrimental. Indeed, many of the links between the dynamic and the backward areas, rather than leading to the latter's development, were likely to hold it back. The construction of roads was one example of these negative effects. While new roads allow a more rapid diffusion of ideas and technology, they also permit new industrial plants to supply the poorer areas with goods previously supplied by the backward regions' own artisan industries. Labour migration, too, while constituting an equalizing force can also lead to the perpetuation of income disparities through the process of selective migration. Emigration from the backward areas may raise labour productivity in those regions, but this occurs only if the previous level of total production can be maintained. If the main body of migrants from the area is made up of the best-qualified, most enterprising and energetic group from the population, the effect on total production and productivity may well be negative. Lastly, a further example of the forces tending towards disparity is exploitation through monopolies. If the supply of new products to the backward areas is in the hands of a monopoly based in the prosperous region, an effective transfer of funds from the poorer to the richer areas will take place, thereby reducing still further the development potential of the former.

The development of the backward areas, therefore, does not depend simply on increasing the level of interaction between the dynamic and the traditional areas. It depends also upon the nature of this interaction, and both Hirschman and Myrdal agreed that although a free-enterprise economy permits development in the backward areas it also allows a faster rate of development in the already dynamic areas. The operation of the market system through time, therefore, is such as to magnify and increase the existing regional-income differentials.

The ideas of the two writers differed, however, over the role that national and state governments could play in rectifying these income disparities. Hirschman believed that once governments begin to play a role in planning development they intervene to reduce inequalities by applying progressive taxation programmes or by giving subsidies to the rural areas. Myrdal on the other hand, while believing that governments do attempt to reduce inequalities, thought that they succeed only in accentuating them. This fundamental difference between the two writers is illustrated in the following two quotations:

Hirschman: 'In other words, if the market forces that express themselves through the trickling down and polarization effects result in a temporary victory of the latter, deliberate economic policy will come into play to correct the situation.'[16]

Myrdal: 'That there is a tendency inherent in the free play of market forces to create regional inequalities, and that this tendency becomes the more dominant the poorer a country is, are two of the most important laws of economic underdevelopment and development under laisser-faire . . . In the next chapter, where I discuss the role of the state, my general point is that the activity of the state will tend rather to support those forces which result in the two broad correlations which I have been discussing.'[17]

In many ways the ideas of these two writers still hold an important position in our understanding of the process of regional-income divergence. Even so, it is obvious that their models do not examine in sufficient detail the nature of the equalizing and polarizing forces. In particular, they do nothing to relate the problem of regional-income divergence to the process of urbanization, or to the interaction between cities and their surrounding rural areas.

To some extent this gap has been filled in recent years by the work of Friedmann, who has related their ideas about regional interaction to a general theory of urbanization.[18] His core/periphery model provides 'a conceptual model that divides the space economy into a dynamic, rapidly growing central region and its periphery. The growth of the centre is viewed as being subsidized in part by the periphery.'[19] The theory develops previous work in that it relates the process of regional-income divergence to the stage of development and to the city system characteristic of that stage. In addition, it provides a strategy for regional-income equalization which is based upon the policy of regional development and the construction of regional growth-poles. By setting up rival centres of dynamism within an economy, the subsidization of the centre by the periphery will be gradually reduced.

The problem with Friedmann's strategy for regional development, however, is that it depends wholly upon government action to initiate the policy of decentralization. What happens if the government is not willing to implement such a policy, or, lacking the funds of Venezuela, is unable to implement such a radical plan? The model is also to be criticized in that it closely follows the stages theory of development evolved by Rostow, a theory which has been rejected by most writers as being factually inaccurate and of little assistance to understanding how 'take-off' can be achieved.[20] Finally, it also neglects the question of what policy should be followed in those cases where equity and efficiency prove to be incompatible objectives.

(IV) INTERNAL COLONIALISM

Friedmann's ideas on regional development are in many ways a logical development from Hirschman's model, especially in their underlying assumption that government action can lead to an eventual solution of regional-income disparities. There is, however, another school of thought which rejects this assumption and whose ideas are more a heritage of the work of Myrdal, Boeke and even Marx.[21] According to these writers most governments should be seen as being undemocratic, élitist and capitalistic and as representing societies with similar characteristics. Under such régimes, therefore, any actions taken will tend to benefit the richer sections of the community rather than to redress the balance between rich and poor. On the problem of regional-income disparities, existing differentials are more likely to increase as a result of government participation than to decrease.

Such writers would also argue that other commentators have tended to misunderstand the whole process of development and underdevelopment, whether at the regional, national or international level of analysis. The dualism theory, for example, is wrong in so far as it fails to recognize that all backward areas have not always been poor. Regions such as the *sierra* of Peru were in fact supporting advanced civilizations before the onset of colonialism. Their backwardness, poverty and traditionalism, rather than being an eternal condition, has been the result of four hundred years of economic and political colonialism. Such areas are backward not because they have failed to develop but because other regions consistently expropriated capital and wealth from them. By such means, the developed nations accelerated their own growth at the expense of the poor nations of the world. Similarly, the backward regions within those poor nations have been handicapped by the transfer of their economic surplus to the more prosperous regions. The resolution of this dilemma cannot be achieved by relying on the actions of governments, who represent the most economically powerful sections of the community and whose policies lead to the benefits of growth by-passing the backward areas. The only long-term solution is to achieve a structural and revolutionary reform of government.

Although this would seem to be an accurate description of the situation in some less-developed countries, it is difficult to believe that it applies to the same extent in all. What is appropriate to all, however, is the manner in which the actions of governments in one field, for example industrialization, tend normally to benefit the richer and urban regions of a nation. These processes by which governments can deliberately or unconsciously exploit the peripheral areas will be examined later, but they undoubtedly represent an important element in the process of regional-income divergence.

The term 'internal colonialism', however, is not restricted to government actions; it is a commentary on the whole social and economic structure of less-developed countries by which the privileged exploit the poorer classes of society. Regional-income disparities are only one aspect of what is essentially a social problem. They are caused by factors such as the high concentration of land and property in relatively few hands, by the élite's control of commercial and economic institutions and by the exclusion of the exploited classes from effective political participation. Such factors are seen to be particularly marked where racial differences augment class differentiation. While these theories are not specifically spatial in character, they are useful in explaining regional differentials in income when the different class and racial groupings are concentrated in specific areas. In fact, much of the literature on 'internal colonialism' has emerged from countries where such spatial concentrations exist; in particular, the studies of González Casanova, Barraclough and Cotler have been based on the Mexican and Peruvian experience.[22] In general the view seems to hold that where such regional disparities do exist they can only widen under the existing social and economic system. No narrowing of these disparities will occur until there is deep-rooted structural change.

Studies of the Latin American experience

Unfortunately, given the sparseness of data, it is very difficult to confirm or reject these different hypotheses. Some information does exist for three countries, however, and the next few pages will examine these data and the different conclusions drawn from them.

(1) BRAZIL

Regional-income data exist in Brazil for the period 1939 to 1966; a longer and more continuous series than for any other Latin American country. Perhaps as a result there have been more studies of regional differentials in Brazil than in the rest of the continent put together. Unfortunately, these numerous studies have often produced conflicting results.

Controversy over the pattern of regional differentials first emerged during the fifties, when several Brazilian studies showed that income disparities were increasing. This evidence was soon refuted by Robock, who argued that between 1950 and 1960 income differentials among the states of Brazil had decreased.[23] He suggested that the previously held idea that they were increasing was an error that had been brought about by the lack of 'objective regional analysis' and by the way such studies had employed point-to-point comparisons or index numbers. Two years later Robock's own conclusions were questioned by Baer, who fanned the controversy by claiming that the differentials had increased and by suggesting that this had occurred largely because of the policies followed by the Brazilian federal government.[24]

Since these first studies, several others have appeared which have clarified the situation in some respects. Even so, they have failed to agree completely on whether the differences are decreasing or not.[25] Gauthier and Semple, for example, have argued that there was a divergent trend in the *rates of growth* of the northern and southern states during the late forties and early fifties, a trend which was reversed during the late fifties and sixties. Graham, on the other hand, has argued that there was a slight convergence in *per capita* income among the states between 1950 and 1960 brought about mainly by an increase in the volume of migration. This last conclusion is supported by Almeida's analysis, in which it is argued that from 1939 to 1966 there was actually convergence in *per capita* income by states. He does add, however, that the tendency was not constant for all years of the period and that the opposite trend occurred during eight of the twenty-eight years.

What is the reader to make of this variety of conclusions? To some extent the differences between the writers can be explained by the fact that their studies encompassed slightly different time periods. An additional problem is that few of them agreed to measure inequality in the same way: several different criteria of inequality were employed and different combinations of states used as bases for measurement. Baer and Robock used the figure of each state's *per capita* income as a percentage of the average for the nation as a whole. Almeida used three coefficients of inequality previously employed by Williamson in the study mentioned on p. 210. Graham used the sums of the differences between income and population shares for selected regional groupings, and Gauthier used an information statistic measure of income-growth inequality. Thus some authors were measuring the inequality between the poorest individual states and the richest, while others were measuring the inequality between groups of states. Some were measuring *per capita* differences in income, and others were analysing differences in rates of growth. Nor was analysis helped by the fact that two commentators managed to calculate different numerical results using identical measures of inequality![26]

Table 32: Brazil's Per Capita Income: Shares by State 1947–66

(Per cent of national average)

North	*1947*	*1950*	*1953*	*1957*	*1960*	*1963*	*1966*
Amazonas	94	76	63	78	68	70	69
Pará	65	58	54	61	56	60	65
North-east							
Maranhão	33	34	32	30	34	30	29
Piauí	37	29	26	28	29	25	29
Ceará	44	47	37	42	45	45	45
Rio Grande do Norte	53	53	43	49	57	60	59
Paraíba	43	48	38	43	54	51	40
Pernambuco	63	61	57	61	60	68	64
Alagoas	46	44	42	49	51	49	45
Sergipe	53	49	52	54	55	53	55
Bahía	53	50	47	49	56	42	53
South-east							
Minas Gerais	77	74	79	81	71	69	81
Espírito Santo	66	79	80	77	64	57	70
Rio de Janeiro	100	102	98	98	95	98	101
Guanabara	330	334	312	311	291	271	249
South							
São Paulo	184	189	190	177	178	194	187
Paraná	103	117	120	99	111	82	81
Sta Catarina	101	84	91	88	90	75	83
Rio Grande do Sul	122	112	121	127	120	119	118
Central West							
Mato Grosso	79	72	105	84	78	78	67
Goiâs	46	54	64	54	55	70	64
Brazil	100	100	100	100	100	100	100

Source: Baer, W. (1964); Robock, S. H. (1963).

Despite the discrepancies, however, there does appear to be a measure of agreement. While differences arise over the pattern during the late forties and early fifties, all the studies seem to support the movement towards convergence in the late fifties. In addition, there seems to be irrefutable evidence that relative differentials have decreased during the period of the early sixties.

Table 33: Brazil's Per Capita Income by State, 1947–66
(U S dollars)

	1947	*1966*
North		
Amazonas	211	218
Pará	146	207
North-east		
Maranhão	74	90
Piauí	83	92
Ceará	99	142
Rio Grande do Norte	119	186
Paraíba	97	127
Pernambuco	142	203
Alagoas	104	143
Sergipe	119	174
Bahía	119	166
South-east		
Minas Gerais	173	257
Espírito Santo	151	221
Rio de Janeiro	225	320
Guanabara	743	789
South		
São Paulo	414	593
Paraná	232	256
Sta Catarina	227	261
Rio Grande do Sul	275	373
Central West		
Mato Grosso	178	213
Goiâs	104	203
Brazil	225*	317†

*Gross domestic product for 1948.
†Gross domestic product – average for 1965–7.

Source: Baer, W. (1964), and *Anuario Estatístico do Brasil*, 1969.

The pattern over the whole 1947 to 1966 period seems to support the idea of convergence. This is best shown by Williamson's V_w and V_{uw} measures both of which reflect a strong decline during the period, from 0·70 to 0·59 in the first and 0·67 to 0·54 in the second. These overall measures are supported by the manner in which the relative differentials between the richest and the poorest states in the country also declined.

Perhaps more important than this convergence in relative differentials is the fact that absolute differentials between the richest and the poorest states increased. This is demonstrated in Table 33, which shows that the *per capita* income of the poorest state in the country improved from 74 dollars in 1947 to 90 in 1966, while the *per capita* income of the richest state increased from 743 dollars in 1947 to 789 in 1966. Although the relative differences between the richest and the poorest states declined, the absolute difference widened from 669 dollars in 1947 to 699 in 1966. It is unfortunate that most observers have concentrated more on the relative differentials than on the important absolute inequalities.

(II) MEXICO

A certain amount of information on regional-income differentials is also available in Mexico. Unlike the Brazilian data this does not form a series but has been calculated for three dates only, 1940, 1950 and 1960. From this data Mendoza has computed measures of inequality for the states using the coefficient of variation (Williamson's V_{uw} measure). He found that the disparity between the states declined gradually from 1940 to 1950 and markedly from 1950 to 1960, the coefficients for the three dates being 0·91, 0·81 and 0·58 respectively.[27]

It is also clear from this data that the differentials between the richest and the poorest states declined during the period. In 1940 it was 18·8 to 1 and, although it had climbed to 21·6 to 1 in 1950, by 1960 it had fallen dramatically to 9·9 to 1. While the changes that have taken place have seen an overall rise in *per capita* income in every state except the wealthiest in 1940, it is quite obvious that the absolute differentials between states have increased over the whole period. In 1940 the difference between the 458 pesos *per capita* in Oaxaca and the 8,621 in Baja California Norte was 8,163 pesos, but by 1960 the difference had risen to 9,863 (1,101 in Oaxaca and 10,964 in the Federal District). As in Brazil, therefore, absolute standards of living have risen, relative differentials have declined and absolute differentials have widened.

Table 34: Poverty Levels in Mexico

	Percentages		
	1940	*1950*	*1960*
Baja California Norte	22·6	19·8	17·1
Chihuahua	36·8	30·9	25·2
Coahuila	32·9	26·6	21·9
Nuevo León	30·5	25·6	18·5
Sonora	33·7	27·1	22·2
Tamaulipas	32·6	27·2	23·0
Aguascalientes	35·9	34·2	27·1
Baja California Sur	38·2	32·9	28·0
Colima	37·8	33·8	30·8
Durango	44·6	40·7	35·9
Jalisco	43·9	39·2	31·5
Nayarit	44·8	41·0	36·2
Sinaloa	47·4	42·1	34·6
Guanajuato	50·5	45·1	39·1
México	55·9	49·7	39·5
Michoacan	50·8	45·0	39·1
Morelos	44·2	34·8	29·7
Hidalgo	58·3	53·0	48·9
Puebla	55·4	49·9	44·1
Querétaro	57·5	52·8	47·3
San Luis Potosí	52·9	47·9	43·3
Tlaxcala	53·9	47·7	42·6
Zacatecas	50·2	47·6	43·5
Chiapas	61·1	55·2	49·7
Guerrero	63·0	56·4	51·7
Oaxaca	63·8	57·4	51·9
Campeche	38·9	33·0	28·4
Quintana Roo	49·0	42·2	38·0
Tabasco	55·0	48·5	42·4
Veracruz	48·0	43·1	35·6
Yucatán	38·4	32·3	30·8
Distrito Federal	11·2	8·8	8·8
Total Mexico	46·0	39·4	33·1

Source: Wilkie, J. W. (1967).

However, the Mexican income data, unlike the Brazilian, have been supplemented by various studies of the changes in social measures during the period. In one of these studies Wilkie produced an index of poverty for the 1940–60 period made up of seven different social measures (Table 34). He claims that they 'represent relative degrees of non-modern standards of living. The items cover the persons actually stating in the census that they (1) are illiterate, (2) speak only an Indian language, (3) live in a community with less than 2,500 persons, (4) go barefoot, (5) wear sandals, (6) regularly eat tortillas instead of wheat bread, and (7) are without sewage disposal.'[28] By calculating the arithmetic average of these variables, he obtains an index from which it is obvious that there has been an overall improvement in basic conditions in every state over the period. It is also clear that relative differentials declined during the two decades.

This evidence has been supported by Mendoza, who used a similar index of welfare calculated as the arithmetic average of five of the previous variables, excluding those who speak only an Indian language and those who wear sandals.

While the use of such a limited number of social variables and their combination through an arithmetic average leaves many doubts about the conclusions of these two studies, there can be little doubt that the overall pattern of regional change in Mexico has been favourable. At the same time the change is not sufficiently great for Wilkie to conclude that 'Mexico need not and should not sacrifice economic development for social expenditure'.[29] For, as Barkin has pointed out in a critique of the work, 'serious problems in the distribution of income still persist, and . . . there has been little or no progress in attacking the sizable regional disparities which continue to characterize Mexico'.[30]

(III) COLOMBIA

Three estimates of regional incomes have been made in Colombia, one for 1951 and 1964, one for 1958 and one for 1964.[31] Unfortunately, these data are inconsistent: according to one estimate the differential in *per capita* income in 1964 between the richest and the poorest departments was 11 to 1, while another estimate for the same date records the difference as 4 to 1.[32]

If we ignore this inconsistency and consider the change that occurred between 1951 and 1964 as recorded in one set of data, we obtain an approximation of the pattern during the period. According to this information there would seem to have been little change in differentials: the coefficient of variation at the two dates was almost identical and the differential between the richest and the poorest department remained at 11 to 1. This pattern, despite its suspect source, is supported by data on fourteen social and economic variables for the same dates. These variables include the number of cars per 1,000 inhabitants, the proportion of houses with different kinds of services, and the proportion of deaths where a death certificate was issued.

From these data indices of 'welfare' have been computed for 1951 and 1964 by a method known as principal components analysis.[33] According to the indices little change occurred in departmental differentials between the two dates (Table 35). The ranking of departments on the indices at both dates is almost identical, and the differ-

Table 35: Index of 'Living Standards' in Colombian Departments 1951 and 1964

Department	*1951*	*1964*
Atlántico	−6·97	−5·07
Cundinamarca	−4·69	−5·73
Valle	−3·10	−3·33
Caldas	−2·77	−0·88
Antioquia	−2·57	−2·47
N. de Santander	0·49	−0·50
Santander	0·59	−0·80
Tolima	1·18	0·94
Bolívar	1·39	1·26
Huila	2·01	1·41
Magdalena	2·03	1·76
Cauca	2·75	3·10
Boyacá	2·92	2·98
Nariño	3·13	2·83
Chocó	3·60	4·48

The higher the value the lower the level of welfare. Mean value of series equals 0·00.

Source: Gilbert, A. G. (1970).

Table 36: Socio-Economic Data for the Most and Least Prosperous Colombian Departments, 1951–64

	Date	*Coefficient of Variation*	*Atlántico*	*Cundina-marca*	*Cauca*	*Nariño*	*Chocó*
% of deaths with	1951	0·55	81·3	50·8	14·3	6·0	18·5
certificate of total deaths	1964	0·14	87·5	67·7	22·7	26·1	20·6
% of houses without	1951	0·23	36·8	61·4	90·4	92·3	95·8
water	1964	0·22	39·4	68·4	82·0	77·7	94·8
% of houses without	1951	0·21	38·3	65·1	89·2	90·6	93·7
electric light	1964	0·24	36·4	46·6	84·1	78·8	94·5
Telephones per	1951	1·03	15·0	23·2	0·9	0·8	2·7
1,000 persons	1964	1·04	34·0	55·8	3·3	3·5	4·0
Cheques cashed *per*	1951	0·93	7·6	8·6	0·6	0·8	0·3
capita ($000)	1964	0·85	17·3	32·1	2·9	2·8	1·3
Cars per	1951	1·02	89·1	88·8	9·7	6·6	0·3
10,000 population	1964	1·02	89·2	136·2	9·7	10·8	0·6

Source: Gilbert, A. G. (1970).

ential between the highest 'score' and the lowest hardly altered. From this index, however, no idea can be gained about the absolute or relative increases in 'welfare' between the two dates. Therefore, a number of variables have been presented in Table 36, which show the changes in the coefficient of variation between the two dates as well as the differential between the highest and the lowest departments. From these it is quite clear that little change took place between the two dates. While there was a greater measure of equality in the distribution of death certificates and cheques, no changes occurred in the distributions of the other variables. In terms of the differential between the richest and the poorest departments, however, there were changes: the gap in terms of death certificates and house services became narrower and that on more economic variables such as cheques, cars and telephones became wider.

The overall pattern in 'welfare', therefore, shows no consistent pattern, either towards or away from convergence. The general tendency was for the extreme differences in 'welfare' to remain throughout the period.

The pattern underlying the changes in regional differentiation in these three countries is thus fairly clear. Firstly, it is certain that absolute standards in most areas have improved through time, even in the poorest regions. Secondly, relative differentials, whether measured as the difference between richest and poorest departments or by an index of overall regional inequality, seem to have been declining slowly. Thirdly, there are some signs that absolute differentials between the poorest and the richest regions have been widening. Lastly, whatever the changes in terms of inequality the basic differentials between rich and poor areas have remained. It is also clear from the rate of convergence that these differentials will remain for many years ahead.

Whether or not this pattern is general to the whole of Latin America, it is impossible to say. In some respects the development experiences of these three countries differ from those of many nations in the continent. The rate of economic expansion in Brazil and Mexico, for instance, has tended to be faster than in other countries. Similarly, all three possess governments which have made some attempt to reduce regional differentials – an attempt which distinguishes them from the handful of states where no action has been taken and from the even smaller number where really effective policies have been implemented. In general, however, while the degree of convergence is likely to vary by country, most of the processes which have led to relative convergence in Brazil, Colombia and Mexico have also been operating elsewhere. We shall consider these processes in the next few pages.

The processes leading to regional differentiation

In examining the underlying causes of regional differentiation, we should be aware that regional disparities are but one aspect of the social and economic polarization which operates throughout Latin American societies. In particular, we must be aware that regional disparities reflect in many ways the dichotomy between rural and urban areas examined in Chapter Five. In explaining the processes which are leading to regional convergence or divergence, therefore, we are also explaining the factors which are modifying the relationship between urban and rural areas. A similar point also applies to the differentiation between class and race. Regional disparities, in fact, form part of the total polarization which exists in all Latin American societies. It is not a separate phenomenon but part and parcel of the polarization between rich and poor, privileged and underprivileged and urban and rural societies.

(I) THE PROCESS OF INDUSTRIALIZATION

Although industrialization has been a necessary process and has brought a variety of benefits for individual Latin American countries, it has tended to accentuate the problem of regional-income disparities. The first and most obvious reason why this has occurred is that modern industrial plants tend to be located in a limited number of areas. And, as was explained in Chapter Three, this phenomenon has been particularly acute in Latin America, where so many countries are dominated by one overwhelmingly large metropolitan centre. The result of this tendency is that a few areas have benefited directly from increased industrial expansion while many other areas previously dependent upon artisan industries have seen those industries decline.

The second reason why it has exacerbated regional differentials is that industrial growth has been financed in part by those areas which have not benefited directly from it. Such a situation is of course an inevitable part of capital mobilization in less-developed nations and is the subject of a vast literature. In part, however, the position of the poorer areas has been worsened by the manner in which Latin American governments have encouraged the development of manufacturing. In particular, the policy of import-substitution has in many cases led to a deterioration in the terms of trade and the prosperity of the rural areas.

Baer has summarized how the process has operated in Brazil, but his argument would seem relevant to many nations in Latin America.[34] He argues that, in the absence of international trade barriers, the poorest regions would be permitted to import from abroad the few manufactured goods they required: the clothing, bicycles, transistors and similar articles consumed in the rural areas would all be freely available from Europe, the USA and Japan. However, once import-substitution becomes the policy and tariffs or quotas are levied on imports, the position of these areas changes. In the place of imported products only manufactured goods produced by national companies in the main industrial centres will be available. If the prices and quality of the new products were identical, there would be no real problem, but this has rarely been true in Latin America. The result is that the rural areas have to pay more for their imported goods than before, and in fact subsidize the industrial growth which is benefiting the urban areas.

However, the situation is far worse for many areas which are themselves producing export goods, such as north-east Brazil, the *sierra* of Peru and the coffee regions of Colombia. For these areas the subsidizing mechanism may be two-fold – not only are they paying the industrial areas higher prices than they would for imported products but they are also often obliged to sell their foreign earnings at an unfavourable exchange rate laid down by the national government. The over-valuation of the national currency discriminates against the areas exporting primary products and effectively subsidizes those regions importing foreign capital equipment.

Apart from the problems caused for the backward areas by governments' attempts to accelerate industrialization, industrial growth generates inequalities in other ways. Unionization tends to occur more rapidly among industrial workers than among workers in most other sectors; industrial labour in most Latin American plants, and especially in Argentina, Chile and Uruguay, belongs to a trade union. Consequently, wage rates in industry tend to rise more rapidly than in other sectors, thereby benefiting the handful of urban centres where manufacturing plants have concentrated. In addition to higher wages, demands for social-security benefits such as hospital treatment are normally conceded, again widening the gap between these centres and the rural areas. So not only is industrial growth financed in part by the rural areas, but the process produces an industrial working élite who are dedicated to advancing their own material position. While the rural areas continue to lack bargaining power, the industrial centres' demands are supported by workers' organizations.

Of course, one solution to these problems would be to encourage industrial development in the rural areas and smaller towns. However, such a solution is difficult to implement in most Latin American countries for, as we have seen, the more successful attempts to encourage industrial dispersal proved expensive and beyond the pockets of most governments. In fact industrial decentralization appears an unlikely panacea for the poorest regions, and industrial development must generally be expected to create further income and welfare differentials.

(II) THE INSTITUTIONAL STRUCTURE

The process of industrialization is not the only mechanism by which certain regions benefit at the expense of other areas of the country. Vitally important, too, are the more direct transfer mechanisms which are related to the institutional structure of the country and which are associated with the concept of 'internal colonialism' mentioned above.

One example of such a transfer mechanism has been observed in the relationship between the *sierra* and the coastal regions of Peru.[35] In this case, the *sierra* has a trade surplus in its dealings with the more prosperous coastal areas. It gains little benefit from this surplus, however, because most of the trade is controlled by a small number of agricultural, mining and commercial enterprises operating from Lima. Consequently the profits from this trade are not reinvested in the *sierra* but are transferred to banks in Lima and abroad. The main benefits in terms of investment and expenditure, therefore, tend to accrue in the region experiencing the trade deficit. Griffin has even suggested that the level of consumption in the *sierra* is 'lower than it would have been had there been no trade'.[36] Although this is an extreme view and has not been supported by other writers, there is no doubting the effect this transfer has had on regional disparities.[37] The fact that the trade surplus represents some 17 per cent of the gross regional product of the *sierra* region, but only 4 per cent of that of the coast, means that the transfer has severely reduced the potential growth rate of the former without critically benefiting that of the latter.

Such a transfer mechanism operates in many areas of Latin America. It is especially important in agricultural regions, however, where landowners live outside those areas. In such cases a large part of the income from trade is transferred out of the region and is spent or invested in the major cities of the country. An additional problem is that taxes are commonly levied on these incomes at the place where the recipients live, so that the areas where the income is produced do not even benefit from the taxes paid on it. The result of this transfer is that the producing region does not have the funds to provide schools, qualified teachers, doctors and other social facilities.

(III) THE ROLE OF GOVERNMENT

The principal difficulty facing governments in Latin America is that many policies devised to accelerate social and economic development are likely to increase regional disparities. The strategy of industrialization accelerates development in certain nodal regions. The improvement of roads tends to encourage migration to the cities by the more enterprising and better-educated rural people. The construction of electricity generators, power systems and other forms of economic infrastructure is destined to support the industrial growth programme.

Unless governments take compensatory action, efforts to accelerate the national growth rate are likely to favour certain areas at the cost of others. In order to counteract this tendency many governments do attempt to introduce programmes which will spread benefits more widely. Most Latin American governments build schools and hospitals to serve the population in all parts of the country. However, even when action is taken to spread the benefits widely, there are factors operating which guarantee that the more prosperous regions will gain most.

The most important of these factors is that the more vociferous and politically aware groups in the society, the middle classes and the industrial workers, are normally concentrated in the urban areas. Any action by the government that threatens to reduce the living standards of these groups is opposed by some form of demonstration or political pressure. A common example is the way in which street demonstrations often erupt when plans are announced to raise city bus-fares. In order to avoid such protests many governments attempt to maintain fares and even food prices at low levels in the cities. They also ensure that the majority of social services are concentrated in the same areas.

Just the opposite situation exists in the rural areas, where policies to improve social services are seldom effectively canvassed by the rural population. Even when such plans are announced, the man-power problem always poses a major restriction on their likely success, since the majority of professional workers live in the major cities and rarely wish to work in the poorer or rural regions. The overall result is that, while these areas normally gain something from government action, this action does little to remove the basic differentials.

(IV) THE ROLE OF MIGRATION

Migration has been a principal factor reducing regional income and welfare differentials throughout Latin America and most writers on Latin America have accepted this.[38] Without such migration to the cities, there can be little doubt that the population explosion, and the limited diffusion of agricultural improvements, would have led to an untenable rural situation. Although it is clear that selective migration does reduce the developmental potential of the rural areas still further, migration has been a vital adjunct of the development process. Whether the exodus need have been so large, and whether it would have been lower given a more equitable land-ownership system, is another question. What migration has achieved, however, is to maintain the levels of living in the rural areas and prevent them deteriorating. By this action migration has helped reduce the effect of forces tending towards regional divergence.

What then are our general conclusions about the direction and magnitude of the processes governing regional-income levels in Latin America? In the first place, it would seem that those writers on dualism who believed that interaction between the developed and traditional sectors of a society would lead to overall growth were too optimistic. It would seem that the ideas of Myrdal and Hirschman and those of the 'internal colonialism' school are correct in as far as the interaction between such areas does in fact harm the poorer regions. Indeed, it is clear that the early characteristics of the growth process, such as the beginnings of manufacturing, do tend to benefit the richer areas at the expense of the poorer. This is true both in terms of relative inequalities and of absolute differences.

In the second place, however, it seems that this divergence of regional incomes does eventually diminish, so that as development proceeds the relative disparities among regions do not actually become larger, although it is clear that absolute differences widen considerably. And while the standards of living in the rural areas do not actually decline, the gap between the rural and urban standards of living does increase absolutely. Although this position is more hopeful than the 'internal colonialism' school would accept, it does mean that the majority of the benefits from growth do accrue in the urban areas. In addition, within these urban areas the benefits tend to reach only limited sections of the community.

Thirdly, it seems that Myrdal's opinion that government action would exaggerate the rural/urban dichotomy is only partially true. Certainly the policies which are designed to encourage urban and industrial development do seem to cause regional-income divergence, but, on the other hand, their activities in the fields of health and education provision represent an improvement on the existing situation. While the overall impact of government policies in most Latin American countries has probably been more beneficial to the urban than to the rural poor, the situation without such intervention would probably have been far worse.

Fourthly, it is quite clear that out-migration from the poor areas has been one of the principal means by which relative differentials have been reduced. Without these vast movements of people to the cities, and even allowing for the negative effects of selective migration, the rural areas would have been even less favourably situated.

Lastly, from the little evidence available it would seem that no government, outside Cuba, has genuinely attempted to even out major regional disparities. Why this has been so and whether this constitutes a major failing on the part of Latin American governments represents the substance of the final two chapters.

8: The Administration of Regional Development

So far, more emphasis has been placed on the effect of government action in increasing regional-income disparities than on their attempts to redress them. This chapter attempts to improve that situation by describing and evaluating recent government attempts at regional planning and development.

The belated establishment of regional agencies

Despite the fact that regional-welfare disparities have long been a pronounced feature of Latin American societies, the appearance of regional planning and development agencies is a comparatively recent phenomenon. The earliest agencies appeared only in the 1940s, when two river-basin projects were established in Mexico, modelled along the lines of the Tennessee Valley Authority in the United States. In the rest of the continent it was not until the late fifties and the establishment of the Venezuelan Corporation for the Guayana (1958) and the Brazilian Superintendency for the Development of the North-east (1959) that multi-functional regional agencies began to appear. Once established, however, they began to proliferate rapidly, until today most nations possess some form of regional-development authority.

Few of these agencies, however, have been concerned specifically with regional planning. Most have been set up to perform a sectoral role within a region or to provide various forms of infrastructure. Very few have had an effective say in the activities or in the investment budgets of other agencies operating within their regions, and they have, therefore, been unable to produce or implement comprehensive plans for development. Even where planning has formed an essential part of agency functions, only in Argentina, Chile and Venezuela has the system of regional agencies been formally integrated into national planning.

Table 37: Abbreviations for Planning and Development Agencies Mentioned in Text

BNDE	National Bank for Economic Development	Brazil
CAR	Autonomous Regional Corporation for the Sabana of Bogotá and the Valleys of Ubate and Chiquinquirá	Colombia
CONZUPLAN	Planning Council for Zulia	Venezuela
CORDIPLAN	Central Office of Coordination and Planning	Venezuela
CORPOANDES	Corporation of the Andes	Venezuela
CORPUNO	Corporation for Development and Social and Economic Promotion of Puno	Peru
CVC	Autonomous Regional Corporation for the Cauca Valley	Colombia
CVG	Venezuelan Corporation for the Guayana	Venezuela
CVM	Autonomous Regional Corporation for the Valleys of the Magdalena and the Sinú. Now known as INDERENA	Colombia
CVSF	São Francisco Valley Commission. Now known as SUVALE	Brazil
DNOCS	National Department of Works against the Drought	Brazil
FUDECO	Foundation for the Development of the Middle-West	Venezuela
IDEA	Institute for the Development of Antioquia	Colombia
IDEBOY	Institute for the Development of Boyacá	Colombia
INDERENA	Institute for the Development of Renewable Natural Resources	Colombia
NOVACAP	Urbanization Company for the New Capital	Brazil
ODEPLAN	National Planning Office	Chile
ORDESUR	Regional Office for Development of the South	Peru
ORPLAN	Regional Planning Offices	Chile
SUDAM	Superintendency for the Development of the Amazonas	Brazil
SUDENE	Superintendency for the Development of the North-east	Brazil
SUVALE	Superintendency of the São Francisco Valley	Brazil
TVA	Tennessee Valley Authority	USA

The late emergence of regional agencies was mainly due to the belated realization within Latin America that the state could play an active role in encouraging development. As we saw earlier, few governments had become actively involved in economic policy making until the world crises of the thirties and forties, and national planning did not begin until the early fifties (Colombia 1951, Nicaragua 1952, Ecuador 1954).[1] Once national planning had been institutionalized, however, regional agencies soon followed. And, by the late sixties, most governments had founded regional agencies and were establishing others. Regional planning, in fact, appears to be gaining support. As Utría has said, 'like import substitution and industrialization in the fifties, and national planning and economic integration in the sixties, regional development appears destined to become one of the principal concerns of planners and strategists of Latin American development.'[2]

If Utría is correct in predicting an increase in the number of agencies, it suggests that regional development has been accepted as an integral part of the development and planning process in the continent. Consequently it is important to ask what the existing agencies have achieved and whether they will be able to foster regional development in the future. Before such an evaluation can be made, however, three other aspects of these agencies need to be considered. Firstly, under what circumstances did the existing agencies evolve? Secondly, what form did they take and how did they complement the existing politico-administrative system? Thirdly, what objectives did they espouse and what criteria were employed to gauge their success?

The evolution of regional agencies

The establishment of any new institution depends on its acceptance by the national government. In turn, this acceptance depends on the creation of an awareness of its importance and often of its popularity. Until the 1950s, there were a number of factors which prevented such an awareness developing in Latin America. After that time, a number of changes took place which made regional development attractive to several political régimes. The next few pages will consider the nature of these changes.

(I) THE POLITICAL CONSENSUS

The establishment of regional-development agencies in Chile, Brazil and Venezuela followed closely upon the election of political parties which had been associated with the idea of administrative decentralization and growth. Each in its way presents a perfect example of why such an evolution took place.

Before 1958, Venezuela had been governed by military dictators for all but three (1945–8) of the preceding sixty-six years.[3] During this period little regard had been paid to the general development needs of the nation, and economic policies were normally instituted which benefited the ruling élite. As a result, the rapid growth of the petroleum industry brought few benefits for most Venezuelans. It employed relatively few people, mostly from the Maracaibo and Caracas areas, and the profits were similarly concentrated. During the Gómez period, most of the funds were spent in the Maracay–Valencia region, and under Pérez Jiménez Caracas was the main beneficiary. By the time that Pérez was deposed, therefore, it is not surprising that considerable feelings had developed in the neglected areas against these arbitrary methods of allocating the oil revenues. The election of Betancourt's Acción Democrática party in 1958 afforded a vehicle through which these feelings could be channelled into popular support for planning and regional development. More accurately, they were channelled into support for a single regional project, the development of Ciudad Guayana, which appealed to a number of popular sentiments.[4] The object of developing the region's iron-ore, bauxite and hydro-electric potential was seen to be in the interest of all sections of society. The participation of the state was acceptable in as far as it meant that certain US corporations which had previously exploited the resources would be displaced. Most important of all was the fact that it indicated what might eventually be done in every region by 'sowing the oil'. Regional-development planning, as exemplified by the Guayana project, represented a new approach to modernization, a means of exploiting the nation's resources and a source of encouragement to every region. In response to this feeling, 'regional planning became all the rage. State governors demanded it; private organizations supported it; and local leadership organized to demand of the central authorities better coordination of development activities within their own areas and funds especially earmarked for regional investments.'[5] Given this popular support for the Guayana programme there were few reasons to delay action by the national government. 'To the extent that Acción Democrática politicians sought support for their programme in the provinces – and the majority of voters lived away from the national capital region – the regional issue came as a god-send.'[6] The CVG was established in Betancourt's first year of power.

A similar consensus in favour of regional development emerged during the fifties in Brazil. Like Betancourt in Venezuela, Kubitschek had espoused a policy closely associated with the development of the nation's resources, with building physical infrastructure and with maintaining a popular consensus. Within this overall strategy the regional plans for establishing Brasília and SUDENE fitted easily. Brasília represented the future and provided new vistas for nationalism. It offered a way of developing the interior, the nation's greatest unutilized resource, and of resolving the interminable conflicts between Rio and São Paulo politicians. Support for SUDENE was based on a national sympathy for the north-east which had been built up through more than a century of poverty and famine. It also offered (as we shall see in a moment) an escape from the older and more corrupt agencies which had been dealing with the problem, and fitted solidly into Kubitschek's policy of making Brazil into a modern nation. By the time the SUDENE legislation was being passed, major opposition was encountered only from supporters of those agencies which would be harmed by the new organization.[7]

Similar examples of new governments accepting regional development as a consensus policy can be seen in several other countries. In Chile the election of Frei's Christian Democratic party in 1964 soon led to the development of a regional-planning programme, and in Peru the Belaúnde government was elected partly on the basis of a promise to bring help to the regions.[8] Such a consensus was not only used by democratic governments, for authoritarian governments in

Colombia (1953–7), in Cuba (1959 to date), in Peru (1968 to date), in Argentina (1966–73) and in Brazil (1964 to date) all developed or are developing regional programmes.

Political backing for regional policies, however, is only one factor explaining their final emergence. That it should have taken so long to emerge is in itself strange since a potential consensus had existed for years founded on the strong regional consciousness characteristic of so many areas in Latin America. Why had no government built upon this regionalism before and why did the issue develop so strongly during the fifties and sixties?

(II) ACCEPTANCE OF REGIONAL PLANNING AS A CONCEPT

A prerequisite for the emergence of regional development and planning agencies was a growth in professional respect for planning in general. Such respect developed during the fifties and sixties when most Latin American nations established national-planning agencies. In turn the process of planning led to an awareness of regional problems. In addition, the introduction of regional-planning studies into the course structures of North American and European universities helped regional planning to achieve academic respectability. As a result, regional planning began to receive political and administrative attention. Whether this in itself would have been sufficient to establish regional agencies is not certain. It is not an important issue, however, since a number of factors emerged during the fifties which gave the demand for regional agencies a point of focus.[9]

(III) SPECIAL FACTORS IN THE EVOLUTION OF REGIONAL AGENCIES

Several special factors encouraged the establishment of regional agencies in a number of countries. It is clear that none of these factors were new phenomena but their re-appearance during a period of changing attitudes to regional development was important.

(a) *Natural disasters.* Few Latin American governments have ever helped their backward regions without the stimulus of strong political pressure. On a number of occasions such pressure has been generated by the incidence of natural disasters. In north-east Brazil, for example, regular stimuli to action have been provided by the periodic droughts which affect the region (1877–9, 1888–9, 1900, 1915, 1919, 1930–32, 1951–3, 1958) and which have invariably led to famine and massive migrations to the cities.[10] On each occasion the droughts have represented a problem which could not be ignored by the federal government, which has duly adopted a mixture of long- and short-term policies of assistance, such as the supply of food, the establishment of employment gangs, the building of reservoirs and the establishment of special agencies (such as DNOCS) to deal with the problem. These actions, however, have never been adequate and, although large sums of money were spent, the droughts always returned. In 1958, however, in an environment favourable to regional development, the appearance of a particularly severe drought led to a new kind of response. This response was the establishment of SUDENE.

A similar process was also evident in the series of events which led to the establishment of regional agencies in Peru. In 1956, there was a drought and subsequent famine in the south of the country, which brought about the signing of an aid agreement with the United States government. Under this agreement the United States sent food to the stricken south and financed a regional study programme. As well as highlighting the problems of the area the droughts accidentally created a political alliance among the normally warring political groups of the south. In the Puno region at least, the droughts were effective in uniting the local élites 'in a common cause that appeared to make of the department a highly integrated and demanding actor in the national system'.[11] The result was that the incoming Prado government were forced to take some action: the founding of regional agencies.

(b) *Corruption, scandal and foreign publicity.* It is possible to argue that the natural disasters alone would have forced the adoption of regional-development programmes. However, in both cases discussed there were additional factors which practically ensured this result: notably the corruption associated with the existing relief administration and the international news coverage given to national emergencies.

Corruption in the administration of public funds is not uncommon on the Latin American scene, but even there it is shamefully exposed when associated with emergency-relief programmes. In Brazil, where the administration of drought relief had been a national scandal for years, a special name, 'the drought industrialists', had been coined, to apply 'to vulgar thieves of relief shipments or corrupt officials in charge of emergency public works and to those who had merely adjusted their economic activity to the dry climate and thus had acquired a vested interest in it and were hostile to irrigation'.[12] After the 1958 emergency the charges of corruption were so vociferous that Kubitschek gave orders for it to be stamped out – a situation which seriously harmed the reputation of DNOCS at a time when the SUDENE legislation was being pushed through Congress.

Further accusations of corruption, in connection with the 1956 emergency food shipment from the United States, also assisted the formation of regional development agencies in Peru.[13] The original aim of the shipments was to distribute free food to the victims of the disaster. But owing to a number of administrative and political difficulties the final decision was to sell it. Such a decision would have been more acceptable had not delays caused by the wrangling led to many of the stocks rotting in the warehouses of Arequipa and Mollendo. This fact, together with the ample evidence of profiteering in which the outgoing national government was implicated, obliged the new government to develop a fresh approach to the regional problem.

The scandals surrounding the emergencies in Peru and Brazil were magnified by the publicity given the problems by the international press. Dew has argued that adverse reports in *Time* magazine about emergency relief in Puno eased the passage of the CORPUNO bill in 1962. 'Without these external pressures and local disasters, it seems possible that continued manipulation of the potential cleavages within the Puno system would have made passage of the CORPUNO bill politically unnecessary for the Prado administration.'[14] Similarly in north-east Brazil, international publicity helped the establishment of SUDENE; publicity that was given added point by the fear in the United States that the peasant leagues then operating in the north-east were the beginnings of a Castro-type revolution.[15]

(c) *Regional personalities as actors on the national scene.* A third factor in establishing regional agencies was the presence within the national power system of persons who were sympathetic to a regional programme. Such, at least, is the argument of Hirschman, who has suggested that north-east Brazil had traditionally obtained help from the national government only when *nordestinos* held important office.[16] The considerable aid received by the area during the 1930s, for example, was associated with the government of Getúlio Vargas, the only *nordestino* ever to have become president. Similarly, the establishment of SUDENE in 1958 was intimately connected with the work of Celso Furtado in the National Bank for Economic Development (BNDE). His activist role within that institution and the publication of a report about the north-east's problems were instrumental in exciting moral indignation and a national consensus in support of a new development agency. SUDENE was established in the same year.

A similar pattern was also apparent with the establishment of the Papaloapan Basin project in Mexico in 1947. The project was conceived and established during the presidency of Miguel Alemán, who was not only a native of the basin but a former governor of the state of Veracruz in which most of the basin lay.[17]

The delimitation, functions and objectives of the regional agencies

These factors guaranteed that regional policies would be politically acceptable to several Latin American governments. The governments, however, still had to formulate the objectives and powers of these agencies. How should the limits of the regions be determined? Should the new agencies complement or replace the existing administrative structure? Should every agency have the same functions and powers? What should be the objectives of the new agencies? In theory these were technical questions; in practice they were answered in a narrow spirit of political compromise.

The problem whether the regional agencies should complement or replace the existing administrative structure was decided in the same way in practically every country. In many cases its early resolution was an essential precondition to an agency's foundation, for, if any threat were made to existing institutions, political opposition would be encouraged. If an attack were made upon existing departments and states, regional pride might be turned against the new agencies. To counter this threat, an expedient policy was to organize the regional agencies in a way that would harmonize with existing institutions.

This attitude of compromise also affected the way in which regional agencies' geographical responsibilities were determined. In virtually every case the existing administrative boundaries were respected – a decision which was a prior condition in many countries for the foundation of the agencies.[18] Even so, some planning departments did go about the task of region-building in a systematic fashion. The national-planning agencies of Chile and Colombia, for example, employed quite sophisticated tools of analysis to delimit development regions, on the basis that each area should demonstrate as much internal homogeneity as possible – a considerable task given that existing boundaries had to be respected.[19] It was complicated further by the major differences that existed in each region between the urban and rural areas. In order to resolve this difficulty a second criterion was usually employed – that of delimiting regions on the basis of nodal characteristics. In the Chilean case each region was to contain one centre that would act as a 'growth pole'. This 'growth pole', it was hoped, would lead to development throughout the whole region. A similar criterion also underlay the Colombian 'Modelo de Regionalización' with its classification of cities into 'metropoli of equilibrium' and 'regional centres'.

Related to the question of how to delimit regions was the problem of how many should be constructed. In part the solution was provided by the boundaries of the existing administrative system, but it is interesting to note that, in practically every case where a complete set of planning regions was devised, the number chosen was almost identical. Despite differences of shape, size and population, Argentina, Colombia and Venezuela each designated eight regions and only Chile was an exception with eleven.[20]

The fundamental question to be resolved, however, concerned the agencies' functions, and perhaps it was the importance of this issue which resulted in the adoption of such a broad spectrum of policies and objectives. These objectives ranged from the regionalization of the national plan, through the development of a backward region, to the performance of a specific task or function within a specific region. Regional agencies were used to develop a resource frontier (Guayana), to maximize the rate of economic growth in a region (Tepalcatepec), to integrate areas into the national economy (Chocó), to equalize regional incomes (north-east Brazil), to prevent an area from seceding to another nation (Arica) and to regionalize nations' investment budgets (Cuba and Chile). In some cases their functions and objectives were irreconcilable within a particular region and in most cases the resources granted them were quite insufficient for the task. In general, political expediency seems to have been a more pervasive motive behind the choice of objectives than administrative viability.

In addition, many agencies were not designed to undertake wide regional development duties or to coordinate the work of other agencies. On the contrary many were set up solely to perform some specific task, such as the development of electricity power, for which there happened to be some special need. The river-basin commissions in Colombia, Brazil and Mexico fall squarely into this category. Instead of helping to integrate planning and development objectives, therefore, they have tended to complicate the matter. Instead of serving to allocate resources more rationally, they have more frequently been used on an *ad hoc* basis to help particular regions or to execute specific tasks.

In defence of this multiplicity of objectives, however, it can be said that different governments will require different results from regional programmes. A communist government's programme will embrace many regional objectives that will not figure in those of right-wing or liberal governments. Apart from differences of ideology regional-development objectives are likely to vary with the level of development in each nation. Regional-planning problems in Britain and the United States will obviously differ from those in any Latin American society. Similarly within Latin America there are many reasons why the regional-development objectives of Brazil will differ from those in Mexico or Ecuador. Friedmann has specifically suggested that the need for regional and spatial planning varies with a nation's level of development. 'Transitional societies are clearly the most directly concerned with regional organization, partly because of the spatial shifts involved in moving from an agrarian to an industrial economy, partly because a large proportion of their potential resources are still unutilized.'[21]

The aims of regional development will vary not only between nations but also between regions. Friedmann has also suggested that there is a need to distinguish between five kinds of region in most developing nations: (a) the core regions – metropolitan areas with a high potential for economic growth; (b) upward-transitional areas – areas whose natural endowments and location relative to core-regions suggest the possibility of a greatly intensified use of resources; (c) downward-traditional areas – areas of old, established settlement whose essentially rural economy is stagnant or in decline and whose peculiar combination of resources suggest as optimal a less-intensive development than in the past; (d) 'resource frontiers', which represent zones of new settlement in otherwise virgin territory; and (e) 'development corridors', which are a type of upward-traditional area connecting two or more core-regions.[22] In each of these regions the objectives of planning and the subsequent strategies devised will vary widely.

Nevertheless, it is difficult to believe that the objectives espoused by most Latin American regional agencies owe as much to careful thought and planning as to the spirit of political compromise. Such a case can be supported by the form in which most regional planning and development agencies have been established.

(I) PLANNING REGIONS WHICH COMPLEMENT THE EXISTING ADMINISTRATIVE STRUCTURE

The most common form of regional agency in Latin America is the regional development and planning unit based upon the existing second-tier authorities, the departments, provinces or states. This form of agency was established in Peru, for example, where each of the six southern departments was permitted its own development agency (Fig. 19). In Chile and Venezuela (Figs. 20 and 21) a similar strategy was followed and many planning units conformed exactly with the boundaries of the existing states. Similarly in Colombia autonomous regional corporations have been set up for the departments of Chocó and Quindío (Fig. 22). A variation of this method has also

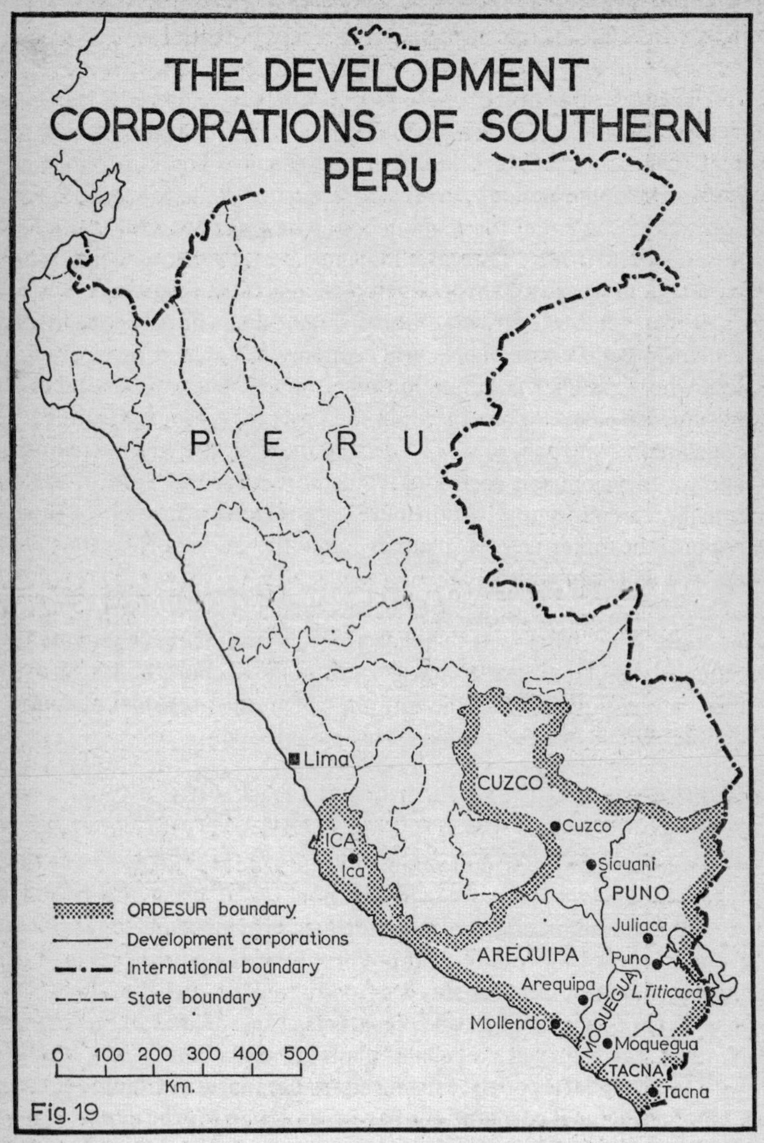
THE DEVELOPMENT CORPORATIONS OF SOUTHERN PERU
P E R U
Lima
CUZCO
Cuzco
ICA
Ica
Sicuani
PUNO
Juliaca
Puno
AREQUIPA
Arequipa
L. Titicaca
Mollendo
MOQUEGUA
Moquegua
TACNA
Tacna
ORDESUR boundary
Development corporations
International boundary
State boundary
0 100 200 300 400 500
Km.

Fig. 19

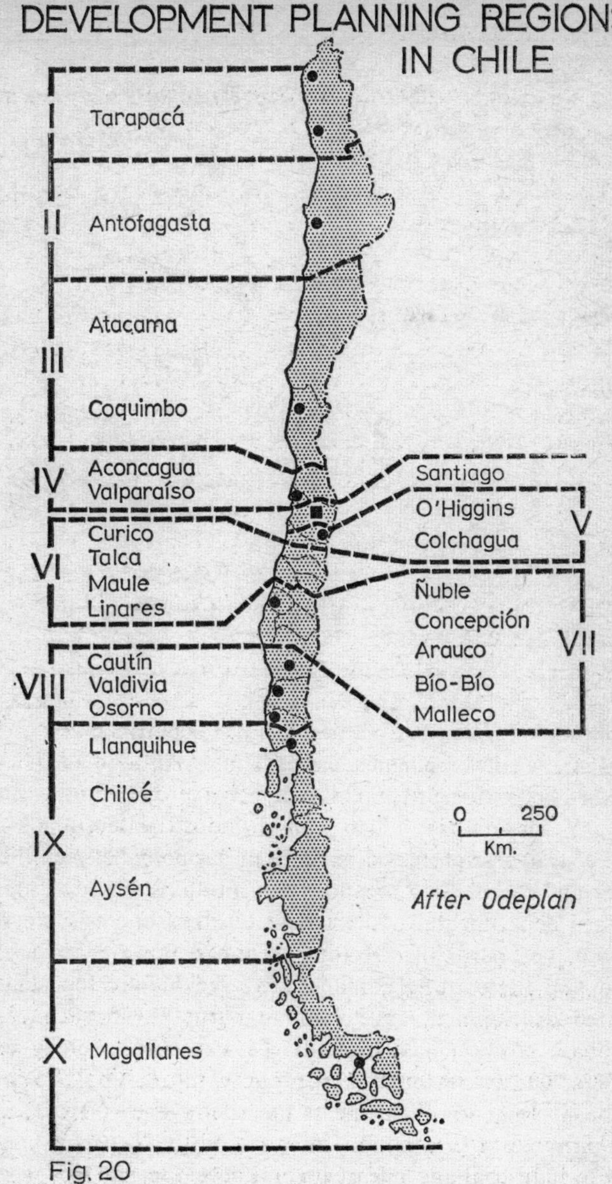

DEVELOPMENT PLANNING REGIONS IN CHILE
I
Tarapacá
II
Antofagasta
Atacama
III
Coquimbo
IV
Aconcagua
Valparaíso
Santiago
O'Higgins
Colchagua
V
VI
Curico
Talca
Maule
Linares
Ñuble
Concepción
Arauco
Bío-Bío
Malleco
VII
VIII
Cautín
Valdivia
Osorno
Llanquihue
Chiloé
IX
Aysén
X
Magallanes
0
250
Km.
After Odeplan

Fig. 20

Fig. 21

been followed in Colombia, where individual departments have established their own development agencies. Thus in Antioquia IDEA was established in 1964 to help to finance municipal projects, and in Boyacá IDEBOY was set up in 1970 to promote industrial development.

Such a stratagem ensures a measure of harmony between the new agencies and the existing second-tier institutions. This is especially true when departmental political and business interests are represented on the boards of directors. At times, however, it has been realized that the existing administrative regions are too small for integrated development and planning purposes. In such cases a compromise position has frequently been reached whereby several second-tier authorities have been grouped into a single region. In Peru the six southern departments have an agency (ORDESUR) which promotes the common interests of the departments with respect to industrial and infrastructural development. In Venezuela,

too, several of the eight planning regions ratified by CORDIPLAN in 1969 embraced several existing states. CORPOANDES, for example, contained the states of Táchira, Mérida, Trujillo, Barinas and part of Portuguesa and FUDECO the states of Falcón, Lara and Yaracuy.[23] Only one state, Zulia, was permitted its own planning council, a concession conditioned by its strong regional pride and by its special problems associated with the declining petroleum industry. Similarly in Brazil, Chile and Argentina the major regional development agencies embraced several states (Figs. 23–25), and only in

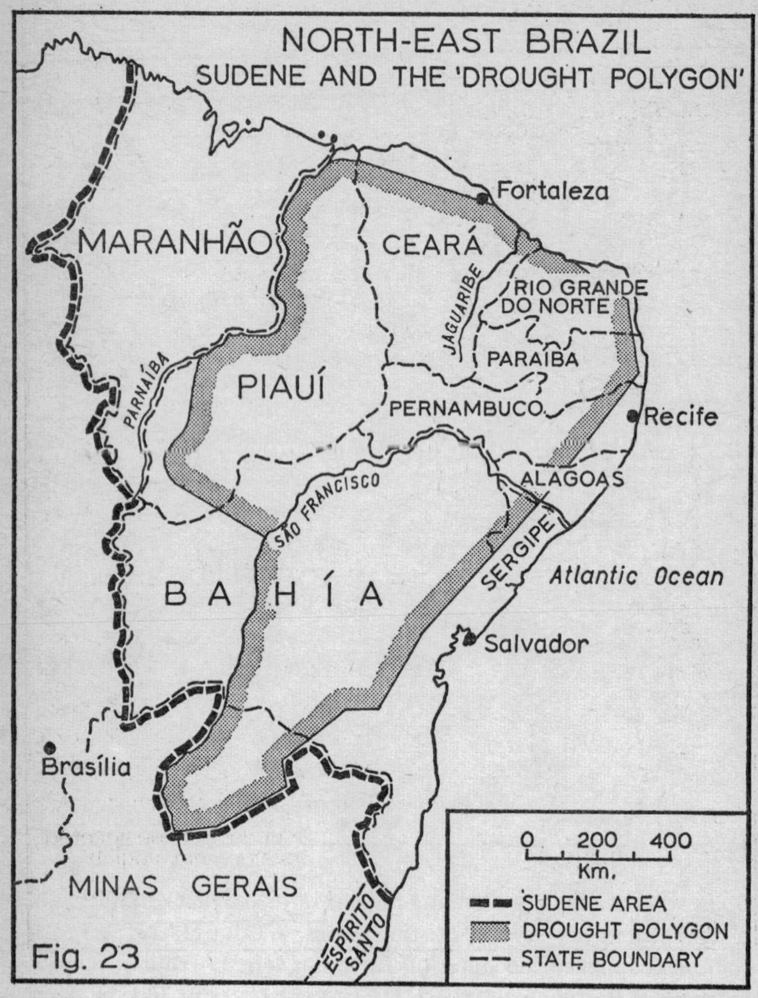

Fig. 23

after Robock, S. H. (1963)

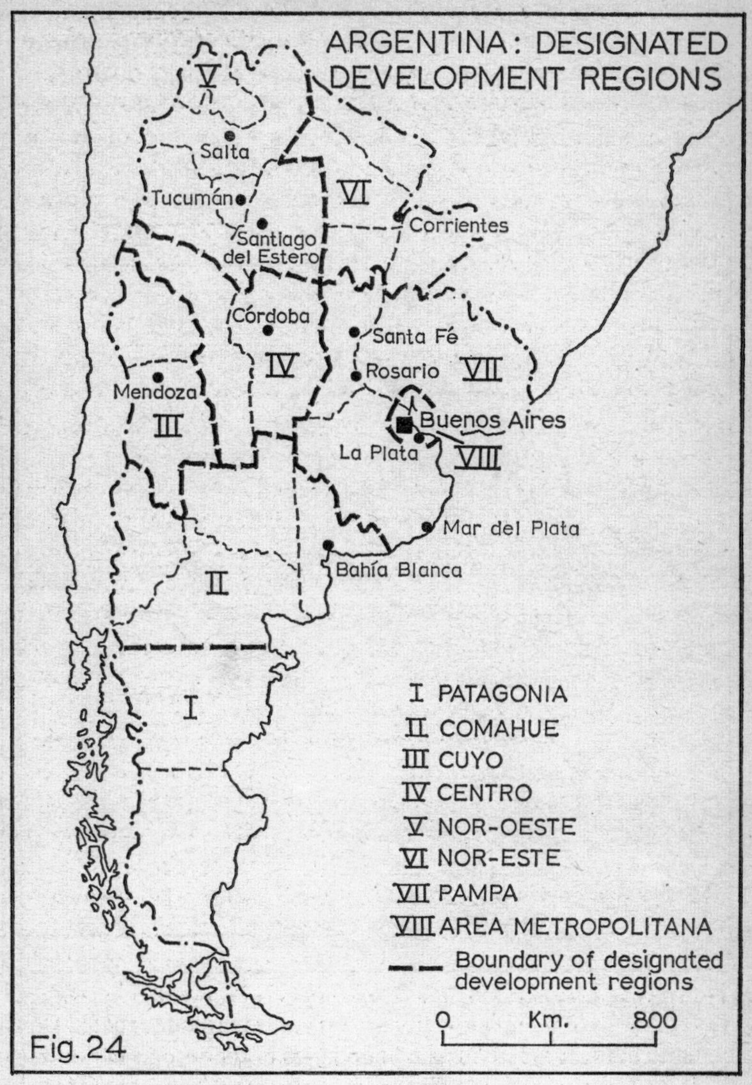
ARGENTINA: DESIGNATED DEVELOPMENT REGIONS
V
Salta
Tucumán
VI
Corrientes
Santiago del Estero
Córdoba
Santa Fé
IV
Rosario
VII
Mendoza
III
Buenos Aires
La Plata
VIII
Mar del Plata
Bahía Blanca
II
I
I PATAGONIA
II COMAHUE
III CUYO
IV CENTRO
V NOR-OESTE
VI NOR-ESTE
VII PAMPA
VIII AREA METROPOLITANA
Boundary of designated development regions
0 Km. 800
Fig. 24

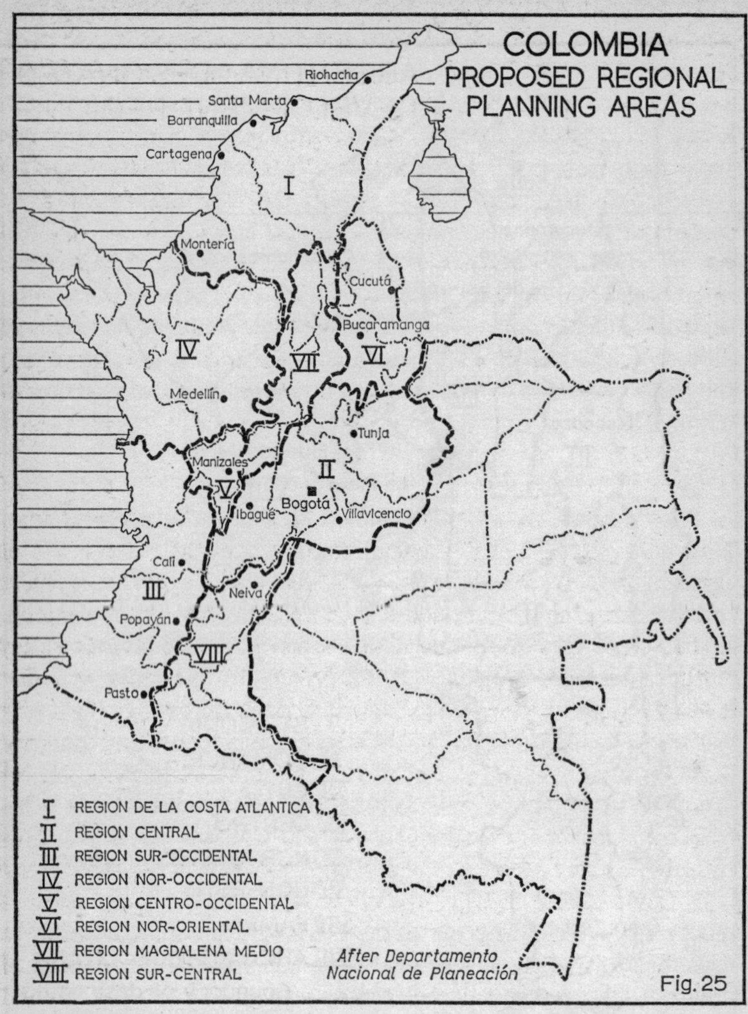

Fig. 25

Colombia have planning regions been consistently designated which do not conform exactly to the boundaries of the second-tier authorities. Even here, 'certain adjustments were introduced to respect, as far as possible, the municipal boundaries'.[24]

To assist administrative harmony still further most of these supra-departmental agencies have also included representatives of local interests. SUDENE was organized so that the governors of the region's states were represented on the agency's board of governors – a representation strengthened by the absence of federal ministers from most meetings.[25] In Venezuela, local interests were strongly represented on the regional agencies. CONZUPLAN's executive committee, for example, was headed by the state governor, and 'all the principal interests active in the state, including government, military, church, business, industry, labour and farmers' were represented.[26] In Colombia, too, the proposed committees for regional development are made up of governors and members of congress for the region who will 'coordinate and promote the regional action of national and departmental entities'.[27]

(II) THE RIVER-BASIN COMMISSIONS

In many ways the river-basin commissions were more independent of local administrative and political interests than the other kinds of agency. In some cases, they were established with the primary purpose of by-passing the existing administrative structure within a region. In this sense they were true descendants of the Tennessee Valley Authority in the USA. But while the principle of the design was clear it was rarely successfully implemented. In those cases where autonomy was achieved the objectives of the commissions tended to be limited to functions such as water control and conservation. In others, where functions were more comprehensive, the commissions were often freed from one set of pressures, such as local interests, but constrained by another, such as the national administrative framework.

In Colombia the goals of the three river-basin corporations were quite narrow. The objectives of the CAR (1961) were laid out in its founding legislation to be simply 'the regulation of water control of floods, irrigation and land reclamation, exploitation of underground water supplies and the transmission of electric energy'.[28] Similarly in the case of the CVC the hard core of the programme was to be concerned with water control and the harnessing of hydro-electric power.[29] And, in the case of the CVM, reorganized in 1968 as INDERENA (Instituto de Desarrollo de los Recursos Naturales

Renovables), the objectives were narrower still, being confined to the conservation of the area's natural resources.

In Mexico and Brazil, on the other hand, the goals of most river-basin corporations were much wider and in the Mexican case at least 'offered a way of planning and coordinating public expenditure in a region that was difficult to do through already established ministries and state governments'.[30] In the case of the Grijalva project (Fig. 26), the commission was entrusted not only with drainage work and building the Malpaso dam but with developing an extensive settlement and irrigation programme. Even wider functions were granted the Tepalcatepec Commission, which was charged with 'planning, proposing, and construction of works for irrigation and for the development of sources of energy, for sanitary engineering, for establishing communications, including roads, railways, telegraphs and telephones, and for the creation and expansion of population centres'.[31] Such wide powers did not apply to all the Mexican agencies, however. The Fuerte Commission, for example, was mainly concerned with exploring the possibilities for

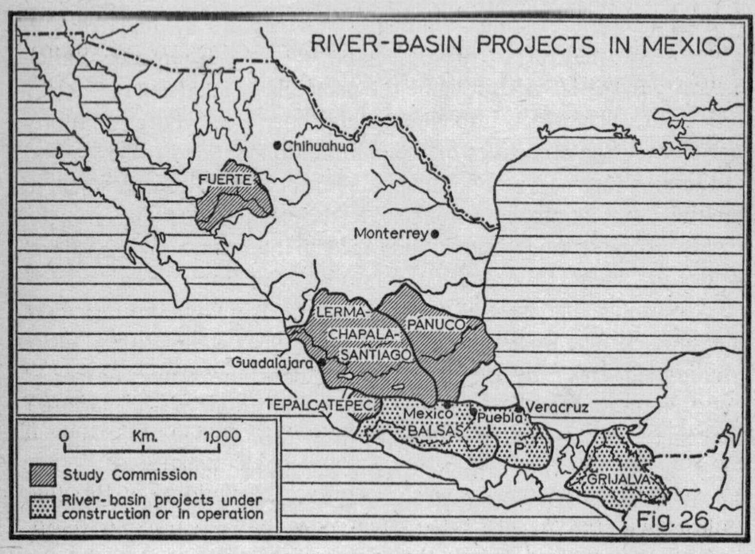

after Barkin, D. and King, T. (1970)

irrigation and with the avoidance of floods in the lower basin.

In Brazil the one river-basin authority to be established (CVSF) had an enormous range of activities to perform. Perhaps as a result it was not a great success and indulged in 'a great policy of small services' such as the building of access roads, provision of water and power supplies, and the construction of hospitals.[32] When at a later date a decision was made to harness the power of the Paulo Afonso Falls, the agency was not entrusted with the project. It was finally reorganized in 1967 as SUVALE and its powers limited to irrigation and basic sanitation.

The ability of these agencies to perform such tasks depended on their position in the administrative system. In Colombia the three corporations were established (like the TVA) as autonomous agencies of the national government; in Brazil the CVSF operated as a traditional government department; and in Mexico they were given less autonomy and were placed under the control of the Ministry of Water Resources. The constraints upon their independence differed, but in each case were severe. More will be said about this later in the chapter.

(III) AGENCIES ENTRUSTED WITH SPECIFIC PROJECTS

In many other cases the above strategies were deemed to be inappropriate, particularly when a project was credited with national importance. In the case of the Guayana programme in Venezuela a different administrative approach was adopted to guarantee the project autonomy and success. In this project, CORDIPLAN, the national planning agency, was isolated from executive responsibility and the new agency granted 'a unique bureaucratic position of great political power; it was the only operational agency attached directly to the President's office'.[33] In order to cement this independence from other agencies, the CVG was given total control in the limited area surrounding the confluence of the Orinoco and Caroní rivers. In addition, and 'this was the novelty – the corporation was legally entitled to undertake investment programmes beyond this zone if their relevance to activities within it could be demonstrated'.[34]

A similar priority project was, of course, the building of Brasília. While such a project constituted much more than a regional development programme it did have the regional objective of reducing the power of São Paulo and Rio de Janeiro and of developing the under-populated Pratinha.[35] And, since it was a project which was fundamental to Kubitschek's plan to bring Brazil fifty years' progress in five, it was given very high priority. Such priority was reflected in the setting-up of a new commission (NOVACAP) with sole responsibility for the project, and the provision of large investment funds to finance it.

Much less important than either of these schemes but also requiring mention are those concerned with fostering regional industrial growth. Some of them were mentioned above and here it is only necessary to remind the reader of their diversity. The approaches varied from the free-trade zones of Arica (Chile), Manaus (Brazil), Barranquilla (Colombia) and the Mexican border, to the industrial development agencies of Colombia, Venezuela and Peru; from the industrial estates throughout the continent to the artisan parks of southern Peru.

(IV) AGENCIES OF NATIONAL PLANNING UNITS

Regional planning agencies have not figured prominently among the regional organizations which have been established. That is to say, there has been little formal contact between most regional agencies and their national-planning offices. One exception to this has been Chile, where under the Frei Government a number of dependencies of ODEPLAN were established in five planning regions.[36] These ORPLAN were intended to stimulate feelings of regional consciousness and to assist in the regionalization of the national plan. In addition, the government introduced a decree which obliged other official agencies to modify their regional administration so as to conform with the ODEPLAN regions. Such deliberate rationalization has been very much the exception in the continent as a whole.

The regional agencies – a success or a failure?

In assessing the contribution of regional agencies to Latin American development, one is faced by a series of problems. The first is that many of the agencies follow a diversity of objectives which makes any evaluation of their different contributions to development an exacting task. This is further complicated by the fact that few of the agencies have specified time periods over which their objectives should be achieved. Even when certain objectives have been accomplished, therefore, it has been impossible to judge the overall efficiency of the agency against a target programme.

An additional difficulty is that there is no single analytical method suitable for evaluating an agency's work. While some writers have claimed that cost–benefit analysis has many virtues in this field, none would claim that it is an adequate method if used alone. Barkin and King, for example, employed it in their evaluation of the Tepalcatepec basin project but pointed out that they considered such an approach valuable 'only with respect to the objectives that are easily expressed in income terms'.[37] Similarly Eckstein has argued that in evaluating 'the developmental impact of different types of projects, all the relevant tools of economic analysis must come into play'.[38] Fundamentally, the problem is that an agency's operations should be judged in the light of many criteria; not only economic but political and social considerations should be included. The only way out of this impasse is to judge performance against specific, previously expressed criteria and to avoid sweeping generalizations relating to an agency's overall success or failure.[39] Such an evaluation will be made below, of the performance of Latin American planning agencies judged against three specific criteria: (1) their ability to reduce regional inequalities in income; (2) their ability to bring about fundamental structural changes in their regions; and (3) their ability (in the case of single-purpose agencies) to achieve their primary-stated objectives. Before doing this, however, we shall consider briefly the grounds upon which other writers have praised or criticized the different regional agencies.

There can be little doubt that a number of agencies have been moderately successful. Several writers have commented on the role of regional agencies in accelerating the rate of economic growth in their areas of influence. In Mexico, Barkin and King concluded that 'a satisfactory return on the investment in a river-basin project, such as we found in the Tepalcatepec project, implies that the project made a satisfactory contribution in increasing aggregate national income. This is probably a sufficient justification of Mexican policies, at least in the Tepalcatepec and Fuerte basins.'[40] And, in the Brazilian north-east, Kleinpenning has praised the way in which SUDENE's activities have helped to expand road mileage in the area, bring about increases in electrical power, train more primary-school teachers and accelerate industrial growth.[41]

In addition, some agencies have been praised for the way they have opened up a resource frontier. Friedmann, for example, has said that 'the Guayana programme represents the major effort of Venezuela's past generation in regional development. This vast public undertaking, scarcely a decade old, is already having a profound impact on the national economy. It is creating a new region on the edge of the effectively settled space in the eastern part of the country; it is expanding the productive capabilities of the nation by bringing new resources into play; it is building the principal base of heavy industry for the further industrialization of the country; it is stimulating economic expansion in other parts of Venezuela; and it is serving as a powerful example of the possibilities of programming for regional development.'[42]

Praise, too, has been conferred on those regional agencies which have helped create a technical, objective and civil-service approach to regional development. Robock has praised the BNB for 'changing the regional mentality and attitudes of regional leaders',[43] and in Colombia the Posadas have praised the CVC for the way it assembled a group of technicians together and developed an objective approach to planning.[44]

Lastly, certain agencies have been praised for the way in which they have accelerated the rate of social transformation. In the case of post-SUDENE Brazil, Hirschman has said that, 'investment boom and profound social transformation were seemingly both in the making and both were promoted and "administered" in various ways by the same agency, SUDENE. The two-pronged undertaking was by no means assured of success, yet the chances for substantial economic and social progress of the region looked brighter than at any previous time in this century.'[45]

On the other hand regional agencies have not been without their critics. Odell has suggested that the CVC did not succeed in its basic task of providing electric energy in the Cauca valley, despite its director's pledge to supply power to any industry establishing itself in the valley.[46] Other critics have commented on the failure of the multipurpose agencies to overcome the principal causes of underdevelopment. Barkin and King have criticized the limited success of the river-basin projects in Mexico as follows: 'The number of people benefiting directly from the projects has been very small indeed in relation to the agricultural population as a whole or even compared with the new entrants to the labour force. As a strategy either for decentralizing the location of economic activity or for stemming the flow of migrants to urban areas, the schemes achieved very little.'[47] A similar criticism was made in an earlier chapter of SUDENE's efforts at industrial development, and it has also been more generally applied to the agency's total activities. Dickenson has stated that in terms of positive achievement its activities have had 'the same consequences as planning at a national level, that is a tendency to favour limited areas within the region'.[48]

Implicit in much of this criticism is the charge that agencies have tended to foster industrial growth at the expense of agricultural development. SUDENE, although 'it has been the most successful of the [Brazilian] regional agencies [has been] less successful in the crucial agricultural sector than in attracting new industry and providing infrastructure in power, transport and education'.[49] As a result of this bias 'not only have the methods of agricultural production remained substantially unaltered but so also has the system of land tenure. Although an important part of the problems originate from the large landed properties, no mention is made of the splitting up of the fazendas in SUDENE's programme.'[50] Similar charges of rural neglect have also been levelled against the CVC, where it has been pointed out that only 21·3 per cent of the agency's budget between 1955 and 1963 was spent upon agriculture.[51] In addition to this charge, it has been claimed that the greater part of the funds devoted to agriculture by the CVC benefited the large landowners of the valley rather than the poor. Neglect of the poor has also been a major charge against the CVG in Venezuela, where Dinkelspiel has argued that agricultural development has been encouraged only in areas where land reform was not a key political issue (see below).[52] Only in a few agencies, such as the Mexican river-basin projects, has agriculture received major attention.

The success and failures of the regional-development agencies, therefore, have been associated with two sets of related but distinct activities. The agencies have been generally praised for their efforts at industrial development and in building physical infrastructure. But they have also been generally condemned for their inability to assist the agricultural sector and for their consequent failure to aid the poorest groups within their regions. While the CVG, CVC, SUDENE, ORDESUR, etc. have been able to build and finance roads, power stations and industrial estates, they have not been able to cure the fundamental problems of their areas.

In terms of the three criteria mentioned above, there have been few overall successes. Firstly, no regional agency has managed to reduce the disparity in *per capita* income or welfare between a poor, backward region and the growth areas. This was made patently clear in the case of three countries by the data presented in Chapter Seven, where it was shown that absolute if not relative differences between regions have continued to widen. While the regional agencies have frequently managed to improve growth prospects for their regions, they have not been able to reverse the general polarizing forces operating within Latin American societies.

Secondly, no regional agency has successfully modified the social and class structure within its region. Thus, while certain modifications have been achieved in the economic structure, these changes have normally benefited élites within and outside the region, rather than the region as a whole. By offering fiscal incentives to manufacturing industry in backward areas, for example, the neglect of agriculture has been encouraged. Had strong employment multiplier effects been generated by these economic changes, then the overall social effect might have been beneficial. In general, however, these modifications have tended only to provide profit opportunities for a privileged minority. Worse still, the few modifications that have been made to the economic structure have covered agencies with a veneer of action that has hidden their inability to institute fundamental changes in fields such as land reform, taxation and market structures.*

*A word should be said at this point about the recent unfavourable experiences of SUDENE. Since 1967, the agency has seen its reputation for efficiency decline, its budget in real terms fall, and its control over other federal agencies

Thirdly, however, regional agencies have been more successful in achieving specific as opposed to diffuse goals. While there have undoubtedly been many disappointments, the majority of these specific goals have been achieved. Despite the enormous costs, Brasília and Ciudad Guayana were built. Regional agencies may have failed to achieve some of their objectives, but nevertheless the CVC did increase electricity generation in the Cauca valley, and SUDENE managed to improve industrial employment in the Brazilian north-east. Whether these partial successes vindicate the overall actions of regional-development agencies is discussed below.

In this evaluation of the success of regional agencies, we have concentrated wholly upon regional-development agencies and have neglected attempts at regional planning. Such neglect has been due mainly to the fact that so few nations have established such agencies, but more importantly to the fact that these attempts have been so recent. The only real comment that can be made is that their success will be determined largely by the aims of national planning. If the latter aims to maximize economic growth rather than foster social and institutional change, the majority of the population will not benefit from the actions of the new agencies. If, however, more ambitious programmes are espoused, every region may well benefit. At their worst, the new planning agencies will merely form another institution supported by the national budget. At best, they will improve the flows of information from the local to the national level and vice versa, will generate economic growth in the regions and will spread the benefits of this growth widely among the regions' populations. If predictions have to be made about their future success from the information available on their foundation and purpose, the former outcome would appear more likely than the latter.

---

disappear. The situation worsened in 1970 when another serious drought hit the north-east. This drought awoke memories of past disasters as large numbers of nordestinos moved towards the cities in search of food and employment. It also raised the spectre of inefficiency as SUDENE showed itself both unwilling and unable to resolve the crisis. As a result of this experience, SUDENE's former control over other agencies operating in the north-east has now been severely weakened. (See Goodman, D. E. (1972).)

Reasons for the limited success of regional agencies

If some regional agencies have been more successful than others, some functions performed and others not, then it is important to understand why. In this section I put forward several reasons for these discrepancies. In many ways they relate to questions of finance, autonomy and image of the agency. Fundamentally, however, I believe successful regional development and planning depends on the support of politicians; in the final analysis it is a question of political commitment and will.

(I) SOURCES OF REVENUE

One factor that has been important in allowing some agencies to be more successful than others is the availability of finance. Those agencies that were guaranteed a steady source of funds have been able to pursue more effective lines of action than others which have been required to request fresh funds for each new project. The best examples of programmes with guaranteed funds of course are SUDENE, CVG and the Operation Bootstrap programme in Puerto Rico. SUDENE, for example, was granted an annual revenue amounting to 2 per cent of federal funds, which, if not an adequate sum, did ensure that the staff would always be paid and an organization maintained. But most agencies have normally been very short of funds. Many of the Mexican river-basin projects have been starved of funds when they were out of favour with particular federal administrations. Similarly, the CVC has not had sufficient funds to support its programme and, between 1956 and 1963, had to borrow approximately 50 per cent of its budget from other institutions (notably from the World Bank).[53] Such problems in financing operations have obviously prejudiced the chances of success of these agencies. Even so, it should not be thought that regular funds are a guarantee of success. The CVSF in Brazil was granted an annual percentage of federal funds for twenty years after 1946, but was still a notable failure.[54]

To some extent, any regional agency in an underdeveloped nation is likely to face financial problems. It is no accident that the regional programmes granted most funds have been those located in the nations with the highest *per capita* incomes. Venezuela had enormous funds from petroleum revenues with which to support the Guayana project; between 1965 and 1975, its income was budgeted at US$3·8 billion, of which US$2·0 billion would come from the national government. The size of this budget can be seen if it is compared to the *total* government budget of neighbouring Colombia, a country with more than twice as many inhabitants. While the Venezuelan government spent US$200 million annually on the Guayana project, the Colombians' total budget was a mere five times higher.

While financial viability is not a guarantee of success, it does make it more probable. Not only does it ensure a greater measure of independence from external pressures, but it also demonstrates to other groups that the programme has the full support of the national government.

(II) THE QUESTION OF AUTONOMY

Administrative autonomy can only be achieved if an agency is free to make or influence decisions on major activities which affect its principal objectives. Unfortunately, few regional agencies have ever been permitted this degree of autonomy. The CVC's electricity generation programme was constrained by its limited control over both coal production (private sector) and supplies of petroleum (private and public sectors).[55] On the other hand, some agencies have been granted complete administrative autonomy. The CVG was freed from this problem as 'its charter was drawn up so as to give it later the freedom largely to exclude other government agencies from the policy-making aspects of the Guayana's development'.[56] As a further insurance of its autonomy, it was the only agency that was attached to the president's office directly rather than through a supervising ministry. Similarly in Brazil, SUDENE was established in a strong administrative position and specifically empowered to 'supervise, coordinate and control' the activities of other federal agencies. Its own autonomy was guaranteed at the expense of those of other agencies.

Many agencies have suffered from interference from other national institutions operating in related fields. By far the greatest threat, however, has come from local politicians and interest groups. The CORPUNO agency in southern Peru, for example, faced a number of major disputes with local political and administrative groups during its first few years of existence. It gave money to the Puno City Council for street paving and the funds were misappropriated. Later the Juliaca municipal authorities spent funds, allocated for paving the city, on buying a *hacienda* for a new airport – land which they had previously agreed to donate for the purpose. On top of these problems the agency was plagued by disputes between the regions' two main towns over the amount of money CORPUNO allocated to each authority. These disputes culminated in 1965 with an outbreak of violence, as the people of Juliaca blocked the road and railway to Puno and demanded the resignation of the head of the agency.[57]

Legitimate, but equally serious, interventions were made in the activities of other regional agencies. The content of the CVC's programme was in large measure influenced by the way in which 'economic groupings with private interests are represented on the directing committee'.[58] Similarly, in the case of IDEA the presence on the board of directors between 1970 and 1972 of representatives of the ANAPO party seriously curtailed its activities. Lastly, political and institutional interference has been an important factor in the declining effectiveness of SUDENE since 1967.

(III) THE IMAGE OF THE REGIONAL AGENCY

The success of a regional agency depends also upon the realization that development planning is primarily a political activity. But while the objective of an agency must be to knit itself into the mainstream of a government's decision-making process it must preserve enough flexibility to survive any changes of administration. To achieve this position Dinkelspiel suggests that an agency must develop an appropriate 'administrative style'. Such a style should embrace a number of characteristics, the most important of which is the establishment of an aura of technical competence, a reputation for honesty and a non-political stance.

In many ways, the CVG, CVC and the SUDENE agencies all achieved such a style. All three agencies made reputations for technical objectivity and honesty, the CVG developing a style 'that embraced anonymity and non-controversiality'.[59] All three also gained a reputation for political neutrality; in the SUDENE case its director, Furtado, 'kept so free of party commitments that both of the 1960 presidential candidates, Jânio Quadros and General Henrique Lott, sent written assurances to Furtado that he would be appointed after the election as head of the Northeast programme'.[60]

Despite the obvious institutional advantages of such an attitude there is a price to pay. This price may be the elimination of a radical element both from the staff and the programme. Dinkelspiel has recognized such an effect on the CVG organization, where 'the staff members tend to range from the centre to the conservative side of the political spectrum', and also on its programme, which was inclined to reject radical projects in favour of non-controversial policies.[61] One example of the latter was the way in which the CVG overcame the problem of providing the new city with a food supply. Providing 'a local food supply could have involved it in the highly volatile and partisan problems of agrarian reform. It has therefore been trying to develop an alternative . . . by exploring the possibility of large-scale commercial food production in the Orinoco Delta region.'[62]

Also important in achieving a successful image has been the selection of a well-known and respected figure to be head of an agency – a strategy of 'the Great Man writing the Plan'.[63] The choice of Celso Furtado ensured that SUDENE would be headed by a man with an international reputation. Another example was the choice of ex-President Lázaro Cárdenas to be head of the Tepalcatepec basin commission and later of the Balsas basin commission. Such a strategy was, in the opinion of Barkin and King, 'a significant factor determining its degree of success in obtaining resources to carry out its work'.[64] It is not one, of course, which will always lead to the acceptance of a radical policy.

(IV) THE POLITICAL WILL

The factors just mentioned have been of considerable importance in determining both whether the regional agencies survived and whether their programmes would be successful. In many ways, however, these factors depend on the willingness of politicians and governments to support an effective regional-development and planning programme.

If politicians are eager to support such a policy then adequate funds will be guaranteed, a respected man will be appointed head of the agency, and no interference with the agency's functions by other state institutions will be permitted. Without this support an agency may be created and may even survive as an institution, but it will not be effective.

Unfortunately, political support for regional development in Latin America has in many ways been ambivalent, which largely explains the relative failure of regional programmes in the continent. This situation is not altogether surprising, for regional-development programmes do involve a number of risks both for national and regional politicians. They involve the national government in a development strategy that promises to include all sectors of society and which may cost it power as new political forces are unleashed. Such programmes may also involve the national government in heavy investment, which may deprive them of funds for other activities or oblige them to contravene previous promises, such as maintaining low levels of taxation.

Neither is regional development likely to be wholly popular with regional politicians. Although it may promise them major injections of investment funds, it may involve political losses too. It may stimulate local demands for policies more radical than local élites wish to countenance. By impinging on the rural sector, for example, such programmes may stimulate demands for land reform and for changes in the system of service provision.

When regional development is allied to regional planning the situation may be even more difficult. For, by replacing the conflict of interest by technical criteria, the process may be modified in a way that will weaken the power base of local politicians. It may even involve the acceptance of a new process of decision-making. It is more likely, however, that the methods of planning as known in the developed world will be modified by local circumstances. Such a process has characterized national planning in Brazil, where it seems 'that *implementation* of central plans is dysfunctional from the point of view of the bureaucracy. This fact is perfectly well understood by such Brazilian politicians as Almino Afonso whose view of planning is quite the reverse of that in the United States. We [Northern

Americans] feel that plan-making [policy] is a political function and that implementation is a technical-administrative matter. Afonso correctly perceives the Brazilian situation to be the reverse. In practice plan-making has been technical, while implementation is patently political.'[65] In Latin America, where few groups are accustomed to resolving their problems according to technical criteria, regional planning and development is likely to be modified in the same way. Alternatively, should such a modification prove impossible, regional development and planning may well prove expendable.

Regional development and planning, therefore, while offering much to local and national groups may also pose difficulties. Unless great care is taken, the fundamental interests of both may be harmed. The only way out of this dilemma is for politicians to support the positive advantages brought by the programmes and pay only lip-service to those aspects which will pose difficulties. Such has been the approach in many Latin American countries. Regional agencies have been established, but their functions have been only vaguely defined, insufficient funds have been allotted to them and political control has been carefully maintained. As long as they function, they provide regional élites with access to national funds and national governments with a means of demanding greater sacrifices of the regions for the national good. Only if such agencies are given powers to evoke fundamental change are political problems likely to appear. But providing that sufficient controls are retained, the existing political power base can be maintained harmoniously.

These comments may appear rather cynical, but there is little evidence to the contrary even in connection with the more successful regional agencies. The Guayana project represented a programme that promised benefits for both regional and national interests; by concentrating on the Guayana region the national objective of fostering development would be served, incipient nationalism was encouraged and political support was strengthened in the regions. Similarly, the programme promised each of the regions a programme for the future, a promise which was eagerly seized by the regions. But, as Friedmann has pointed out, the Venezuelan government responded to this regional demand 'with something less than spontaneous enthusiasm. Its evident reluctance derived partly from a recognition that institutionalizing regional development might lead to far-reaching changes in the political structure, as political power became displaced from a single national centre to be reconstituted around a number of regional loci.'[66]

Thus regional development is frequently held back by the national government against the wishes of the regions. It is part and parcel of the total political system and must tailor its aims to that system. Such a situation is as true of regional agencies as of local government; both are likely to be weak for the same institutional reasons. As Mariátegui has said of the provinces of Peru: 'The provinces are right when they condemn centralism, its methods and its institutions. They are right when they denounce an organization which concentrates the administration of the Republic in the capital. But they are completely wrong if, deceived by a mirage, they believe that decentralization will be sufficient to solve their major problems. "Gamonalismo" inside the centralized and unitary republic is the ally and the agent of the capital in the regions and in the provinces.'[67]

Regional agencies are fundamentally weak because they have generally lacked political support from the central government and have been used by local politicians for their own purposes. One can, in fact, generalize Daland's view about the planning process in Brazil to regional programmes generally. 'We have now arrived at the frustrating point of noting that planning . . . is politically useful, but not for the purpose of achieving development goals.'[68]

In general, therefore, regional agencies have been unsuccessful in as far as they have failed to bring structural changes to backward regions. Most have failed to change agrarian structures radically, to impart real dynamism to the rural sector or to alter the distribution of income. Even in north-east Brazil and the Venezuelan Guayana highly respected agencies such as SUDENE and the CVG have concentrated on physical improvements and have neglected distributional goals. That regional agencies should have failed to act in such controversial areas, however, merely reflects the political environment in which they have been forced to operate.

On the other hand, there can be no doubt that some areas have gained more through the actions of regional agencies than might have been achieved otherwise. Many regions have benefited from investment in roads, power and industrial projects. Often, this has created new employment opportunities and raised *per capita* incomes. While such actions will not solve the fundamental problems of the poorer regions, they do show that regional agencies can achieve incremental changes. These changes will be more pronounced should regional planning be actively encouraged. Effective regional planning will help decentralize employment opportunities, will improve the infrastructure in peripheral areas and will improve the flow of information between the regions and the national government. Given the limited possibility of fundamental changes occurring in the political environment, these incremental changes should be encouraged.

9: Spatial Alternatives for the Future

The previous chapters have described and explained a number of spatial patterns associated with Latin America's recent development experience. This concluding chapter will attempt to summarize those patterns and suggest ways in which they may change in the future. It will argue that national governments should consider spatial tendencies more carefully than they have in the past, especially when undertaking major developmental projects. Finally, it will suggest several spatial approaches which might form the basis of effective regional-development planning in the future.

The need for a spatial component in development planning

Major changes in the organization of the space-economy are essential to the process of economic growth and development. Just as development involves a transformation in the structure of employment and in the social environment, so too it stimulates changes in the location of economic activity and in the distribution of population. The introduction of more complex technology, of larger-scale operations and of a more specialized division of labour into the manufacturing sector encourages the spatial concentration of employment and production. The creation of a more sophisticated government bureaucracy and increases in the number of white-collar workers lead to a similar pattern of spatial concentration in the tertiary sector. Improvements in the transport network increase the volume of interregional trade and encourage a higher level of geographical mobility in the population.

These spatial changes are as universal and as integral a part of the development process as modifications in social attitudes or patterns of employment. Any failure to understand and plan for these spatial phenomena, therefore, may lead to major social problems and serious mis-allocations of investment. Such difficulties are especially likely to occur when spatial change is associated with large capital investments or when it affects large numbers of people. What is required to avoid these problems is the acceptance and implementation of a process of regional planning far more comprehensive than that which has been practised in Latin America. Such comprehensive regional planning should be concerned with more than the mere allocation of infra-structure or the establishment of regional-development agencies. It should play a key role in decisions relating to investment priorities and budget allocation. Decisions to favour region A rather than region B should be considered as carefully and as objectively as the decision to develop the steel industry before the plastics sector.

This form of regional or spatial planning should serve two important functions. Firstly, it should help to smooth and encourage spatial changes which are consequent upon essential sectoral changes. Secondly, and more ambitiously, it should establish whether or not spatial processes are beneficial to a society's long-term development. This latter control function is particularly important during periods of rapid growth, for it is clear that economic transformation may stimulate forms of spatial change which are inappropriate to long-term goals and objectives. When this occurs some mechanism should be established to modify, retard or prevent such change.

But under what circumstances should spatial processes be modified? Firstly, it is possible that a conflict may appear between a country's immediate and longer-term requirements. As has been suggested in Chapters Four and Seven the debate over the appropriate location of economic and urban development may fall into this category. Should rapid economic growth be encouraged whatever its spatial effect or should a slower but more regionally balanced growth policy be espoused? Such a decision is especially important in those countries where the source of rapid growth may disappear. Venezuela, for example, is becoming a relatively high-cost source of petroleum and within the next ten years its world importance could decline.[1] The product which has supported the Venezuelan economy over the past thirty years will then have to be replaced or a slower rate of economic growth will ensue. In these circumstances it is appropriate to ask whether planners should check the continuing tendency towards economic concentration in the Caracas and oil-producing regions. Should a regional policy be adopted that encourages the development of new export products, as for example in the Guayana programme? Alternatively, should greater emphasis be laid on rural development and increasing agricultural production? These are fundamental questions which should be considered in spatial as well as in sectoral terms.

Secondly, planning is required when spatial processes harm the economies of populous regions. In such cases a decision has to be made whether to encourage substantial migration from those areas or to help them by means of regional-development policies. *Prima facie*, there would seem to be a social case for slowing down large-scale migrations as far as possible. It is true that migration frequently provides an individual with greater economic and social opportunities. On the other hand, it may also loosen family ties, weaken local cultures and undermine the residual communities. While there may be economic and social gains from migration there are undoubtedly losses as well. In such cases, the net cost involved in discouraging migration should be considered. Additional infrastructure will be required if people move to the cities; is it very much more expensive to provide these services in the rural areas or in local market-towns? Can employment opportunities be created locally if government incentives are offered, and how costly are such incentives likely to prove? Naturally there are circumstances when the answers to both questions are negative. There are areas where high population-to-land ratios are associated with few local resources and with poor accessibility. Here there is no real alternative to out-migration. Equally, some areas' problems are caused by institutional factors, such as inequitable land-tenure systems, that force the population to leave unnecessarily. In such circumstances a spatial perspective to planning will underline the need for a different kind of government response.

A third and related opportunity for spatial decision-making arises when spatial tendencies encourage the 'undesirable' use of resources. It could be argued, for example, that the preference for urban living so common among Latin American élites is inhibiting agricultural development and the evolution of small towns. Such a preference encourages investment in questionable urban activities, such as real-estate speculation and the building of urban motorways, draws capital away from other projects, and occupies the attention of scarce entrepreneurial and administrative personnel. In this case, the objective of regional planning might be to reverse this tendency by fostering rural development projects and increasing the social prestige to be gained from professional work in rural areas.

Recent spatial tendencies in Latin America

Existing tendencies form a backcloth against which future planning decisions will be made. Before examining the possible spatial alternatives facing Latin American governments, therefore, it may be useful to summarize the most important spatial changes which have been occurring in the region.

(I) THE SPATIAL CONCENTRATION OF POPULATION AND ECONOMIC ACTIVITY

The present pattern of economic growth has encouraged rapid urban expansion in the largest cities. During the post-war period most of these centres have more than trebled their populations through the joint forces of migration and natural increase. Industrial and commercial activities have blossomed and the construction of motorways and skyscrapers has changed the faces of many city centres. The spatial impact of this change has been to concentrate both population and economic activity more than ever before. In many cases, existing regional-income disparities have widened because rural areas have been by-passed by the growth process.

(II) DISPERSAL OF ACTIVITIES AND POPULATION WITHIN THE 'CORE-REGION'

The sheer growth in population and in the number of economic activities has forced the larger cities to expand over a wider physical area. This expansion has been particularly marked as urban growth has been associated with a decline in population density. The introduction of large numbers of cars, the adoption of suburban life-styles and the decline of élite housing in the city centres have been particularly important in encouraging this tendency. Despite the increase of central-city densities through vertical development, average densities have declined in most metropolitan areas. This has caused many cities to develop into large, unplanned, urban sprawls. Such a tendency has been particularly marked in cities such as Mexico City, Santiago and Lima where there have been few physical constraints to development. In such cities the urban area has spread in all directions, largely owing to the weakness of local-planning agencies. Only in cities such as Rio and Caracas, where there were major topographical constraints, has multi-directional growth been limited. Even here sprawl has continued, being channelled by the ingenuity of engineers into linear or multiple-centre forms.

In addition to the physical spread of cities, the concentration of population has stimulated the growth of nearby towns and villages. This process has been encouraged by the way in which industrial companies have tried to escape the higher taxes, land prices and congestion of the central cities. As we saw in Chapter Three, this process has been particularly strong in Mexico City, São Paulo and Buenos Aires, but it has been very apparent in most large cities. The overall result has been that the rapidly growing 'core-areas' of most Latin American countries have covered a larger geographical area.

(III) THE PROCESS OF SPATIAL INTEGRATION

Increasing regional integration has characterized Latin America since the time of the Incas. It is a process, however, that has been accelerating as major improvements have been made in transport technology. The development of primary-export products and the introduction of railways in many areas during the nineteenth and early twentieth centuries brought about the first dramatic increases in spatial integration. More recently the road revolution which has swept the continent has encouraged still higher levels of integration. Today, most cities are connected with surrounding rural areas and with other regional centres, and traffic plies the routes between them. These improvements in transport networks have encouraged, and been stimulated by, a higher degree of regional economic specialization. Manufacturing industry has tended to produce for a national market, and individual cities have frequently become specialized along particular product lines. Rural areas have begun to supply factories with raw materials and slowly demanded more manufactured products.

While spatial integration is clearly continuing, increases in the movement of goods and services are more difficult to document. There are few road-traffic data, unlike the situation in many developed countries and certain Third World nations such as India.[2] This is unfortunate, for, with the exception of mineral traffic, road transport represents the largest and most ubiquitous form of transportation today. Even so it is quite clear from the rapid expansion in vehicle numbers (Table 27, p. 179) that every Latin American country is experiencing a similar process. Despite common falls in the tonnage carried by railway systems, inter-regional trade has increased greatly over the past twenty years.

A further manifestation of spatial integration is the way that people in general have become more mobile. The introduction of roads into rural areas has allowed more people to travel regularly to the cities. Such mobility has encouraged migration, has helped the diffusion of new ideas and products to the rural areas and has increased the feeling of national identity. Improvements in other forms of communication have obviously accelerated these trends. The introduction and adoption of the transistor radio over wide areas has had a pronounced effect on attitudes, especially feeling of national identity. The growing ability of rural people to read has helped the diffusion of new ideas and practices. In many countries these trends have only recently begun, but they are certain to grow in importance.

(IV) THE SETTLEMENT OF PREVIOUSLY UNEXPLOITED AREAS

Although a higher proportion of economic activities and population has become concentrated in the core-areas, there has also been an expansion in the effectively settled area. Large land areas are populated today which were previously unsettled and neglected. This expansion has been brought about by two separate forces, the process of colonization, and the establishment of new cities.

The increase in the area of agricultural land since 1945 has been considerable. As a result of irrigation, large areas of Mexico, Peru and Venezuela have been farmed for the first time. Similarly, road-building and colonization have opened up vast new areas for exploitation in many Latin American countries, especially Brazil.

The construction of new cities has been a less-common process, but one that has brought important changes where it has occurred. The building of Brasília and Ciudad Guayana has induced major changes in the regional structure of Brazil and Venezuela. The former has given a focus to Brazilian colonization and road-building programmes and has helped to create a new frontier spirit in that country. In Venezuela, the new city has led to the exploitation of large mineral deposits, to the development of huge electric-power resources and to the creation of a major new industrial centre.

All of these tendencies are likely to continue in the future. And, although individual countries will experience different combinations of them, everywhere the same tendencies will challenge spatial planners. But, since so many of these processes are well established, any attempt to alter them will be difficult. Unless governments are prepared to adopt radical and at times unpopular measures, the effect on the spatial structure will be limited.

Spatial alternatives for the future

A number of alternative spatial policies are open to Latin American governments. None of the policies are original for all have been discussed from various academic viewpoints and many have been adopted by different Latin American governments. Nor are all the policies equally suitable for every country; differences in size, wealth and ideology mean that particular policies may be inappropriate in certain places. All that is being suggested is that spatial alternatives exist whose adoption could benefit the overall development of individual countries.

The possibilities range in scale from methods to promote rural development to strategies designed to accelerate international integration. They are as follows:

- extension of the settled area
- rural-based development policies
- establishment of new central-places in rural areas
- deliberate urbanization policies – metropolitan growth versus growth-centre strategies
- international integrationist measures.

(I) EXTENDING THE SETTLED AREA

Over the past hundred years, road construction and agricultural colonization have led to the effective settlement of extensive land areas. Today, however, many writers have complained that too little backing has been given to colonization programmes. Planned schemes have been few in number and spontaneous movements have seldom received effective support. Outside Brazil and Mexico the numerous efforts at land-opening have been limited both in scope and conception. Similarly, criticism has been directed at recent attempts to extend the frontier through mineral-resource development. In places such as the Venezuelan Guayana it has been highly effective, but in general, its success has been limited by the way many mining enterprises have developed into local enclaves which have had little impact on the surrounding region. Where minerals have been exported without prior processing, employment has been limited. And it is only where secondary development has been encouraged, as in the establishment of smelters in the Cerro de Pasco complex in central Peru, that more employment has been created.

Both methods of land opening represent effective ways of accelerating Latin American development, although the success of both kinds of project depends greatly upon the land, mineral and financial resources available. Where such projects have been strongly encouraged in the past they have made a major impact on the spatial structure and the whole philosophy of national development. This has been clearly shown in the Brazilian and Venezuelan programmes. Not only did these projects stimulate agricultural colonization and mineral development, they also led to the establishment of important new urban centres and to the creation of a feeling of national pride.

In the Brazilian case it could be argued that the anticipated psychological effect was a major motivating force behind both the building of Brasília and the trans-Amazonian roads. Skidmore has argued that Kubitschek's Brasília policy was intended 'to generate a sense of self-confidence among Brazilians'.[3] Similarly the road-building programmes of the military government have appealed to the same kind of 'developmental nationalism'. In many ways, attempts to create this kind of spirit have definite virtues. At the same time, such strategies contain a strong element of political opportunism. As Skidmore has said, Brasília was a *tour de force* that promised something for everyone. It was therefore useful 'to divert attention from many difficult social and economic problems, such as reform of the agrarian system and the universities'.[4] In Chapter Five a similar argument was made with respect to the present road-building projects.

Even so, the Brazilian efforts do represent spatial policy writ large. They have succeeded in expanding the present area of occupation, and in developing agricultural and mineral resources which might otherwise have been neglected. While in the Brazilian case the policy has been closely associated with a capitalistic model of development, it does represent a form of spatial planning that might be followed, on a less ambitious scale, in most other countries. While few governments are likely to wish to construct a new capital (although one tiny country is doing so at the moment) or build trans-continental roads, all could usefully encourage agricultural colonization through road expansion and related measures.

The Venezuelan Guayana programme is also a guide for other nations. Again few could attempt to carry out a policy on quite the same scale; the Guayana project involved great expense and was permitted by a particularly favourable concentration of mineral and power resources. It does illustrate, however, the possible national and regional benefits to be gained from trying to process mineral products rather than exporting them directly.

(II) RURAL-BASED DEVELOPMENT POLICIES

A major opportunity facing some Latin American governments is to shift the balance of their attention from urban to rural development strategies. Such a change of emphasis is particularly important for two reasons. Firstly, because, in a number of countries, the major part of the population live in the rural areas and will continue to do so for many years ahead. Secondly, because employment opportunities in the cities are growing more slowly than the number of people requiring jobs.[5] Despite this situation, few governments outside Cuba have adopted policies designed to improve the general welfare of the poorer members of society. It is true that throughout the continent many measures have been introduced to encourage agricultural development. But, on the whole, these policies have benefited commercial and export producers rather than the rural population in general. Only on rare occasions have attempts been made to help these communities directly, most notably in the land redistributions which occurred in Mexico, Peru, Bolivia and Chile.

In Cuba and in other parts of the world, however, the rural sector has been at the forefront of developmental efforts. In Tanzania this was clearly recognized in the Arusha Declaration of 1967, which set the country on a path towards greater national self-reliance and socialism.[6] Such a policy was adopted because the government recognized the country's limited opportunities for industrialization and because a social gap was growing between the rural and the urban areas. Major changes were made which involved greater help for the rural areas, more emphasis on community service and greater attempts to even out differences in living standards between the towns and the country. Such a policy clearly underlay President Nyerere's order in 1971 that any unemployed persons living in Dar es Salaam should return to the rural areas and work on the land.

In Cuba, the early acts of the Castro administration were designed to make the nation more self-reliant and the society more equitable. These aims were to be achieved through land redistribution, the diversification of agriculture and a policy of import-substituting industrialization. In addition, social policies were introduced, notably the establishment of comprehensive education, the construction of rural roads and the opening of state shops. During the middle-sixties rural programmes were emphasized still further as the direction of economic policy altered and more resources were devoted to the production of export products such as sugar. This policy was underlined by Castro's decree that all urban workers should help in the sugar fields for two months of the year.

While in both Cuba and Tanzania such rural-based policies have been used for socialist ends, there are a number of reasons why a similar strategy might be useful throughout Latin America. The first reason is that it can help to reduce the gulf that presently exists between urban and rural areas. In many Latin American societies this gulf is acute and may well have distorted the allocation of economic resources. The effect of urban aspirations on the larger landowners, which was discussed in Chapter Five, is one aspect of this problem.

A second factor is that the policy can be used to maintain or even re-create local traditions. Such a role is important given that urban activities are not expanding quickly enough to absorb the potential work-force. Should such a situation continue, then some viable alternative ought to be offered, and rural-based programmes allied with land redistribution may represent one such alternative. By providing better welfare standards in the countryside, the movement of people to the cities may be slowed.

Unfortunately, such a policy requires that the government reject certain forms of material advancement. The production of many consumer-durable items such as television sets and cars does not fit squarely with a rural-based policy. For a government that was prepared to accept these consequences, the goals of higher local self-sufficiency and equity might well prove attractive.

(III) ESTABLISHMENT OF NEW CENTRAL-PLACES IN RURAL AREAS

Both the strategies of agricultural colonization and rural-based development represent means of developing nations from the bottom up. Both recognize that the resources and the population in rural areas must be employed in the process of developmental change. Both to some extent accept that it is in the rural sector that more equitable forms of development may emerge. At the same time, it is clear that outside stimuli are required to encourage change in rural areas. The need for agricultural-extension officers, better education and social-service facilities, better incentives for production and so on is generally accepted. So, too, is the need for land redistribution in some areas. In addition, however, some commentators have suggested that these incentives can be introduced successfully only by superimposing a system of urban centres on the rural areas.

Such a policy has been strongly recommended by Johnson, as follows: 'The really great developmental potentials of underdeveloped countries are not going to be found in a few glamorous projects but in the systematic improvement of the productivity and the spending power of the rural areas and the mass of the rural people. It is the argument of this essay that in countries which for historical reasons have inherited village-structured economic landscapes, a transition to a modern economy will require the creation of a network of intermediate agro-urban centres to provide incentives capable of tempting producers to raise more and better farm crops, to induce them to sell relatively more products, so that they can spend more yet save more, invest more, and thereby raise their productivity. The critical link in this chain will be the visible supply of incentive goods that can indirectly and silently persuade farmers to produce more.'[7]

What Johnson is suggesting is a means of improving the system of marketing and retailing as well as providing an efficient mechanism for diffusing innovations. All these functions can be performed more successfully in towns than in small villages, which may be as traditional and institutionally rigid as the rural areas themselves.

The role of particular marketing and retail systems in stimulating or retarding development has been recognized for a long period.[8] Certainly its negative influence is very important in Latin America, where peasant exploitation poses a major limit on any kind of rural improvement and change. One blatant example of exploitation has been reported by Burgos in Ecuador. 'In the La Concepción market square of Riobamba at stalls selling cloth by the length to both Indian countryfolk and mestizo townspeople two wooden rules are used to measure a vara of cloth (normally 83 cm.). One rule is 7 or 8 cm. shorter than the other and is used to measure cloth sold to Indians, while the other is used to measure cloth for the mestizos.'[9]

In another context, Preston has shown that the establishment of new market centres can aid rural development.[10] In Bolivia the formation of new peasant towns after the 1952 revolution led to the development of small villages which were socially distinct from the traditional mestizo towns. These new villages were inhabited mainly by local farmers who wished to provide for themselves the services formerly offered in the old-established towns. Since the personnel engaged in the activities were different, this process automatically removed some of the more blatant examples of exploitation. This was true not only in the marketing and retail systems but also in the local administration of justice and government.

It is quite clear, however, that the general application of such a policy would involve difficulties. Firstly, there is no guarantee that the marketing system can be made more honest by means of new towns. If, unlike the situation in Bolivia, the same merchants should establish themselves in the new towns, little change would take place. To prevent this, it might be necessary to introduce some form of control over trading practices, such as the establishment of government-controlled markets as in many parts of India. A major problem in introducing such a policy in Latin America is that in many areas local-government officials are as corrupt and dishonest as the merchants. Government intervention might only introduce other hands into the exploitive process.

Secondly, it is not clear where in the urban hierarchy the new towns should be established. The kind of new towns discussed by Johnson and Preston are different – the former is referring to towns which operate above the existing villages, the latter to smaller settlements where the functions are performed largely by the peasants themselves. In part, this variation is due to the differences between Indian* and Bolivian society and culture, but it is also a result of the fact that Johnson is emphasizing ways to stimulate greater production while Preston is particularly concerned with removing forms of exploitation. One interesting feature of the new towns in Bolivia, however, is that they seem to have had little influence on local agriculture. This suggests that while small settlements based on local farming communities may reduce exploitation they do not function well as receivers of information. A key factor, therefore, is the manner in which information is transmitted from and received by the town. In theory, the town would appear to have many advantages as a place from which to diffuse information, especially where it serves as a

*Johnson's ideas were based largely on work carried out in India.

daily or periodic market. If, however, the agents of diffusion do not operate efficiently, the information will not be spread. This is the situation in parts of Bolivia, where opportunities for communication provided by the Sunday market are wasted because most agricultural-extension officers do not work on that day. This whole question of diffusion is now receiving considerable academic attention and would seem to be a priority area for future research.[11]

New or expanded central-places may also be useful as a means for providing rural areas with social services. At present the poor working and living conditions in these areas dissuade professional workers such as doctors and teachers from moving there. One possible way of attracting them, therefore, is to provide adequate facilities in a limited number of small urban centres. In these centres basic facilities such as electricity, fresh water and modern housing could be provided and small professional communities established. From this centre the surrounding rural areas could be serviced either by attracting the population to the centre or, more effectively, by providing ambulatory services. Such a method would not be particularly cheap, but it is perhaps the only real alternative to compulsory rural service. And, since few governments seem prepared to adopt the latter policy, such centres may provide the only viable method of servicing these areas.

Agro-urban centres could also play a part in industrializing the rural areas. Such industrialization would be based not on large-scale manufacturing but on what has become known as intermediate technology.[12] This form of industry has a major advantage for less-developed countries in that it is less capital-intensive than manufacturing, thereby reducing the need for expensive capital imports and creating more employment. Since it is also intended to use local resources, there are greater advantages to be derived from small centres. This type of process is illustrated by recent efforts in Colombia to establish local artisan industries engaged in pottery, metal-working and weaving. In this case there is an obvious foreign market for the products, but other activities could be easily encouraged for internal consumption. Such a policy would seem to offer many possibilities for both the rural areas and less-developed countries in general.

(iv) Deliberate Urbanization Policies

A theory emerged during the 1950s and 1960s which suggested that the less-developed nations were suffering from over-urbanization. It was argued that, given their limited economic development, too many people were congregating in the Third World cities, the principal symptom of which was the growth of slums and urban unemployment. It was suggested that planning should attempt to slow this rate of urban growth, otherwise the effect on economic development would be negative.

As shown in Chapter Four, however, the balance of opinion shifted in the late sixties. More and more studies appeared which showed the advantages to be gained from urban expansion. Certain work even began to suggest that urbanization should be positively encouraged. Among such studies the writing of Friedmann and Currie was particularly important.[13] Both believed that urbanization encouraged the process of development, although there was an interesting difference between them over its effect on economic growth *per se*.

Friedmann's attitude had been strongly influenced by his work in Chile. In a comparative study of seventy countries he had found that Chile had approximately twice the population in urban areas than might have been expected given its *per capita* product.[14] This 'hyper-urbanization' had had positive political and social effects for the country. In particular, it had allowed substantial numbers of the organized middle and working classes greater access to power and had encouraged 'a general drift to the left in the political orientation of the country as a whole'.[15] Like other writers, however, he accepted that the imbalance might have reduced the rate of economic growth that might have been attained with a more 'normal' rate of urbanization. Indeed he argued that hyper-urbanization had played a role in 'encouraging a shift of resources from investment to consumption, by reinforcing incipient tendencies to inflation, and by leading to the summary neglect of agriculture as a productive sector'.[16] In general, however, these losses were less important than the positive effects of social and political change. He recommended that governments and planners should consider adopting a policy of deliberate urbanization.

Such a view provides an interesting contrast to that of Currie, who argues that urban growth represents a means by which the rate of national growth can be accelerated. He believes that rapid urbanization can be used to widen the effective demand for housing and thereby generate employment in construction and related industries. It will create employment opportunities in the cities and allow rural workers to move from low-income agricultural occupations to higher-income urban activities.

Such ideas are particularly interesting in that they have been largely adopted by the Colombian government in its latest development plan.[17] The bare outline of this plan is to generate a higher rate of saving in the Colombian economy and to channel this saving into housing investment. The new savings will be stimulated by guaranteeing investors a reasonable return over and above the rate of inflation. In turn these savings will be lent to home buyers, who will repay the loan plus some proportion of the increased value in their land and property. The demand for housing will stimulate the construction industry, and through the multiplier mechanism, the rest of the economy. Local industries producing construction materials such as bricks, glass, tiles, ceramics and wood will immediately benefit, and higher personal incomes should stimulate the demand for home-manufactured consumer goods such as textiles, clothing and electrical products. Providing that national industries are able to satisfy this higher demand, neither inflation nor the balance of payments should pose problems. In addition, there should be a positive incentive for agriculture. Larger numbers of migrants will be attracted to the cities by the increased opportunities for employment. This will reduce pressure on the land which, together with credit provided through the state, will help the development of more efficient commercial producers.

Such a strategy is not without its risks. If agriculture or the building-supply industries are unable to cope with the upward shift in demand, there will be a rapid increase in prices. Inflation would directly hit the poorer groups and the overall result might be to increase income disparities. A similar result might also be caused by any failure to tax increases in land and property values accruing principally to the upper-income groups.

The plan is also likely to induce major changes in spatial organization. In particular, several factors are likely to lead to population and economic activity concentrating still further in the largest centres.[18]

Firstly, demand for improved housing will be greatest in the largest cities. Already a large share of house-building takes place in these areas, and companies are likely to accelerate their programmes in these centres. In 1971, for example, 46 per cent of loans from the Central Mortgage Bank went to Bogotá and its surrounding area. Similarly 60 per cent of commercial-bank loans to the construction industry went to companies in the Bogotá area.

Secondly, if the plan succeeds in stimulating manufacturing industry, Bogotá and the other large cities will be the main beneficiaries. Already Bogotá contains approximately 26 per cent of manufacturing employment and the largest four centres together 70 per cent. Any expansion in manufacturing activity therefore is certain to benefit these cities *vis-à-vis* the smaller centres and the rural areas.

Thirdly, the process by which agriculture and the rural sector will benefit from the plan has not been explained in detail. It is assumed that urban growth will stimulate agricultural production, but little study has been made of supply constraints in that sector. Even if the agricultural sector can produce the required food, increased production is likely to come principally from large- and medium-sized commercial holdings, rather than from smaller producers.

The results of this plan, therefore, should be to accelerate the growth of the largest cities and to widen welfare disparities still further. In many ways this will merely exaggerate the tendencies existing in Colombia and in most Latin American countries. In terms of urban growth it will turn Bogotá into a metropolitan centre of some 8–9 million people by 1990. But, as we have already seen, many people believe that the growth of such large cities is not beneficial to Latin American development. These arguments were discussed in Chapter Four, but they are of such importance that it is worth repeating them.

The basic criticisms against metropolitan growth have been summarized by the Economic Commission for Latin America as follows: 'The lack of checks on the growth of metropolitan areas has caused a decline in urban living conditions and has made huge investments necessary to permit the smooth running of activities in those areas and to remedy deficiencies provoked by the same lack of checks. At the same time, excessively high and uncontrolled land values in the metropolitan area have caused the cost of urbanization to soar to unprecedented levels.'[19] In addition there are 'serious doubts as to the validity [of the assumption] that the growth and consolidation of the central development nucleus would transform it into a dynamic element promoting the development of the rest of the economy'.[20]

There is therefore a two-fold criticism against the growth of metropolitan centres. Firstly, it is argued that major diseconomies develop once a city reaches a particular size. Over-crowding in terms of housing and social facilities, traffic congestion and pollution, rising land values, and possibly social alienation are among the more obvious. These problems require major investments to remove them, such as the building of motorways and popular housing estates. In some cities, such as Rio de Janeiro, topographical features make these diseconomies particularly obvious.

Secondly, there is the criticism that other forms of urban system are better suited to the task of encouraging development in the rest of the nation. For example, regional-development programmes will be more successful if they are centred on viable regional centres. In these centres scale-economies will develop which may attract commercial and industrial enterprise. This new activity will in turn stimulate the surrounding regions.

There are a number of planners, however, who believe that there is nothing inherently wrong with a policy of metropolitan growth. While they do not deny that diseconomies develop, they suggest that the worst problems can be avoided by better urban planning. If many economic activities which now concentrate in city centres were encouraged to develop in semi-autonomous sub-centres, traffic and other congestion problems might be reduced. This is the opinion of the Colombian government, which has had a planning team working on the viability of this strategy in Bogotá.[21]

The defenders of metropolitan growth also point out that while there are costs to increasing size there are also many benefits. Metropolitan societies allow concentrations of skills, enterprise and innovation that can accelerate the generation and application of new ideas.

Concentration also permits administrators and managers to meet regularly and reduce their travelling time.[22] In addition there are many direct economic advantages. The agglomeration of industries allows ancillary economic activities to develop which help the process of growth and development. With respect to the impact of metropolitan growth on the rest of society there is a double argument. The first is that while some areas may be neglected as a result of concentration, the nation as a whole gains more from faster growth in the centre. If regional inequality worsens there is no reason why more people from the poorer areas should not move to the metropolitan centres. Secondly, it is doubtful whether the diffusion of ideas, technology and new products to rural areas occurs more rapidly when there are many regional centres. There is little point, therefore, in advocating a regional-centre policy to accelerate diffusion processes when these may not develop.

Unfortunately there is no way of measuring all the advantages and disadvantages of metropolitan growth. Some estimates can be made of the costs of expanding individual centres, but different *per capita* cost levels are as likely to be associated with physical features of the site as with population size. Similarly the form of urban growth can affect costs. Some cities' structures allow cheaper forms of expansion than others. If there are difficulties in measuring the costs of city growth, estimating the benefits is still more complex. A few attempts have been made but none have been wholly successful.

Despite this difficulty alternatives to metropolitan growth have many advocates. The most popular of these alternatives is some form of growth-pole strategy.[23] Such a strategy involves setting up or stimulating existing, medium-sized cities. In such centres many agglomeration economies can be obtained, while the worst metropolitan diseconomies can be avoided. In addition, such centres are more likely to stimulate local agriculture and rural activities than distant metropolitan centres.

The difficulty with a growth-centre strategy lies in its application. Normally it is associated with industrial growth and fiscal or other incentives are introduced to attract companies to the centres. But, as we saw in Chapter Three, it is difficult to attract industry away from the metropolitan centres. One alternative is to encourage the development of other forms of activity. Commercial development, the establishment of government offices or even the setting-up of technological universities might provide some form of economic stimulus. Whatever its difficulties, however, decentralization policies and, implicitly, a growth-pole strategy are becoming more common. The efforts of SUDENE in creating industrial employment in Salvador, Fortaleza and Recife, the expansion of Arequipa, and the growth of certain Mexican and Argentinian cities testifies to this fact.

(V) INTERNATIONAL INTEGRATIONIST MEASURES

The formation of LATFA, CACM and the Andean Pact reflects the desire in Latin America to accelerate the rate of international economic integration. Should such integration prove successful, national governments will be presented with further spatial alternatives. The principal opportunity will be to encourage development in those areas which will benefit from greater inter-regional trade.

In general the larger ports and metropolitan cities will be the principal beneficiaries of international integration.[24] The former will gain because most forms of trade will be carried by sea. The latter will benefit since manufacturing products are likely to be the main object of tariff reduction. There is, however, a possibility that international integration will encourage governments to help certain poorer regions as well. The regions concerned will be those which border international frontiers, among which are many of the continent's poorest areas. The Nariño department of Colombia, which borders on Ecuador, the Puno area of Peru, which adjoins Bolivia, and north-west Argentina, which borders on both Bolivia and Chile, are obvious examples.

For these regions to benefit some form of frontier-development programme will be required. The potential of such programmes, of course, is greatest when poor and rich areas are juxtaposed, as in the case of the Mexico–United States frontier. There is, however, an opportunity to accelerate the rate of development in poor areas even when they border on other poor areas.

The border between Colombia and Venezuela seems a particularly likely candidate for a frontier programme now that Venezuela has decided to join the Andean Pact. Even before this decision Colombia was experiencing certain benefits owing to its location. The towns of Maicao and Cúcuta had developed into contraband centres supplying both the Colombian and the Venezuelan markets. More respectably, a major attempt was being made to encourage Venezuelan tourists to Colombian resorts. In 1971 a road was completed from Maicao to the main Colombian tourist centres of Santa Marta and Cartagena.

How far similar benefits are likely to develop in other regions is difficult to judge. Success will depend upon the particular characteristics of the areas – in scenically beautiful areas tourism could be developed. The principal limit on success is the present slow rate of international integration. All border schemes will tend to founder unless there is genuine government commitment to integration.

The fact that there is a range of spatial approaches does not mean that every country is free to follow them all. Differences in population, level of development, resources and geographical area mean that some countries have a far wider choice of policies than others.

Among these 'structural' limits on choice the availability of resources is very important. The shortage of unsettled land in many parts of the Caribbean and Central America means that large-scale colonization is not possible. In other countries unpopulated areas abound, but unfavourable climatic and soil conditions make colonization equally impossible. Similarly the opportunity to develop resource-frontiers depends on the availability, quantity and accessibility of mineral deposits. Where major deposits are found, as for example in the recent discovery of oil in north-east Ecuador, resource-frontier development presents an exciting possibility.[25] (See Appendix Two.)

A further limitation on choice is the poverty of so many Latin American nations. Many spatial strategies require large-scale investment that may simply not be available. On occasions foreign capital may be forthcoming, but this can occur only where there are major mineral deposits or where developed nations are prepared to invest for ideological reasons. In other cases a government may be hostile to foreign investment or may have nothing with which to attract it. In the absence of such funds, many poor countries will be forced to reject certain kinds of policies. Closely related to this point is the question of growth potential. A government which expects the economy to grow annually by 7 or 8 per cent has a wider range of alternatives than one where the economy is growing at only 1 or 2 per cent. The former may allow spatial concentration for ten years, until it has sufficient funds to introduce a genuine decentralization policy. The latter, however, is less able to reach such a decision and whatever it does decide will affect it for much longer.

Lastly, both population and geographical size pose 'structural' limitations on choice. There is little reason why countries of the size of El Salvador or the Dominican Republic should adopt a growth-centre policy. While the decentralization of economic activity outside the principal city may be beneficial for reasons of congestion and pollution, these countries are not faced by the same range of choices as a large country like Brazil. In the latter, reduced growth in São Paulo or Rio may be achieved by stimulating new centres near by, by encouraging more industry in the distant north-east or by a colonization programme. Both its geographical and economic size allow a wider range of choice. Anyone discussing decentralization in Brazil and Central America therefore should be aware of this difference in scale.[26]

Acceptance of particular policies is also limited by political factors. Support for a declining region through a radical policy of land redistribution is not open to a government dependent on right-wing civilian or military support. Similarly adoption of a rural-based policy is difficult for governments whose political support comes from the cities. Governments dependent on the urban working class have little choice but to devote most of their attention to the urban areas. Political ideology, too, can be limiting even for a totalitarian government. Continued urban expansion, for example, was considered inappropriate to the emergence of a socialist Cuba. Similarly a policy of rapid industrialization supported by foreign investment is not likely to be furthered by a policy of land redistribution or nationalization. Intermediate positions do exist, as is illustrated by the Peruvian approach, but the presence of foreign capital does pose difficulties.

While there are limits on the ability of each country to adopt different spatial policies, the range of choice is probably greater than most governments would admit. Frequently alternative spatial policies have not been adopted, simply because planners have given them insufficient thought. This situation is unfortunate in two respects.

Firstly, the spatial modifications which have occurred during the past two or three decades have represented large-scale changes. The concentration of activity in the core-areas has involved the migration of large numbers of people and the investment of huge sums in infrastructural improvements such as transportation. Such changes will continue in the future and merely by their size they demand that governments pay them careful attention. This is especially important, since every country will be forced to live with the emerging spatial structures for many years ahead.

Secondly, spatial approaches may provide a partial solution to some of today's problems. Just as a readjustment of the sectoral pattern of investment may accelerate the rate of development, so support for a different pattern of regional investment may achieve a similar result. Regional needs should be considered just as carefully as the needs of industry, education or agriculture, and may provide excellent opportunities for faster economic and social change.

This is not to say that the inclusion of a spatial dimension to planning will provide a panacea for underdevelopment; economic and social backwardness is too complex a phenomenon for anyone to believe in simple solutions. All that is being suggested is that a spatial approach to planning decisions might offer a more reliable route to equitable and balanced development than several of those now being followed.

Appendix One: Cost–Benefit Analysis

Is the cost–benefit technique as competent in evaluating investment decisions in South America as in the United States or Western Europe? In the author's opinion there are several additional complications involved in making such calculations in developing countries, but which studies normally ignore. *Firstly*, investments in transportation in developing countries frequently induce fundamental changes in the society. The building of roads into 'backward' rural areas, for example, is likely to bring about major alterations in societal behaviour. If these changes are sufficiently great, then it will be impossible to predict the reactions of the society beforehand. Any attempt to calculate the stream of discounted benefits arising from the investment is likely to be subject to a large margin of error. *Secondly*, transport development may fail to stimulate an area to the point of 'take-off' and may merely point to a further, and perhaps previously unrealized, bottleneck to development. For example, the only effect of a road improvement in a backward agricultural area may be to indicate that the region is alarmingly short of lorries, or that more fertilizer is needed, or that agricultural development must await changes in the land-tenure situation. In these circumstances the estimation of costs and benefits from a transport improvement is very difficult. *Thirdly*, developing countries normally possess less equitable income distributions than developed countries (see Chapter Two). As such cost–benefit calculations must be very careful to take into account who gains from investments and who pays for them. Otherwise, it is quite possible that while the poorer sections of society gain little from a new airport, it has been their taxes on beer and tobacco which have paid for the investment. In societies where the inequalities between rich and poor are already too great, any cost–benefit study which does not take this point into account may perpetuate or increase those income differentials.

These difficulties for cost–benefit analysis could have been supplemented by several others. However, the point is not to show that this type of analysis is inherently bad, but rather that even more care must be taken in calculating the results in developing societies than in the developed world.

Appendix Two: Natural Resource Development

The part natural resources have played in influencing Latin American development has already been described in several parts of this book. The strong association between export commodities and natural resources was described in Chapter Two. The dynamic role played by resource exploitation in stimulating economic growth in Argentina and southern Brazil was sketched in Chapter Three. And the influence of resource exploitation on the nature and orientation of transport networks throughout the continent was examined in Chapter Six. The importance of natural-resource development to Latin America's past and future growth, however, is so great that it is worth emphasizing further.[1]

Ever since the Conquest, Latin America's exports have consisted mainly of mineral and agricultural products. Ever since independence, national rates of economic growth have depended upon the success with which natural resources could be exported. The present high levels of *per capita* income in Argentina and Venezuela, for example, were achieved largely as a result of growing world demands for those countries' exports. In Argentina, abundant temperate grasslands permitted the development of agricultural and meat products which could be exported to the industrialized nations. In turn, these agricultural exports generated strong multiplier effects which stimulated other sectors of the economy, at least up to the World Depression of the 1930s. On the other hand, countries like Honduras, Guatemala and Nicaragua were unable to develop export products which could stimulate their economic development. Lacking extensive temperate grasslands and mineral deposits, all were forced to develop exports based upon tropical agricultural products. With the exception of coffee, most of these crops generated few growth stimuli.

Naturally the different natural resources have not only influenced levels of *per capita* income. They have also affected patterns of social development and economic organization in each society. This has occurred because the exploitation of different natural resources has involved different kinds of technology, labour skills and employer–worker relationships. The social and economic consequences of banana plantations have been very different from those associated with the mining of copper or tin. Political awareness and social mobility have developed more rapidly in regions of large-scale mining than in plantation areas. In the former, integrated workers' organizations have frequently emerged which have helped to mould the course of national politics. In the latter, the social systems that have evolved have generally stifled political movements. Natural-resource endowments and their exploitation, therefore, have led to different kinds of societies emerging throughout the continent. In Brazil, the social differences which exist between the small-holding areas of the south, the coffee regions of São Paulo and the plantation areas of the north-east have come about largely in this way. Naturally, such an association does not constitute an inviolable rule. The differences that exist in social organization between the coffee areas of Colombia and Brazil make this clear. Even so it is obvious that different economic and social forms have emerged in close association with different kinds of resource development.

Despite these differences, every nation's experience of resource development has been similar in certain respects. Every country has experienced difficulties from fluctuating world prices for its products.[2] Some countries have suffered from this problem throughout their history; the classic example is Brazil, which has experienced trade cycles, over the past four centuries, involving sugar, cotton, gold, rubber and, to a lesser extent, coffee. Recently, this continuing difficulty has encouraged certain Latin American governments to collaborate with other Third World countries in improving the bargaining position of primary-good producers *vis-à-vis* that of the consuming countries. In some cases, most notably with the petroleum producers, this policy has met with spectacular success.[3] In general, however, the constant problem of fluctuating prices and the slow expansion of import revenues have limited economic growth prospects throughout the continent.

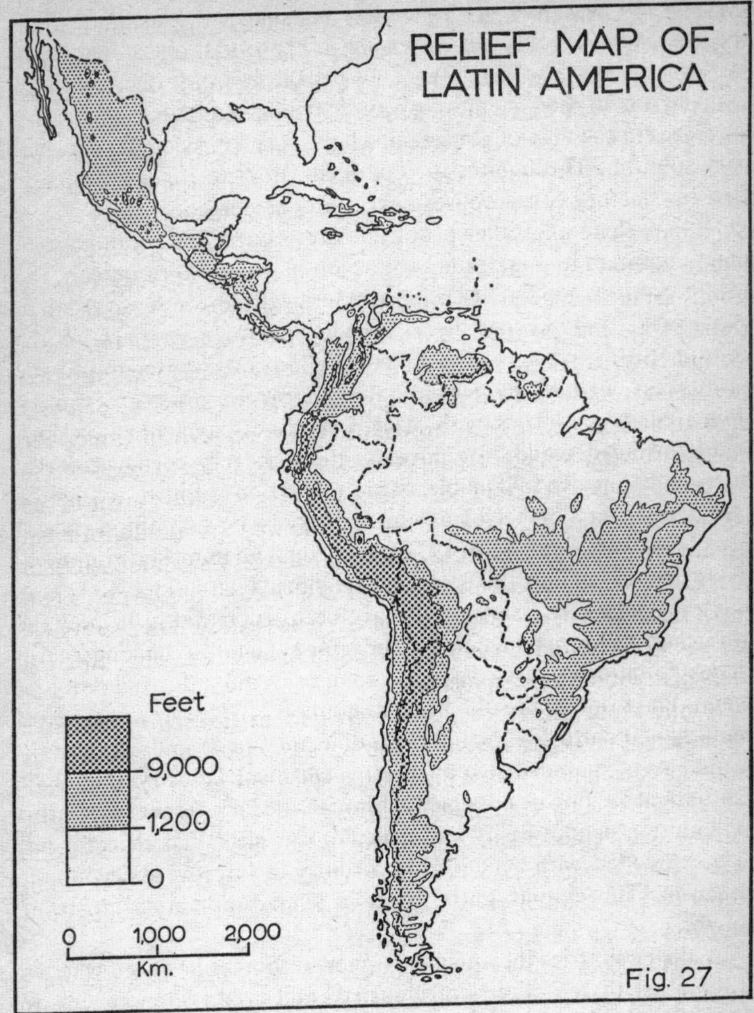

Fig. 27

Another common problem facing governments has been their dependence on foreign companies to develop their resources. While foreign involvement has provided capital and technology, it has frequently led to a conflict of interests developing between national and business objectives. This conflict of interests has frequently reached the headlines of the world's newspapers. Sometimes these disputes have resulted in government expropriation of company facilities, as happened in the cases of petroleum in Mexico, Peru and Bolivia, tin in Bolivia and copper in Chile. On other occasions, increases in the cost of concessions have been considered a satisfactory solution. Throughout the continent, however, it is quite clear that satisfactory compromises have seldom emerged.

Despite these and other problems, every Latin American government continues to search for and exploit new natural resources. The exploration of minerals is being encouraged more intensively than ever before and prospecting is taking place in most parts of the continent. For, whatever the difficulties, mineral exports do provide the easiest method by which national growth prospects can be improved. In countries with weak balance-of-payments situations and growing demands for imports, the discovery of new mineral deposits can prove invaluable. Such a situation is illustrated by the recent discovery of petroleum in Ecuador. The first shipments of petroleum were exported in 1972 and brought an immediate improvement in the country's balance-of-payments situation. Revenues accruing from concession rights have been a godsend in helping the government reduce its recurrent budgetary deficit. In the longer term the exploitation of these deposits promises to aid industrial development. Plans have already been announced to construct a petrol refinery at Puerto Balao (Province of Esmeraldas) and the government has recommended that a petro-chemical industry should be established as soon as possible.[4] Although the long-term effect of this exploitation cannot easily be predicted, it is clear that Ecuador has been presented with a major opportunity to improve its economic situation. Throughout Latin America similar bonanzas are being sought.

In most countries the appetite for new resources has been whetted still further by the process of industrial and urban development. In particular the growing demands for energy, both by manufacturing industry and by domestic consumers, has led to a greater emphasis being laid on the development of electricity supplies. Between 1958 and 1967, the generation of electricity rose by 7·7 per cent per annum. Fortunately, a large part of this increase could be obtained by develop-

Fig. 28a

ing some of the continent's vast hydro-electric power potential. The extent of these resources is indicated by the fact that, although 53 per cent of the region's electricity came from this source in 1967, ECLA calculated that only 2 per cent of the continent's potential was being utilized at that time.[5] On a continental scale, therefore, there are

Fig. 28b

ample supplies for the future. There are, however, a number of areas which will be forced to use other sources of electricity because they lack suitable water resources or because these resources are inconveniently located. Argentina is developing a nuclear power station to cover part of its future needs, a decision which has been helped by the discovery of uranium in that country. Other areas which cannot develop hydro-electric power are more likely to rely on conventional thermal plants.

The demand for petroleum, like that for electricity, has increased rapidly during the past decade. This expansion has been stimulated by the demands of thermal-electric plants, by the growth of manufacturing industry and by the massive rise in the number of road vehicles. Unfortunately few countries have adequate supplies, and practically every country will be forced to import petroleum in the

Table 38: Mineral Exploitation

Iron Ore (000 m. tons)	*1960*	*1965*	*1970*
Argentina	58	54	133†
Brazil	6,355	14,122	15,447†
Chile	3,804	7,763	6,940
Colombia	178	370	538*
Dominican Republic	82	—	—
Mexico	521	1,593	2,511
Peru	3,947	6,009	7,100
Venezuela	12,474	11,296	14,080
Tin (tons)			
Argentina	242	1,225	2,162
Bolivia	20,542	23,406	30,099
Brazil	1,581	1,219	2,842
Mexico	371	511	533
Peru	25	20	20
Copper (000 m. tons)			
Bolivia	2	5	9
Brazil	2	4	5*
Chile	536	585	700
Honduras	1	4	2*
Mexico	60	69	61
Peru	184	180	212
Lead (000 m. tons)			
Argentina	27	32	31
Bolivia	21	18	26
Brazil	10	16	19
Chile	2	1	1
Guatemala	9	1	1
Honduras	5	10	18
Mexico	191	170	176
Peru	131	154	155
Zinc (000 m. tons)	*1960*	*1965*	*1970*
Argentina	35	30	39
Bolivia	4	14	47
Chile	1	1	1
Guatemala	10	1	0
Honduras	4	11	16
Mexico	262	224	266
Peru	157	255	317

Table 38 (contd)

Coal (000 m. tons)			
Argentina	271	374	615
Brazil	2,330	3,137	5,127†
Colombia	2,600	3,072	3,000*
Chile	1,365	1,629	1,382
Mexico	1,771	2,006	188
Peru	162	129	165
Venezuela	35	30	39
Petroleum (000 m^3)			
Argentina	10,213	15,849	22,803
Bolivia	568	541	
Brazil	4,709	5,539	9,534
Chile	1,150	2,049	1,976
Colombia	8,867	11,721	12,728
Cuba	17	62	
Ecuador	434	460	230
Mexico	15,749	19,026	26,500
Peru	3,062	3,714	
Venezuela	165,632	204,452	215,170

* 1968 figures
† 1969 figures

Sources: *UN Statistical Yearbook,* 1971; Grunwald, J., and Musgrave, P. (1970).

near future. Even countries such as Colombia which are exporting oil at the present time will be forced to import supplies if increases in demand continue at current rates. Such a situation is especially difficult for these countries in as far as the success of the OPEC agreements will force them to pay higher prices to the petroleum producers. The policies which are favouring certain less-developed nations, therefore, are going to harm many others in the near future.

Another resource in short supply on the continent is coal. Brazil, Chile, Mexico and Peru have deposits, but none is large and most are unsuitable for coking. Only Colombia, in fact, possesses large deposits of good coking coal, but to date these have not been fully exploited. Recently coal has begun to be exported to Europe and Brazil and further shipments are probable but a great deal of investment is required before large-scale exports can be considered.

As regards other minerals, the continent is relatively rich. Various countries produce large quantities of lead, zinc, copper, manganese, gold, emeralds and iron ore, much of which is exported. (See Table 38 and Map 28.) In addition, new deposits are being discovered at regular intervals. Within the last three years, for example, major nickel and copper deposits have been discovered in Colombia.

Equally, over the continent as a whole, agricultural land is not in short supply. Admittedly there are areas where the number of farmers exceeds the available land. There are areas, too, where shortages of water mean that expensive irrigation schemes are required before land may be used for agriculture. In general, however, it is institutional rather than physical factors which limit the amount of available land and these could be overcome by radical land-redistribution measures.

Compared to many less-developed areas, Latin America's natural-resource base does not present a major barrier to development. While there are countries which possess few minerals and little free land, the majority of Latin American countries find themselves in a position where natural resources offer opportunities for development. One obvious example of an area where this is occurring is the Santa Cruz region of Bolivia. The region is rich in petroleum and its agricultural potential has encouraged the development of large-scale rice, sugar, cotton and cattle farming in recent years.[6] For areas such as these the future is bright. For the continent in general it is less promising, but, if major difficulties are encountered, they will not derive principally from the shortage of resources.

Bibliography

The following bibliography is neither a select nor a comprehensive list of the enormous literature now available on aspects of development in Latin America. It is not a select list because I hope that it will be of use to various kinds of reader: to the interested layman, to the undergraduate geographer and to the non-geographer concerned with less-developed areas and their problems. By including a long list, I hope to have provided all kinds of reader with a number of titles from which to follow his particular interests. In addition, I am well aware that the stocks of many libraries are limited, so that by including a wide range of titles I may be increasing the general availability of relevant work. Despite its length, however, it is not a comprehensive list simply because the recent flood of literature makes such a list impossible to compile. In this respect I should apologize to those authors whose work may be highly relevant but which has been omitted because of my unawareness of its existence. I hope that such authors may take the trouble to advise me of these omissions.

Asterisks are used to indicate works mentioned in the text.

*Abrams, C. (1964), *Housing in the Modern World: Man's Struggle for Shelter in an Urbanizing World*, Faber, London.

*Abu-Lughod, J. L. (1965), 'Urbanization in Egypt: Present State and Future Prospects', *Economic Development and Cultural Change*, 13, April, 313–43.

Achurra Larrain, M. (1972), 'Chilean Regional Development Policy', in Geisse, G., and Hardoy, J. E. (1972), 133–42.

Acosta, M., and Hardoy, J. E. (1972), 'Urbanization Policies in Revolutionary Cuba', in Geisse, G. and Hardoy, J. E. (eds,) (1972), 167–78.

Adams, D. W. (1964), 'Land Ownership Patterns in Colombia', *Inter-American Economic Affairs*, 17, Winter, 77–86.

(1966), 'Colombia's Land Tenure System: Antecedents and Problems', *Land Economics*, 42, February, 43–53.

*(1969), 'Rural Migration and Agricultural Development in Colombia', *Economic Development and Cultural Change*, 17, October, 527–39.

*Adams, J. G. U. (1970), 'The Spatial Structure of the Economy of West Africa', Ph.D. thesis, University of London.

Agarwala, A. N., and Singh, S. P. (eds.) (1963), *The Economics of Underdevelopment*, Oxford University Press, New York.

Alisky, M. (1969), *Uruguay: A Contemporary Survey*, Pall Mall, London.

*Almeida Andrade, T. (1971), *Disparidades regionais de desenvolvimento no Brasil*, I.G.U. Commission on Regional Aspects of Economic Development, Colloquium on Regional Inequalities of Development, Vitória, Espírito Santo.

Alonso, W. (1968a), *Industrial Location and Regional Policy in Economic Development*, Center for Planning and Development Research, University of California, Berkeley, Working Paper no. 74.

(1968b), *Equity and Its Relation to Efficiency in Urbanization*, Center for Planning and Development Research, University of California, Berkeley, Working Paper no. 78.

*(1969), 'Urban and Regional Imbalances in Economic Development', *Economic Development and Cultural Change*, 17, October, 1–14.

Amato, P. W. (1969), 'Environmental Quality and Locational Behaviour in a Latin American City', *Urban Affairs Quarterly*, 5, September, 83–101.

(1970), 'Elitism and Settlement Patterns in the Latin American City', *Journal of the American Institute of Planners*, 36, March, 96–105.

Andrade Lleras, G. (1963), *El papel de la planificación regional, departmental, local y de las corporaciones de fomento en Colombia como instrumentos del desarrollo*, Escuela Superior de Administración Pública, Bogotá, Documento 40.

Andrews, F., and Phillips, G. W. (1970), 'The Squatters of Lima: Who They Are and What They Want', *The Journal of Developing Areas*, 4, January, 211–24.

*Aranda, S. (1968), *La revolución agraria en Cuba*, Siglo XXI Editores S.A., Mexico.

*Araujo, O. (1969), *Situación industrial de Venezuela*, Universidad Central de Venezuela, Caracas.

*Arriaga, E. E. (1968), 'Components of City Growth in Selected Latin American Countries', *Milbank Memorial Fund Quarterly*, 46, April, 237–52.

(1970), 'A New Approach to the Measurement of Urbanization', *Economic Development and Cultural Change*, 18, January, 206–18.

Artle, R. (1971), 'Urbanization and Economic Growth in Venezuela', *Papers and Proceedings of the Regional Science Association*, 27, January, 63–93.

Augelli, J. P. (1958), 'Cultural and Economic Change of Bastos, a Japanese Colony on Brazil's Paulista Frontier', *Annals of the Association of American Geographers*, 48, March, 3–19.

*Bachmura, F. T. (ed.) (1968), *Human Resources in Latin America: An Interdisciplinary Focus*, The Bureau of Business Research, Graduate School of Business, Indiana University.

*Baer, W. (1964), 'Regional Inequality and Economic Growth in Brazil', *Economic Development and Cultural Change*, 12, July, 268–85.

*(1965), *Industrialization and Economic Development in Brazil*, Irwin, Homewood, Illinois.

(1969a), *The Development of the Brazilian Steel Industry*, Vanderbilt University Press, Tennessee.

(1969b), 'Socio-Economic Imbalances in Brazil', in Baklanoff, E. (ed.) (1969), 137–54.

Baerresen, D. W. (1971), *The Border Industrialization Program of Mexico*, Heath Lexington, Lexington, Massachusetts.

Baerresen, D. W., Carnoy, M., and Grunwald, J. (1965), *Latin American Trade Patterns*, Brookings Institution, Washington.

*Bain, J. S. (1966), *International Differences in Industrial Structure: Eight Nations in the 1950s*, Yale University Press, New Haven.

Baklanoff, E. (ed.) (1969), *The Shaping of Modern Brazil*, Louisiana State University Press, Baton Rouge.

*Balan, J. (1969), 'Migrant-Native Socio-Economic Differences in Latin American Cities: A Structural Analysis', *Latin American Research Review*, 4, Fall, 3–29.

Barkin, D. (1972a), 'Cuban Agriculture: A Strategy of Economic Development', *Studies in Comparative International Development*, 6, Spring, 19–38.

*(1972b), 'Public Expenditures and Social Change in Mexico: A Methodological Critique', *Journal of Latin American Studies*, 4, May, 105–12.

*Barkin, D., and King, T. (1970), *Regional Economic Development: The River Basin Approach in Mexico*, Cambridge University Press, London.

Barna, T. (ed.) (1963), *Structural Interdependence and Economic Development*, Macmillan, London.

Barraclough, S. (1970a), 'Alternate Land Tenure Systems Resulting from Agrarian Reform in Latin America', *Land Economics*, 46, August, 215–28.

(1970b), 'Rural Development and Employment Prospects', in Field, A. J. (ed.) (1970), 97–120.

(1972), 'Agrarian Reform and Structural Change in Latin America: The Chilean Case', *Journal of Development Studies*, 8, January, 163–81.

*Barraclough, S., and Domike, A. L. (1966), 'Agrarian Structure in Seven Latin American Countries', *Land Economics*, 42, November, 391–425.

Bassols Batalla, A. (1967), *La división económica regional de México*, Universidad Nacional Autónoma de México, Mexico City.

*Bauer, P. T. (1954), *West Africa Trade: A Study of Competition, Oligopoly, and Monopoly in a Changing Economy*, Cambridge University Press, London.

(1957), *Economic Analysis and Policy in Underdeveloped Countries*, Duke University Press, Durham, North Carolina.

*Bauer, P. T., and Yamey, B. S. (1957), *The Economics of Underdeveloped Countries*, James Nisbet, London.

*Bazant, J. (1970), *Alienation of Church Wealth in Mexico: Social and Economic Aspects of the Liberal Revolution, 1856–1875*, Cambridge University Press, London.

Benham, F. C. C., and Holley, H. A. (1960), *A Short Introduction to the Economy of Latin America*, Oxford University Press, London.

*Berg, E. J. (1961), 'Backward-Sloping Supply Functions in Dual Economies – the African Case', *Quarterly Journal of Economics*, 75, August, 468–92.

*Bergmann, B. R. (1966), 'The Cochabamba–Santa Cruz Highway in Bolivia', in Wilson, G. W., et al. (1966), 17–54.

*Bergsmann, J. (1970), *Brazil: Industrialization and Trade Policies*, Oxford University Press, London.

*Berry, B. J. L. (1961), 'City Size Distributions and Economic Development', *Economic Development and Cultural Change*, 9, July, 573–88.

(1964), 'Cities as Systems within Systems of Cities', in Friedmann, J., and Alonso, W. (eds.) (1964), 116–37.

(1966), *Essays on Commodity Flows and the Spatial Structure of the Indian Economy*, University of Chicago, Department of Geography, Research Paper No. 111.

*(1969), 'Relationships between Regional and Economic Development and the Urban System: The Case of Chile', *Tijdschrift voor Econ. en Soc. Geografie*, 60, September/October, 283–307.

Beyer, G. H. (ed.) (1967), *The Urban Explosion in Latin America*, Cornell University Press, Ithaca, New York.

*Bird, R. (1963), 'The Economy of the Mexican Federal District', *Inter-American Economic Affairs*, 17, Autumn, 19–52.

(1970), 'Income Distribution and Tax Policy in Colombia', *Economic Development and Cultural Change*, 18, July, 519–35.

*Blakemore, H. (1971), 'Chile', in Blakemore, H., and Smith, C. T. (eds.) (1971), 475–566.

*Blakemore, H., and Smith, C. T. (eds.) (1971), *Latin American Geographical Perspectives*, Methuen, London.

Blaug, M. (ed.) (1969), *Economics of Education*, Penguin Books, Harmondsworth, Middlesex.

*Board, C., Davies, R. J., and Fair, T. J. D. (1970), 'The Structure of the South African Space Economy: An Integrated Approach', *Regional Studies*, 4, October, 367–92.

Boeke, J. H. (1953), *Economics and Economic Policy of Dual Societies as Exemplified by Indonesia*, Willink, Haarlem.

*Boisier, S. (1970), *An Information System for Regional Planning. Chile: Experiences and Prospects*, United Nations Research Institute for Social Development, Geneva.

*Boorstein, E. (1968), 'The Economic Transformation of Cuba: A First-hand Account', *Monthly Review Press*, New York.

Bor, W. (1969), 'Venezuela', *Architectural Design*, 39, August, 425–47.

(1972), *The Making of Cities*, Leonard Hill, London.

Bor, W., and Smulian, J. (1970), *Planning in Venezuela – with Special Reference to the Recent Development of Three New Cities*, Regional Studies Association, Conference on Urbanization and Regional Change, Balliol College, Oxford.

*Borah, W. (1963), 'Colonial Institutions and Contemporary Latin America: Political and Economic Life', *Hispanic American Historical Review*, 43, August, 371–9.

*Borts, G. H. (1960), 'The Equalization of Returns and Regional Economic Growth', *American Economic Review*, 50, June, 319–47.

*Borts, G. H., and Stein, J. L. (1964), *Economic Growth in a Free Market*. Columbia University Press, New York.

*Bos, H. C. (1961), Discussion paper in Isard, W., and Cumberland, J. H. (eds.) (1961), 369–73.

*(1965), *Spatial Dispersion of Economic Activity*, Rotterdam University Press, Rotterdam.

*Bottomley, A. (1965), 'Imperfect Competition in the Industrialization of

Ecuador', *Inter-American Economic Affairs*, 19, January, 83–94.
(1966), 'Planning in an Underutilization Economy: The Case of Ecuador', *Social and Economic Studies*, 15, December, 305–13.
Boudeville, J. R. (1966), *Problems of Regional Economic Planning*, Edinburgh University Press, Edinburgh.
Bourricaud, F. (1970), *Power and Society in Contemporary Peru*, Faber and Faber, London.
Bradshaw, B. S. (1969), 'Fertility Differences in Peru: A Reconsideration', *Population Studies*, 23, March, 5–19.
*Brandenburg, F. R. (1964), *The Making of Modern Mexico*, Prentice Hall, Englewood Cliffs, New Jersey.
Brazil, Conselho de Desenvolvimento do Nordeste (1959), *A Policy for the Economic Development of the Northeast*, Rio de Janeiro.
Breese, G. (ed.) (1972), *The City in Newly Developing Countries: Readings on Urbanism and Urbanization*, Prentice Hall, Englewood Cliffs, New Jersey.
*Bromley, R. J. (1971), 'Markets in the Developing Countries: A Review', *Geography*, 56, April, 124–32.
*(1972), 'Agricultural Colonization in the Upper Amazon Basin: The Impact of Oil Discoveries', *Tijdschrift voor Econ. en Soc. Geografie*, 63, Jan./Feb., 278–94.
Brooks, R. H. (1971), 'Human Response to Recurrent Drought in Northeastern Brazil', *Professional Geographer*, 23, January, 40–44.
Brown, L. A. (1968), *Diffusion Processes and Location: A Conceptual Framework and Bibliography*, Regional Science Research Institute, Philadelphia, Pennsylvania.
(1969), 'Diffusion of Innovation: A Macroview', *Economic Development and Cultural Change*, 17, January, 189–211.
Brown, R. T. (1965), 'The "Railroad Decision" in Chile', in Fromm, G. (ed.) (1965).
*(1966), *Transport and the Economic Integration of South America*, Brookings Institution, Washington D.C.
*Browning, D. (1971), *El Salvador: Landscape and Society*, Clarendon Press, Oxford.
*Browning, H. L. (1958), 'Recent Trends in Latin American Urbanization', *Annals, American Academy of Political and Social Science*, 316, March, 111–20.
Browning, H. L., and Feindt, W. (1969), 'Selectivity of Migrants to a Metropolis in a Developing Country. A Mexican Case Study', *Demography*, 6, November, 347–57.

*(1971), 'The Social and Economic Context of Migration to Monterrey, Mexico', in Rabinovitz, F. F., and Trueblood, F. M. (eds.) (1971), 45–71.

Bryant, J. (1969), *Health and the Developing World*, Cornell University Press, Ithaca, N.Y.

Burgos Guevara, H. (1970), *Relaciones interétnicas en Riobamba: dominio y dependencia en una región ecuatoriana*, Instituto Indigenista Interamericano, Mexico City.

Burke, M. (1970), 'Land Reform and Its Effect upon Production and Productivity in the Lake Titicaca Region', *Economic Development and Cultural Change*, 18, April, 410–50.

Cable, V. (1969), 'The "Football War" and the Central American Common Market', *International Affairs*, 45, October, 658–71.

*Cameron, J., and Dodd, W. A. (1970), *Society, Schools and Progress in Tanzania*, Pergamon Press, Oxford.

Cardona, R. (1969), *Las Invasiones de Terrenos Urbanos*, Ediciones Tercer Mundo, Bogotá.

(1972) (ed.), *Las Migraciones Internas*, ASCOFAME, Bogotá.

Carmin, R. L. (1953), *Anápolis, Brazil, Regional Capital of an Agricultural Frontier*, University of Chicago, Department of Geography Research Paper 35, Chicago.

Carnoy, M., and Katz, M. L. (1971), 'Explaining Differentials in Earnings among Large Brazilian Cities', *Urban Studies*, 8, February, 21–38.

Castro, J. de (1966), *Death in the Northeast*, Random House, New York.

Chapman, M. (1969), 'Geography and the Study of Development', *Journal of Developing Areas*, 3, April, 319–38.

Chenery, H. B. (1960), 'Patterns of Industrial Growth', *American Economic Review*, September, 624–54.

*Childe, G. V. (1941), *Man Makes Himself*, Watts, London.

*Chile, ODEPLAN (1965), *Mapas básicos sobre la regionalización y descentralización de Chile*, Santiago.

Chonchol, J. (1965), 'Land Tenure and Development in Latin America', in Veliz, C. (ed.) (1965), 75–90.

Chorley, R. J., and Haggett, P. (eds.) (1967), *Models in Geography*, Methuen, London.

*Clark, C. (1951), *Conditions of Economic Progress*, Macmillan, London.

Clarke, J. I. (1971), *Population Geography and the Developing Countries*, Pergamon, Oxford.

*Cline, W. R. (1970), *Economic Consequences of a Land Reform in Brazil*, North Holland Publishing Company, Amsterdam.

Cochrane, J. D. (1972), *Regional Integration in Central America*, Lexington Books, Lexington, Massachusetts.

*Cole, J. P. (1965), *Latin America: An Economic and Social Geography*, Butterworth, London.

*Colombia, COLPUERTOS – Empresa 'Puertos de Colombia' (1969), *Boletín Informativo*.

*Colombia, Departamento Nacional de Planeación (1970), 'Políticas de desarrollo regional y urbano: modelo de regionalización', *Revista de Planeación y Desarrollo*, 2, October, 303–52.

*(1972), *Las Cuatro Estrategias*, Bogotá.

*Colombia, Ferrocarriles Nacionales de Colombia (1961), *Ferrocarril del Atlántico*, Bogotá.

*(1966), *Los ferrocarriles en cifras: Boletín anual*, Bogotá.

Colombia, Ministerio de Educación Nacional (1971), *Programa de concentraciones de desarrollo rural*, Bogotá.

*Colombia, Ministerio de Agricultura (1971), *Informe del comité evaluador de la reforma agraria*, Banco Ganadero, Bogotá.

*Colombia, Ministerio de Salud Pública (1970), *Ley 39 de 1969: Plan Hospitalario Nacional 1970–72*, Bogotá.

Comité Interamericano de Desarrollo Agrícola (1966), *Tenencia de la tierra en Colombia*, Washington.

*Consuegra, J. (1960), *Doctrina de la planeación colombiana*, Thesis of the Faculty of Architecture, Fundación Universidad de América, Bogotá.

*Contreras, V. (1962), *Financiación pública del transporte; Carreteras nacionales en Colombia*, Centro de Estudios de Desarrollo Económico, Universidad de los Andes, Bogotá.

*Cotler, J. (1967–8), 'The Mechanics of Internal Domination and Social Change in Peru', *Studies in Comparative International Development*, 3, December.

*(1970–71), 'Political Crisis and Military Populism in Peru', *Studies in Comparative International Development*, 6, May, 95–113.

Couto, A. J., and King, R. A. (1969), *The Agricultural Development of Peru*, Praeger, New York.

Crapper, D. B. (1968), 'A Location Study of Some British Based Industrial Firms in East Africa', *East African Geographical Review*, 6, April, 51–61.

Crease, D. (1964), 'Brasília: Brazil Looks West', *Geographical Magazine*, 36, March 1964, 633–48.

Crist, R. (1952), *The Cauca Valley*, Waverley Press, Baltimore.

Crossley, J. C. (1971), 'The River Plate Countries', in Blakemore, H., and Smith, C. T. (eds.) (1971), 475–566.

Curle, A. (1963), *Educational Strategy for Developing Societies*, Tavistock Publications, London.
*Currie, L. L. (1954), *Operación Colombia*, Cámara de Comercio, Barranquilla.
(1965), *Una política urbana para los paises en desarrollo*, Ediciones Tercer Mundo, Bogotá.
(1966), *Accelerating Development: The Necessity and the Means*, McGraw-Hill, New York.
*Daland, R. T. (1967), *Brazilian Planning and Development: Politics and Administration*, University of North Carolina Press, Chapel Hill.
*Darwent, D. J. (1969), 'Growth Poles and Growth Centres in Regional Planning', *Environment and Planning*, 1, 1969, 5–32.
*Davis, K. (1962), 'Las causas y efectos del fenómeno de primacía urbana con referencia especial a América Latina', Instituto de Investigaciones Sociales, XIII Congreso Nacional de Sociología, Mexico, 361–79.
*Davis, K., and Hertz, H. (1954), 'Urbanization and the Development of Pre-industrial Areas', *Economic Development and Cultural Change*, 4, October, 6–26.
*Davis, L. H. (1970), 'The Structure and Operation of Rural Local Government', in Flinn, W. L., and Havens, A. E. (eds.) (1970), 81–92.
*Daza Roa, A. (1967), 'La repartición de los ingresos', Banco de la República, *Revista Mensual*, 40, 1967, 880–89.
De Vries, E. (ed.) (1962), *Essays on Unbalanced Growth. A Century of Disparity and Convergence*, Institute of Social Studies, The Hague.
*Delgado, C. (1969), 'Three Proposals Regarding Accelerated Urbanisation Problems in Metropolitan Areas: The Lima Case', in Miller, J. P., and Gakenheimer, R. A. (eds.) (1971), 269–310.
*Dell, S. (1966), *A Latin American Common Market?*, Oxford University Press, London.
*Deutschman, P. J., and McNelly, J. T. (1964), 'Characteristics of Latin American Countries', *American Behavioral Scientist*, 8, September, 25–9.
*Dew, E. (1969), *Politics in the Altiplano. The Dynamics of Change in Rural Peru*, University of Texas Press, Austin.
Dickenson, J. P. (1967), 'The Iron and Steel Industry in Minas Gerais, Brazil, 1695–1965', in Steel, R. W., and Lawton, R. (eds.) (1967).
(1970), 'Industrial Estates in Brazil', *Geography*, 55, July, 326–9.
*(1971), 'Regional Implications of Economic Development Programmes in Brazil', paper given to the British Association for the Advancement of Science, Annual Meeting.

(1973), 'A Survey and Bibliography of British Geographical Work on Latin America', *Bulletin of the Society for Latin American Studies*, 16, January, 3–18.

Dillman, C. D. (1970a), 'Recent Developments in Mexico's National Border Programme', *The Professional Geographer*, 22, September, 243–7.

*(1970b), 'Urban Growth along Mexico's Northern Border and the Mexican National Border Programme', *Journal of Developing Areas*, 4, July, 487–508.

*Dinkelspiel, J. R. (1969), 'Administrative Style', in Rodwin, L. (ed.) (1969), 301–14.

*Dix, R. H. (1967), *Colombia: The Political Dimensions of Change*, Yale University Press, New Haven.

Dobyns, H. F., and Vásquez, M. C. (eds.) (1963), *Migración o integración en el Perú*, Estudios Andinos, Lima.

Dozier, C. L. (1956), 'Northern Paraná, Brazil; An Example of Organized Regional Development', *Geographical Review*, 46, July, 318–33.

*(1969), *Land Development and Colonization in Latin America: Case Studies of Peru, Bolivia and Mexico*, Praeger, New York.

Drekonja, G. (1971), 'Religion and Social Change in Latin America', *Latin American Research Review*, 6, Spring, 53–72.

Duff, E. A. (1966), 'Agrarian Reforms in Colombia. Problems of Social Reform', *Journal of Inter-American Studies*, 8, January, 75–88.

*Dumont, R. (1970), *Cuba: Socialism and Development*, Grove Press, New York.

*Easterlin, R. A. (1965), 'Long-Term Regional Income Changes: Some Suggested Factors', *Papers and Proceedings*, Regional Science Association, 4, 313–25.

*Eckaus, R. S. (1955), 'The Factor Proportions Problem in Underdeveloped Areas', *American Economic Review*, 45, September, 539–65.

*Eckstein, O. (1963), 'Benefit-Cost Analysis and Regional Development', in Isard, W., and Cumberland, J. H. (eds.) (1961), 359–68.

Edelmann, A. T. (1967), 'Colonization in Bolivia: Progress and Prospects', *Inter-American Economic Affairs*, 20, Spring, 39–54.

*Eidt, R. C. (1962), 'Pioneer Settlement in Eastern Peru', *Annals of the Association of American Geographers*, 52, April, 255–78.

(1966), 'Economic Features of Land Opening in the Peruvian Montana', *Professional Geographer*, 18, May, 146–50.

(1968), 'Japanese Agricultural Colonization: A New Attempt at Land Opening in Argentina', *Economic Geography*, 44, January, 1–20.

*Elizaga, J. C. (1966), 'A Study of Migration to Greater Santiago', *Demography*, 3, 2, 352–77.

Ellis, H. S. (ed.) (1969), *The Economy of Brazil*, University of California Press, Berkeley.

Erickson, E. E., et al. (1970), *Area Handbook for Ecuador*, American University, Washington, D.C.

*Estall, R. C., and Buchanan, R. O. (1961), *Industrial Activity and Economic Geography*, Hutchinson, London.

Fals Borda, O. (1969), *Subversion and Social Change in Colombia*, Columbia University Press, London.

Farmer, B. H. (1971), 'The Environmental Sciences and Economic Development', *Journal of Development Studies*, 7, April, 257–70.

*Feder, E. (1970), 'Counterreform', in Stavenhagen, R. (ed.) (1970), 173–224.

Felix, D. (1966), *Beyond Import Substitution: A Latin American Dilemma*, Harvard University Press, Cambridge, Massachusetts.

Ferns, H. S. (1969), *Argentina*, Benn, London.

Ferrer, A. (1967), *The Argentine Economy*, University of California Press, Berkeley.

Field, A. J. (ed.) (1970), *City and Country in the Third World: Issues in the Modernization of Latin America*, Schenkman, Cambridge, Massachusetts.

Fifer, V. J. (1967), 'Bolivia's Pioneer Fringe', *Geographical Review*, 57, January, 1–23.

(1972), *Bolivia: Land, Location and Politics since 1825*, Cambridge University Press, London.

Fillol, T. R. (1961), *Social Factors in Economic Development. The Argentinian Case*, MIT Press, Cambridge, Massachusetts.

Flinn, W. L., and Cartano, D. (1970), 'A Comparison of the Migration Process to an Urban Barrio and to a Rural Community: Two Case Studies', *Inter-American Economic Affairs*, 24, Autumn, 37–48.

*Flinn, W. L., and Converse, J. W. (1970), 'Eight Assumptions Concerning Rural-Urban Migration in Colombia: A Three-Shantytowns Test', *Land Economics*, 46, 456–66.

Flinn, W. L., and Havens, A. E. (eds.) (1970), *Internal Colonialism and Structural Change in Colombia*, Praeger, New York.

Flores, E. (1954), 'Land Reform in Bolivia', *Land Economics*, 30, May, 112–24.

*(1965), 'The Economics of Land Reform', in Stavenhagen, R. (ed.) (1970a), 139–58.

Flores Moncayo, J. (1965), 'Bases of the Agrarian Reform in Bolivia', in Smith, T. L. (ed.) (1965), 120–28.

*Fluharty, V. L. (1957), *Dance of the Millions*, University of Pittsburgh Press, Pittsburgh.

*Forni, F., and Mármora, L. (1967), *Migración diferencial en comunidades rurales*, Cuadernos del Centro de Estudios Urbanos y Regionales, Instituto Torcuato di Tella, Buenos Aires.

*Fox, D. J. (1971), 'Mexico', in Blakemore, H., and Smith, C. T. (eds.) (1971), 19–72.

(1972a), 'Mexico, the Transport System', *Bolsa Review*, 6, February, 60–69.

(1972b), 'Patterns of Morbidity and Mortality in Mexico City', *Geographical Review*, 62, April, 151–85.

*Frank, A. G. (1968), *Capitalism and Underdevelopment in Latin America*, Monthly Review Press, New York.

*(1970), *Latin America: Underdevelopment or Revolution; Essays in the Development of Underdevelopment and the Immediate Enemy*, Monthly Review Press, New York.

*(1971), *The Sociology of Development and the Underdevelopment of Sociology*, Pluto Press, London.

Frieden, B. J., and Nash, W. W. (eds.) (1969), *Shaping an Urban Future*, MIT Press, Cambridge, Massachusetts.

Friedlander, S. L. (1965), *Labor Migration and Economic Growth: A Case Study of Puerto Rico*, MIT Press, Cambridge, Massachusetts.

Friedmann, J. (1965), *Venezuela: From Doctrine to Dialogue*, Syracuse University Press, Syracuse, New York.

*(1966), *Regional Development Policy: A Case Study of Venezuela*, MIT Press, Cambridge, Massachusetts.

(1968), 'The Strategy of Deliberate Urbanization', *Journal of Institute of American Planners*, 26, November, 364–73.

(1969a), 'The Guayana Program in a Regional Perspective', in Rodwin, L. (ed.) (1969), 147–59.

(1969b), 'The Future of Urbanization in Latin America: Some Observations on the Role of the Periphery', *Papers and Proceedings*, Regional Science Association, 23, 161–76.

(1971), 'The Role of Cities in National Development', in Miller, J. P., and Gakenheimer, R. A. (eds.) (1971), 167–88.

Friedmann, J., and Alonso, W. (eds.) (1964), *Regional Development and Planning: A Reader*, MIT Press, Cambridge, Massachusetts.

Friedmann, J., and Lackington, T. (1967), 'Hyper-Urbanization and National Development in Chile: Some Hypotheses', *Urban Affairs Quarterly*, 11, June, 3–29.

Friedmann, J., and Stöhr, W. (1966), *The Uses of Regional Science: Policy Planning in Chile*, mimeo.

Fromm, G. (ed.) (1965), *Transport Investment and Economic Development*, Brookings Institution, Washington D.C.

*Furtado, C. (1963), *Economic Growth of Brazil, A Survey from Colonial to Modern Times*, University of California Press, Berkeley.

(1965), 'The Experience of National and Regional Planning in Brazil', in UN Department of Economic and Social Affairs (1965), 1–18.

*(1968), 'The Industrialization of Brazil', in Veliz, C. (ed.) (1968).

(1970) (ed.), *Brazil hoy*, Siglo XXI Editores SA, Mexico.

*(1971), *Economic Development of Latin America: A Survey from Colonial Times to the Cuban Revolution*, Cambridge University Press, London.

Galbraith, J. K. (1958), *The Affluent Society*, Hamish Hamilton, London.

*Gallo, E., and Katz, J. (1968), 'The Industrialization of Argentina', in Veliz, C. (ed.) (1968), 597–604.

*Galloway, J. H. (1971), 'Brazil', in Blakemore, H., and Smith, C. T. (eds.) (1971), 335–400.

Galvis, F. (1964), *El municipio colombiano*, Imprenta departamental 'Antonio Nariño', Bogotá.

*García, A. (1964), 'Agrarian Reform and Social Development in Bolivia', in Stavenhagen, R. (ed.) (1970), 301–46.

(1967), *Reforma agraria y economía empresarial en América Latina*, Editorial Universitario, Santiago.

(1969), *La estructura del atraso en América Latina*, Editorial Pleamar, Buenos Aires.

(1970), *Dinámica de las reformas agrarias en América Latina*, Editorial La Oveja Negra, Medellín.

García, C. (1968), *Características de los inmigrantes en cinco ciudades colombianas. Bogotá, Bucaramanga, Manizales, Medellín, Popayán*, Centro de Estudios de Desarrollo Económico, Universidad de los Andes, Bogotá.

*Gauthier, H. L. (1968), 'Transportation and the Growth of the São Paulo Economy', *Journal of Regional Science*, 8, September, 77–94.

(1970), 'Geography, Transportation and Regional Development', *Economic Geography*, 46, October, 612–19.

(1971), *Trends in Regional Inequalities in the Brazilian Economy*, Commission on Regional Aspects of Economic Development, Colloquium on Regional Inequalities of Development, Vitória, Espiritó Santo.

*Gauthier, H. L., and Semple, R. K. (1971), *An Information Analysis of Income Growth Inequalities in Brazil*, Commission on Quantitative Methods, Colloquium, Rio de Janeiro.

Geisse, G., and Hardoy, J. E. (eds.) (1972), *Latin American Urban Research*, Volume Two, Sage Publications, Beverly Hills.

*Germani, G. (1963), 'El proceso de urbanización en la Argentina', *Revista Interamericana de Ciencias Sociales*, 2, 287–345.

(1969–70), 'Stages of Modernization in Latin America', *Studies in Comparative International Development*, 5, 8, 155–78.

(1970), *Social Modernization and Economic Development in Argentina*, United Nations Research Institute for Social Development, Geneva.

*Gibson, C. (1963), 'Colonial Institutions and Contemporary Latin America: Social and Cultural Life', *Hispanic American Historical Review*, 43, August, 380–89.

Gibson, J. R. (1971), *A Demographic Analysis of Urbanization: Evolution of a System of Cities in Honduras, El Salvador and Costa Rica*, Cornell University Latin American Studies Series, Ithaca, New York.

*Gilbert, A. G. (1970), *Industrial Growth in the Spatial Development of the Colombian Economy between 1951 and 1964*, doctoral thesis, London University.

*(1974), *Industrial Concentration and the Growth of Colombian Cities*, Occasional Paper No. 24, Department of Geography, University College, London.

(1975), *Industrialization and Urban Growth in Colombia, 1951–1970*, Cambridge University Press, London, forthcoming.

Gillette, A. (1972), *Cuba's Educational Revolution*, Fabian Research Series 302, London.

Ginsburg, N. (ed.) (1960), *Essays on Geography and Economic Development*, University of Chicago, Department of Geography Research Paper 62, Chicago.

(1962), *Atlas of Economic Development*, University of Chicago Press, Chicago.

González, A. (1971), 'Population Growth and Socio-Economic Development: The Latin American Experience', *Journal of Geography*, 70, January, 36–46.

González Casanova, P. (1964–5), 'Internal Colonialism and National

Development', *Studies in International Comparative Development*, 1, 4, 27–37.

*(1965), *La democracía en México*, Ediciones Era, Mexico City.

González Navarro, M. (1965), 'Mexico: The Lop-Sided Revolution', in Veliz, C. (ed.) (1965), 206–29.

*Goodman, D. E. (1972), 'Industrial Development in the Brazilian North-east: An Interim Assessment of the Tax Credit Scheme of Article 34/18', in Roett, R. J. A. (ed.) (1972), 231–74.

*Gould, P. R. (1960), *The Development of the Transportation Pattern in Ghana*, Northwestern University Studies in Geography 5, Evanston, Illinois.

(1970), 'Tanzania 1920–63: The Spatial Impress of the Modernization Process', *World Politics*, 22, January, 149–70.

*Graham, D. H. (1970), 'Divergent and Convergent Regional Economic Growth and Internal Migration in Brazil, 1940–1960', *Economic Development and Cultural Change*, 18, April, 362–82.

*Griffin, K. B. (1966), 'Reflections on Latin American Development', *Oxford Economic Papers*, 18, March, 1–18.

*(1969), *Underdevelopment in Spanish America: An Interpretation*, Allen and Unwin, London.

Grunig, J. (1969), 'The Minifundio Problem in Colombia: Development Alternatives', *Inter-American Economic Affairs*, 23, Winter, 3–23.

*Grunwald, J. (1970), 'Some Reflections on Latin American Industrialisation Policy', *Journal of Political Economy*, 78, July-August, 826–56.

*Grunwald, J., and Musgrave, P. (1970), *Natural Resources in Latin American Development*, Johns Hopkins Press, Baltimore.

Guhl, E. (1966), 'Anotaciones sobre población, poblamiento, posición y estructura demográfica en Colombia', *Academía Colombiana de Ciencias Exactas, Físicas y Naturales*, 12, July, 377–89.

Guhl, E., and Fornaguera, M. (1969), *Colombia: ordenación del territorio en base del epicentrismo regional*, Universidad Nacional, Facultad de Ciencias Humanas, Bogotá.

Gutelman, M. (1967), *L'agriculture socialisée à Cuba*, François Maspero, Paris.

*(1967), 'The Socialization of the Means of Production in Cuba', in Stavenhagen, R. (ed.) (1970), 347–68.

Guzmán, G., Fals, O., and Umaña, E. (1962 and 1964), *La violencia en Colombia*, Ediciones Tercer Mundo, Bogotá, 2 volumes.

Hagen, E. E. (1962), *On the Theory of Social Change*, The Dorsey Press, Homewood.

*Hägerstrand, T. (1952), 'The Propagation of Innovation Waves', Lund Studies in Geography, Series B, *Human Geography* no. 4, 3–19.

(1967), *Innovation Diffusion as a Spatial Process*, Chicago University Press, Chicago.

*Haggett, P. (1965), *Locational Analysis in Human Geography*, Arnold, London.

Haggett, P., and Chorley, R. J. (1967), 'Models, Paradigms and the New Geography', in Chorley, R. J., and Haggett, P. (eds.) (1967) 19–41.

Hall, P. G. (1970), *The Theory and Practice of Regional Planning*, Pemberton Books, London.

*Hanke, L. (ed.) (1967), *History of Latin American Civilization: Sources and Interpretation*, Little Brown, Boston, 2 volumes.

*Hanna, F. A. (1959), *State Income Differentials, 1919–1954*, Duke University Press, Durham, North Carolina.

*Hansen, N. M. (1965), 'Unbalanced Growth and Regional Development', *Western Economic Journal*, 4, Fall, 3–14.

Hansen, R. D. (1971), *The Politics of Mexican Development*, Johns Hopkins Press, Baltimore.

Hardoy, J. E., and Schaedel, R. P. (eds.) (1969), *The Urbanization Process in America from Its Origins to the Present Day*, Editorial del Instituto Torcuato di Tella, Buenos Aires.

Harris, W. D. (1971), *The Growth of Latin American Cities*, Ohio University Press, Athens.

*Hauser, P. M. (ed.) (1957), *Urbanization in Asia and the Far East*, Calcutta.

(1960), *Urbanization in Latin America*, UNESCO, Geneva.

*Hauser, P. M., and Duncan, O. D. (eds.) (1959), *The Study of Population: An Inventory and Appraisal*, University of Chicago Press, Chicago.

*Havens, A. E., and Usandizaga, E. (1966), *Tres barrios de invasión: estudio de nivel de vida y actitudes en Barranquilla*, Ediciones Tercer Mundo, Bogotá.

*Hayter, T. (1971), *Aid as Imperialism*, Penguin Books, Harmondsworth.

Heath, D. B. (1959), 'Land Reform in Bolivia', *Inter-American Economic Affairs*, 12, Spring, 3–27.

Heath, D. B., and Adams, R. (eds.) (1965), *Contemporary Cultures and Societies of Latin America*, Random House, New York.

Heath, D. B., Erasmus, C. J., and Buechler, H. C. (1968), *Land Reform and Social Revolution in Bolivia*, Praeger, New York.

*Heaton, L. E. (1969), *The Agricultural Development of Venezuela*, Praeger, New York.

Hegen, E. E. (1966), *Highways into the Upper Amazon Basin: Pioneer Lands in South Colombia, Ecuador and Northern Peru*, Florida University Press, Gainesville.

Herbert, J. D., and Van Huyk, A. P. (eds.) (1968), *Urban Planning in the Developing Countries*, Praeger, New York.

*Herrick, B. H. (1965), *Urban Migration and Economic Development in Chile*, MIT Press, Cambridge, Massachusetts.

*Higgins, B. (1956), 'The Dualistic Theory of Underdeveloped Areas', *Economic Development and Cultural Change*, 4, January, 99–112.

(1967), 'Urbanization, Industrialization and Economic Development', in Beyer, G. T. (ed.) (1967), 117–74.

Hildebrand, J. R. (1967), 'The Central American Common Market: Economic and Political Integration', *Journal of Inter-American Studies*, 9, July, 383–95.

Hirsch, L. V. (1966), 'The Littoral Highway in El Salvador', in Wilson, G. W., et al. (1966), 87–126.

*Hirschman, A. O. (1958), *The Strategy of Economic Development*, Yale University Press, New Haven.

(ed.) (1961), *Latin American Issues – Essays and Comments*, Twentieth Century Fund, New York.

*(1965), *Journeys toward Progress: Studies of Economic Policy Making in Latin America*, Anchor Books, New York.

(1968a), 'The Political Economy of Import-Substituting Industrialization in Latin American Countries', *Quarterly Journal of Economics*, 82, January, 1–32.

*(1968b), 'Industrial Development in the Brazilian Northeast and the Tax Credit Scheme of Article 34/18', *Journal of Development Studies*, 5, October, 1–28.

(1971), *A Bias for Hope: Essays on Development and Latin America*, Yale University Press, New Haven.

*Hodder, B. W., and Ukwo, U. I. (1969), *Markets in West Africa: Studies of Markets and Trade among the Yoruba and Ibo*, Ibadan University Press, Ibadan.

Hoffmann, W. G. (1958), *The Growth of Industrial Economies*, Manchester University Press, Manchester.

*Hoover, E. M. (1948), *The Location of Economic Activity*, New York.

Hopkins, J. W. (1967), *The Government Executive of Modern Peru*, University of Florida Press, Gainesville.

Hoselitz, B. F. (1953), 'The Role of Cities in the Economic Growth of Underdeveloped Countries', *Journal of Political Economy*, 61, June, 195–208.

(1955a), 'The City, the Factory and Economic Growth', *American Economic Review*, 45, May, 166–84.

*(1955b), 'Generative and Parasitic Cities', *Economic Development and Cultural Change*, 3, April, 278–94.

*(ed.) (1960), *Sociological Aspects of Economic Growth*, Free Press, Glencoe, Illinois.

*Humphreys, R. A. (1969a), 'The Caudillo Tradition', in Humphreys, R. A. (1969b), 216–28.

(1969b), *Tradition and Revolt in Latin America and Other Essays*, Weidenfeld and Nicolson, London.

*Humphreys, R. A., and Lynch, J. (eds.) (1965), *The Origins of the Latin American Revolutions, 1808–1826*, Alfred Knopf, New York.

*Hurtado Ruiz-Tagle, C. (1966), *Concentración de población y desarrollo económico – el caso chileno*, Instituto de Economía, Universidad de Chile, Santiago.

Hurtado, O. (1969), *Dos mundos superpuestos: ensayo de diagnóstico de la realidad ecuatoriana*, Instituto Ecuatoriana de Planificación para el Desarrollo Social, Quito.

Inter-American Development Bank (1969), *The Process of Industrialization in Latin America*, Round Table, Guatemala City.

*International Bank for Reconstruction and Development (1955), *The Autonomous Regional Corporation of the Cauca and the Development of the Upper Cauca Valley*, Washington D.C.

(1972), *Economic Growth of Colombia: Problems and Prospects*, Johns Hopkins Press, Baltimore.

*Isard, W., et al. (1960), *Methods of Regional Analysis: An Introduction to Regional Science*, MIT Press, New York.

Isard, W., and Cumberland, J. H. (eds.) (1961), *Regional Economic Planning: Techniques of Analysis for Less Developed Areas*, OECD, Paris.

James, P. E. (1969), *Latin America*, Odyssey, New York.

*James, P. E., and Faissol, P. (1956), 'The Problem of Brazil's Capital City', *Geographical Review*, 46, July, 301–17.

Johnson, A. W. (1971), *Sharecroppers of the Sertão: Economics and Dependence on a Brazilian Plantation*, Harvard University Press, Cambridge, Massachusetts.

*Johnson, E. A. J. (1970), *The Organization of Space in Developing Countries*, Harvard University Press, Cambridge, Massachusetts.

*Johnson, L. L. (1967a), 'Problems of Import Substitution: The Chilean Automobile Industry', *Economic Development and Cultural Change*, 15, January, 202–16.

*(1967b), 'Problems in Evaluating Latin American Development', *Oxford Economic Papers*, 19, July, 221–34.

*Jones, E. (1964), 'Aspects of Urbanization in Venezuela', *Ekistics*, 18, December, 420–25.

Jorgenson, H. T. (1968), 'Impending Disaster in Northeast Brazil', *Inter-American Economic Affairs*, 22, Summer, 3–22.

Kahl, J. A. (1968), *The Measurement of Modernism: A Study of Values in Brazil and Mexico*, University of Texas Press, Austin.

*Kamerschen, D. R. (1969), 'Further Analysis of Overurbanization', *Economic Development and Cultural Change*, 17, April, 235–53.

*Kansky, K. J. (1963), *Structure of Transportation Networks*, University of Chicago, Department of Geography Research Paper 84, Chicago.

*Keeble, D. E. (1967), 'Models of Economic Development', in Chorley, R.J., and Haggett, P. (eds.) (1967), 243–302.

King, L. J. (1969), *Statistical Analysis in Geography*, Prentice Hall, Englewood Cliffs.

*King, M. H. (1966), *Medical Care and Developing Countries*, Oxford University Press, Nairobi.

*King, T. (1970), *Mexico: Industrialization and Trade Policies since 1940*, Oxford University Press, London.

Kiser, C. V. (ed.) (1968), 'Current Research on Fertility and Family Planning in Latin America', *Milbank Memorial Fund Quarterly*, 46, July.

Klein, M. S. (1966), 'The Atlantic Highway in Guatemala', in Wilson, G. W., et al. (1966), 55–86.

*Kleinpenning, J. M. G. (1971a), 'Objectives and Results of the Development Policy in Northeast Brazil', *Tijdschrift voor Econ. en Soc. Geografie*, 62, Sept./Oct., 271–84.

*(1971b), 'Road Building and Agricultural Colonization in the Amazon Basin', *Tijdschrift voor Econ. en Soc. Geografie*, 62, Sept./Oct., 285–9.

Kuklinski, A. (ed.) (1972), *Papers on Growth Poles and Growth Centres in Selected Countries*, UNRISD, Mouton Publishers, The Hague.

*Kuznets, S. (1966), *Modern Economic Growth: Rate, Structure and Spread*, Yale University Press, New Haven.

*Lambert, J. (1967), *Latin America: Social Structures and Political Institutions*, University of California Press, Berkeley.

*Landsberger, H. A. (ed.) (1970), *The Church and Social Change in Latin America*, University of Notre Dame Press, Indiana.

*Lasuen, J. R. (1969), 'On Growth Poles', *Urban Studies*, 2, June, 137–61.

*Lavell, A. M. (1971), *Industrial Development and the Regional Problem: A Case Study of Central Mexico*, doctoral thesis, University of London.

*(1972), 'Regional Industrialization in Mexico: Some Policy Considerations', *Regional Studies*, 6, September, 343–62.

*Lebret Mission (1958), *Estudio sobre las condiciones del desarrollo de Colombia*, Bogotá.

*Lefeber, L. (1958), *Allocation in Space: Production, Transport, and Industrial Location*, North Holland Publishing Company, Amsterdam.

(1964), 'Regional Allocation of Resources in India', in Friedmann, J., and Alonso, W. (eds.) (1964), 642–53.

*Lehmann, D. (1971), 'Political Incorporation versus Political Stability: The Case of the Chilean Agrarian Reform, 1965–70', *Journal of Development Studies*, 7, July, 365–95.

*Leiserson, A. (1966), *Notes on the Process of Industrialization in Argentina, Chile, Peru*, University of California Press, Berkeley.

Lerner, D. (1964), *The Passing of Traditional Society: Modernizing the Middle East*, The Free Press, New York.

*(1967), 'Comparative Analysis of Processes of Modernization', in Miner, H. (ed.) (1967), 21–38.

*Levin, J. V. (1960), *The Export Economies: Their Pattern of Development in Historical Perspective*, Harvard University Press, Cambridge, Massachusetts.

Levy, F. D. Junior (1968), *Economic Planning in Venezuela*, Praeger, New York.

*Lewis, W. A. (1954), 'Economic Development with Unlimited Supplies of Labour', in Agarwala, A. N., and Singh, S. P. (eds.) (1963), 400–449.

*(1957), *The Theory of Economic Growth*, Allen and Unwin, London.

*(1966), *Development Planning*, Allen and Unwin, London.

Lieuwen, E. (1954), *Petroleum in Venezuela: A History*, University of California Press, Berkeley.

*(1961), *Venezuela*, Oxford University Press, London.

Linke, L. (1960), *Ecuador – Country of Contrasts*, Oxford University Press, London.

*Linsky, A. (1965), 'Some Generalizations Concerning Primate Cities', *Annals of the American Association of Geographers*, 55, September, 506–13.

Lipman, A. (1963), *El empresario bogotano*, Tercer Mundo, Bogotá.

*Livesey & Henderson (in association with Maxwell Stamp Associates Ltd) (1969), *Feasibility Study for Port Development in the Region of Matarani*, London.

Logan, M. I. (1972), 'The Spatial System and Planning Strategies in Developing Countries', *Geographical Review*, 62, April, 229–44.

*López, T. A. (1968), *Migración y cambio social en Antioquia durante el siglo diez y nueve*, Universidad de los Andes, Centro de Estudios de Desarrollo Económico, Monografía 25.

*Lowder, S. (1970), 'Lima's Population Growth and the Consequences for Peru', in Roberts, B. R., and Lowder, S. (1970), 21–33.

Ludwig, A. K. (ed.) (1969a), 'The Kubitschek Years, 1956–1961: A Massive Undertaking in a Big Rush', in *Cultural Change in Brazil*, papers for Midwest Association for Latin American Studies, Ball State University, 101–13.

(1969b), 'The Planning and Creation of Brasília: Toward a New and Unique Regional Environment', in Baklanoff, E. (ed.) (1969), 179–204.

Mabogunje, A. L. (1965), 'Urbanization in Nigeria – a Constraint on Economic Development', *Economic Development and Cultural Change*, 8, April, 413–38.

MacDonald, J. S., and L. E. (1968), 'Motives and Objectives of Migration: Selective Migration and Preferences Toward Rural and Urban Life', *Social and Economic Studies*, 17, December, 417–34.

McGinn, N., and Davis, R. (eds.) (1969), *Build a Mill, Build a City, Build a School: Industrialization, Urbanization and Education in Ciudad Guayana*, MIT Press, Cambridge, Massachusetts.

*McGreevey, W. P. (1968), 'Causas de la migración interna en Colombia', in CEDE, *Empleo y desempleo en Colombia*, Universidad de los Andes, Bogotá.

Mamalakis, M., and Reynolds, C. W. (1965), *Essays on the Chilean Economy*, Irwin, Homewood, Illinois.

Mangin, W. (1967), 'Latin American Squatter Settlements: A Problem and a Solution', *Latin American Research Review*, 2, Spring, 65–98.

(1970), *Peasants in Cities; Readings in the Anthropology of Urbanization*, Houghton Mifflin, Boston.

*Marabelli, F. (1966), *Tentativa de distribución del producto bruto interno de Colombia por secciones administrativas del país, 1964*, mimeo, Bogotá.

*Marchand, B. (1966), 'Les ranchos de Caracas, contribution à l'étude de bidonvilles', Cahiers d'Outre-Mer, 105–43.

Marett, R. (1969), *Peru*, Benn, London.

*Margulis, M. (1967), 'Análisis de un proceso migratorio rural urbano en Argentina', *Aportes* 3, January, 73–128.

(1970), *Migración y marginalidad en la sociedad argentina*, Editorial Paídos, Buenos Aires.

*Mariátegui, J. C. (1952), *Siete ensayos de interpretación de la realidad peruana*, Ed. Arauta, Lima.

Martin, K., and Knapp, J. (eds.) (1967), *The Teaching of Development Economics – Its Position in the Present State of Knowledge*, Frank Cass, London.

Matos Mar, J. (1968), *Urbanización y barriadas en América del Sur*, Instituto de Estudios Peruanos, Lima.

Mehta, S. K. (1964), 'Some Demographic and Economic Correlates of Primate Cities: A Case for Revaluation', *Demography*, 1, 1, 136–47.

*Meier, G. M. (ed.) (1964), *Leading Issues in Development Economics*, Oxford University Press, New York.

*Mendoza Berrueto, E. (1969), 'Implicaciones regionales del desarrollo económico de México', *Demografía y Economía*, 3, 25–67.

Meyer, J. (1963), 'Regional Economics: A Survey', *American Economic Review*, 53, 19–54.

*Miller, J. P., and Gakenheimer, R. A. (eds.) (1971), *Latin American Urban Policies and the Social Sciences*, Sage Publications, Beverley Hills.

Miner, H. (ed.) (1967), *The City in Modern Africa*, Pall Mall, London.

*Mishan, E. J. (1967), *The Costs of Economic Growth*, Staples Press, London.

Momsen, R. P. (1968), *Brazil: A Giant Stirs*, Van Nostrand, Princeton.

Morris, A. S. (1972), 'The Regional Problem in Argentine Economic Development', *Geography*, 57, November, 289–306.

*Morse, R. (1958), *From Community to Metropolis, a Biography of São Paulo, Brazil*, University of Florida Press, Gainesville, Florida.

(1965), 'Recent Research on Latin American Urbanization: A Selective Survey with Commentary', *Latin American Research Review*, 1, Fall, 35–74.

(1971), 'Trends and Issues in Latin American Urban Research, 1965–1970', *Latin American Research Review*, Spring, 3–52, and Summer, 19–76.

Mountjoy, A. B. (ed.) (1971), *Developing the Underdeveloped Countries*, Macmillan, London.

*Mumford, L. (1938), *The Culture of Cities*, Harcourt Brace, New York.

Mutchler, D. E. (1971), *The Church as a Political Factor in Latin America: With Particular Reference to Colombia and Chile*, Praeger, New York.

*Myrdal, G. M. (1957), *Economic Theory and Underdeveloped Regions*, Gerald Duckworth, London.

*(1968), *Asian Drama: An Inquiry into the Poverty of Nations*, Pantheon, New York.

*(1970), *The Challenge of World Poverty: A World Anti-Poverty Programme in Outline*, Allen Lane The Penguin Press, London.

Neglia, A., and Hernández, F. (1970), *Marginalidad, población y familia*, Instituto de Desarrollo de la Comunidad, Bogotá.

*Nelson, R. R., Schultz, T. P., and Slighton, R. L. (1971), *Structural Change in a Developing Economy: Colombia's Problems and Prospects*, Princeton University Press, Princeton, New Jersey.

Nicholls, H. (1961), 'Industrialization, Factor Markets and Agricultural Development', *Journal of Political Economy*, 69, August, 319–40.

*Nicholls, W. H. (1969), 'The Agricultural Frontier in Modern Brazilian History: The State of Paraná, 1920–1965', in *Cultural Change in Brazil*, papers of the Midwest Association for Latin American Studies, Ball State University, Muncie, Indiana.

*Nichols, V. (1969), 'Growth Poles: An Evaluation of Their Propulsive Effect', *Environment and Planning*, 1, 2, 193–208.

*Odell, P. R. (1966), 'The Demand for Energy in a Developing Region; A Study of the Upper Cauca Valley of Colombia, *Journal of Development Studies*, 2, January, 120–34.

*(1968), 'Economic Integration and Spatial Patterns of Economic Development in Latin America', *Journal of Common Market Studies*, 6, 3, 267–87.

*(1970), *Oil and World Power: A Geographical Interpretation*, Penguin Books, Harmondsworth, Middlesex.

*(1971), 'A European View on Regional Development and Planning in Latin America', *International Review of Community Development*, 25–6, 3–22.

*Odell, P. R., and Preston, D. A. (1973), *Economies and Societies in Latin America: A Geographical Interpretation*, John Wiley, London.

*Okun, B., and Richardson, R. W. (1961), 'Regional Income Inequality and Internal Population Migration', *Economic Development and Cultural Change*, 9, April, 128–43.

*Olden, D. (1971), *The Spatial Distribution of Population in Relation to Wealth and Welfare in Colombia, Mexico and Peru*, M. Phil. thesis, University of London.

Ortiz, S. (1970), 'The Human Factor in Social Planning in Latin America', *Journal of Development Studies*, 6, July, 152–62.

Owens, R. J. (1963), *Peru*, Oxford University Press, London.

Padilla Aragon, E. (1969), *México: desarrollo con pobreza*, Siglo XXI Editores, Mexico City.

Paredes Manrique, R. (ed.) (1968), *La profesión médica*, Asociación Colombiana de Facultades de Medicina, Ministerio de Salud Pública, Bogotá.

*Parker, F. D. (1964), *The Central American Republics*, Oxford University Press, London.

Parsons, J. J. (1967a), *Antioqueño Colonization in Western Colombia*, University of California Press, Berkeley.

(1967b), *Antioquia's Corridor to the Sea: An Historical Geography of the Settlement of Urabá*, University of California Press, Berkeley.

*Payne, J. L. (1968), *Patterns of Conflict in Colombia*, Yale University Press, New Haven.

*Pearse, A. (1966), 'Agrarian Change: Trends in Latin America', *Latin American Research Review*, 1, Summer, 45–69.

*(1973), 'Structural Problems of Education Systems in Latin America', in Brown, R. (ed.) (1973), *Knowledge, Education and Cultural Change*, Tavistock Publications, London, 113–40.

*Pearson, L. B. (ed.) (1969), *Partners in Development: Report of the Commission on International Development*, Pall Mall Press, London.

Peattie, L. (1968), *The View from the Barrio*, University of Michigan Press, Ann Arbor, Michigan.

*Pedersen, P. O. (1970), 'Innovation Diffusion within and between National Urban Systems', *Geographical Analysis*, 2, July, 203–54.

Pendle, G. (1952), *Uruguay: South America's First Welfare State*, Royal Institute of International Affairs, London.

(1954), *Paraguay: A Riverside Nation*, Royal Institute of International Affairs, London.

*(1963), *A History of Latin America*, Penguin Books, Harmondsworth, Middlesex.

Pérez Lopez, E., et al. (1967), *Mexico's Recent Economic Growth: The Mexican View*, University of Texas Press, Austin.

Petras, J., and Zeitlin, M. (eds.) (1968), *Latin America: Reform or Revolution?*, Fawcett, Greenwich, Connecticut.

Pincus, J. (1968), *The Economy of Paraguay*, Praeger, New York.

Pinto, A., et al. (1970), *Chile Hoy*, Siglo XXI Editores, Mexico City.

*Pirenne, H. (1925), *Mediaeval Cities*, Princeton University Press, Princeton.

Poleman, T. (1964), *The Papaloapan Project: Agricultural Development in* the Mexican Tropics*, Stanford University Press, Stanford, California.

Poppino, R. E. (1968), *Brazil: The Land and the People*, Oxford University Press, London.

*Posada, A. J. and J. (1966), *The C.V.C.: Challenge to Underdevelopment and Traditionalism*, Tercer Mundo, Bogotá.

Pred, A. (1967), *Behaviour and Location. Foundations for a Geographic and Dynamic Location Theory*, Lund, Sweden.

Preston, D. A. (1969a), 'The Revolutionary Landscape of Highland Bolivia', *Geographical Journal*, 135, March, 1–16.

*(1969b), 'Rural Emigration in Andean America', *Human Organization*, 28, Winter, 279–86.

*(1970), 'New Towns – A Major Change in the Rural Settlement Pattern in Highland Bolivia', *Journal of Latin American Studies*, 2, January, 1–28.

(1972), *Internal Domination: Small Towns, the Countryside and Development*, University of Leeds, Department of Geography, Working Paper 17.

*(1973), *Farmers and the Town: Rural-Urban Interaction in Highland Bolivia*, Institute of British Geographers Annual Conference, Birmingham.

*Quijano, A. (1971), *Nationalism and Capitalism in Peru: A Study in Neo-Imperialism*, Monthly Review Press, New York.

Rabinovitz, F. F., and Trueblood, F. M. (eds.) (1971), *Latin American Urban Research*, Volume One, Sage Publications, Beverly Hills.

Rama, C. M. (1962), 'De la singularidad de la urbanización en el Uruguay', *Revista de Ciencias Sociales*, 6, June, 95–112.

Randall, L. R. (1962), 'Labour Migration and Mexican Economic Development, 1940–1950', *Social and Economic Studies*, 2, March, 73–81.

*Ranis, G., and Fei, J. C. H. (1961), 'A Theory of Economic Development', *American Economic Review*, 51, September, 533–65.

*Ray, T. F. (1969), *The Politics of the Barrios of Venezuela*, University of California Press, Berkeley.

Redding, D. C. (1967), 'The Economic Decline of Uruguay', *Inter-American Economic Affairs*, 20, Spring, 55–72.

Reyes Carmona, Marco F. (1965), 'Estudio socio-económico del fenómeno de la inmigración a Bogotá', *Economía Colombiana*, January, 1–31.

Reynolds, C. W. (1965), 'Chilean Copper and Economic Growth, 1925–1959', in Mamalakis, M., and Reynolds, C. W. (1965), 203–398.

*(1971), *The Mexican Economy: Twentieth Century Structure and Growth*, Yale University Economic Growth Center, New Haven.

*Richardson, H. W. (1969), *Elements of Regional Economics*, Penguin Books, Harmondsworth, Middlesex.

Riddell, J. B. (1971), *The Spatial Dynamics of Modernization in Sierra Leone: Structure, Diffusion and Response*, North-Western University Press, Evanston, Illinois.

Rippy, J. F. (1931), *The Capitalists and Colombia*, Vanguard Press, New York.

*(1944), *Latin America and the Industrial Age*, G. P. Putnam, New York.

Rivarolf, D. (1967), *Migración paraguaya: aspectos preliminares*, Centro Paraguayo de Estudios Sociológicos, Asunción.

Rivera, J. (1971), *Latin America: A Socio-Cultural Interpretation*, Appleton-Century-Crofts, New York.

*Roberts, B. R. (1970), 'Migration and Population Growth in Guatemala City: Implications for Social and Economic Development', in Roberts, B. R., and Lowder, S. (1970).

Roberts, B. R., and Lowder, S. (1970), *Urban Population Growth and Migration in Latin America: Two Case Studies*, University of Liverpool, Centre for Latin-American Studies, Liverpool.

Robinson, D. J. (1971), 'Colombia and Venezuela', in Blakemore, H., and Smith, C. T. (eds.) (1971), 179–246.

Robinson, D. J., and Fox, D. (1969), *Cities in a Changing Latin America: Two Studies of Urban Growth in the Development of Mexico and Venezuela*, Latin American Publications Fund, London.

Robinson, J. (1964), *Economic Philosophy*, Pelican Books, Harmondsworth, Middlesex.

Robinson, R. (ed.) (1971), *Developing the Third World: The Experience of the 1960s*, Cambridge University Press, London.

*Robock, S. H. (1963), *Brazil's Developing Northeast: A Study of Regional Planning and Foreign Aid*, The Brookings Institution, Washington D.C.

*Rocca, C. A. (1970), 'Productivity in Brazilian Manufacturing', in Bergsmann, J. (1970), 222–41.

Rodriguez Mariño, T. (1970), *Descentralisar es gobernar*, Eduardo Salazar e Hijos, Bogotá.

Rodwin, L., and Associates (ed.) (1969), *Planning Urban Growth and Regional Development*, MIT Press, Cambridge, Massachusetts.

Roemer, M. (1970), *Fishing for Growth: Export-Led Development in Peru, 1959–1967*, Harvard University Press, Cambridge.

Roett, R. J. A. (ed.) (1972), *Brazil in the Sixties*, Vanderbilt Press, Nashville.

Rogers, E. M. (1969), *Modernization among Peasants: The Impact of Communication*, Holt, Rinehart and Winston, New York.

Rogler, L. (1967), 'Slum Neighbourhoods in Latin America', *Journal of Inter-American Studies*, 9, October, 507–28.

*Romero, E. (1949), *Historia económica del Perú*, Editorial Suramericana, Buenos Aires.

(1966), *Geografía económica del Perú*, Tipografía Peruana, Lima.

Romero, E., and Liévano, C. (1969), *Regionalismo y centralismo*, Biblioteca Amauta, Lima.

*Rostow, W. W. (1960), *The Stages of Economic Growth: A Non-Communist Manifesto*, Cambridge University Press, London.

*(ed.) (1963), *The Economics of Take-Off into Sustained Growth*, Macmillan, London.

Ruddle, K., and Hamour, M. (eds.) (1970), *Statistical Abstract of Latin America*, Latin American Center, University of California, Los Angeles.

Ruddle, K., and Obermann, D., (eds.) (1972), *Statistical Abstract of Latin America*, Latin American Center, University of California, Los Angeles.

Ruiz, R. E. (1969), *Cuba: The Making of a Revolution*, University of Massachusetts Press, Amherst.

*Rummell, R. J. (1967), 'Understanding Factor Analysis', *Journal of Conflict Resolution*, 11, December, 444–80.

*Safford, F. (1967), *Significación de los antioqueños en el desarrollo económico colombiano*, Imprenta Nacional, Bogotá.

Sahota, G. S. (1968), 'An Economic Analysis of Internal Migration in Brazil', *Journal of Political Economy*, 76, March–April 218–43.

*Schaedel, R. P. (1965), 'Land Reform Studies', *Latin American Research Review*, 1, Fall, 75–122.

(1967), *La demografía y los recursos humanos del sur del Perú*, Instituto Indigenista Interamericano, México.

Schmitter, P. (1970), 'Central American Integration: Spillover, Spills-around or Encapsulation', *Journal of Common Market Studies*, 9, September, 1–48.

*Schultz, T. W. (1964), *Transforming Traditional Agriculture*, Yale University Press, New Haven.

*Schumacher, E. F. (1965), 'Industrialization through Intermediate Technology', in Robinson, R. (ed.), *Industrialization in Developing Countries*, Cambridge Conference on Developing Countries, 91–9.

*Scitovsky, T. (1969), *Prospects for Latin American Industrialization within the Framework of Economic Integration: Bases for Analyses*, Inter-American Development Bank (1969), 7–29.

*Scobie, J. R. (1964a), *Revolution on the Pampas: A Social History of Argentine Wheat, 1860–1910*, University of Texas Press, Austin.

*(1964b), *Argentina: A City and a Nation*, Oxford University Press, New York.

Scott, J. F. (1971), 'A Self-Financing Strategy of Agrarian Reform: The Case of the Peruvian Sierra', *Socio-Economic Planning Sciences*, 5, August, 347–62.

*Seers, D. (1963), 'The Limitations of the Special Case', *Bulletin of the Oxford University Institute of Statistics*, 25, May, 77–98.

*Seers, D., and Joy, L. (eds.) (1971), *Development in a Divided World*, Penguin Books, Harmondsworth, Middlesex.

*Sepulveda Niño, S. (1970), *El atraso rural colombiano*, Editorial El Catolicismo, Bogotá.

*Sharpston, M. J. (1972), 'Uneven Geographical Distribution of Medical Care: A Ghanaian Case Study', *Journal of Development Studies*, 8, January, 205–22.

Simmons, A. B. (1970), *The Emergence of Planning Orientations in a Modernizing Community: Migration, Adaptation, and Family Planning in Highland Colombia*, Cornell University, Latin American Studies Program, dissertation series 15, Ithaca.

*Sjoberg, G. (1966), 'Rural-Urban Balance and Models of Economic Development', in Smelser, N. J., and Lipset, S. M. (eds.) (1966), 235–61.

Skidmore, T. E. (1967), *Politics in Brazil 1930–1964: An Experiment in Democracy*, Oxford University Press, New York.

Slawinski, Z. (1965), 'Structural Changes in Development within the Context of Latin America's Economic Development', *Economic Bulletin for Latin America*, 10, October, 163–87.

Smelser, N. J., and Lipset, S. M. (eds.) (1966), *Social Structure and Mobility in Economic Development*, Routledge and Kegan Paul, London.

Smith, C. T. (1968), 'Problems of Regional Development in Peru', *Geography*, 53, July, 260–87.

(1970), 'The Central Andes', in Blakemore, H., and Smith, C. T. (1971), 263–334.

*Smith, D. M. (1971), *Industrial Location: An Economic Geographical Analysis*, John Wiley, New York.

Smith, T. L. (1963), *Brazil: People and Institutions*, Louisiana State University, Baton Rouge.

(ed.) (1965), *Agrarian Reform in Latin America*, Alfred Knopf, New York.

(1966), 'The Racial Composition of the Colombian Population', *Journal of Inter-American Studies*, 8, April, 213–35.

(1967), *Colombia: Social Structure and the Process of Development*, University of Florida Press, Gainesville, Florida.

*(1969), 'Studies of Colonization and Settlement', *Latin American Research Review*, 4, Spring, 93–123.

Snyder, D. E. (1962), 'Commercial Passenger Linkages and the Metropolitan Nodality of Montevideo', *Economic Geography*, 38, April, 95–112.

Soberman, R. M. (1966), *Transport Technology for Developing Regions: A Study of Road Transportation in Venezuela*, MIT Press, Cambridge, Massachusetts.

*Soja, E. W. (1968), *The Geography of Modernization in Kenya: A Spatial Analysis of Social, Economic, and Political Change*, Syracuse University Press, Syracuse, New York.

*Solow, A. A. (1967), 'Housing in Latin America: The Problem of the Urban Low Income Families', *Town Planning Review*, 38, July, 83–102.

*Sovani, N. V. (1964), 'The Analysis of Over-Urbanization', *Economic Development and Cultural Change*, 7, January, 113–22.

*Spengler, O. (1928), *The Decline of the West*, Allen and Unwin, London.

Stavenhagen, R. (1968), 'Seven Fallacies about Latin America', in Petras, J., and Zeitlin, M. (eds.) (1968), 13–31.

*(ed.) (1970a), *Agrarian Problems and Peasant Movements in Latin America*, Doubleday, Anchor Books, New York.

(1970b), 'Social Aspects of Agrarian Structure in Mexico', in Stavenhagen, R. (ed.) (1970a), 225–70.

Steel, R. W. (1971), 'The Challenge of the Tropics in our Teaching of Geography', *Geography*, 56, January, 15–23.

Steel, R. W., and Lawton, R. (eds.) (1967), *Liverpool Essays in Geography*, Longmans Green, London.

*Stein, S. J., and B. H. (1970), *The Colonial Heritage of Latin America: Essays on Economic Dependence in Perspective*, Oxford University Press, New York.

Steiner, H. M. (1966), 'Mexican Social Roads', *International Development Review*, September, 21–4.

*Stephenson, G. V. (1970), 'Two Newly Created Capitals: Islamabad and Brasília', *Town Planning Review*, 41, October, 317–32.

*Sternberg, M. (1962), *Chilean Land Tenure and Land Reform*, doctoral thesis, University of California, Berkeley.

(1972), *The Latifundista: The Impact of His Income and Expenditure*

Patterns on Income and Consumption, Studies in Comparative International Development, 7, Spring, 1–18.

Steward, J. H. (ed.) (1967), *Contemporary Change in Traditional Societies*, Volume 3, *Mexican and Peruvian Societies*, Illinois University Press, Urbana.

*Stewart, J. Q., and Warntz, W. (1958), 'Physics of Population Distribution', *Journal of Regional Science*, 1, 99–123.

*Stewart, N. R. (1965), 'Migration and Settlement in the Peruvian Montaña: The Apurimac Valley', *Geographical Review*, 55, April, 143–57.

(1967), *Japanese Colonizationi n Eastern Paraguay*, National Academy of Sciences, Washington.

(1968), 'Some Problems in the Development of Agricultural Colonization in the Andean Oriente', *Professional Geographer*, 20, January, 33–8.

Stoddart, D. R., and Trubshaw, J. D. (1962), 'Colonization in Action in Eastern Colombia', *Geography*, 47, January, 47–53.

*Stöhr, W. (1967), *The Definition of Regions in Relation to National and Regional Development in Latin America*, mimeographed, Santiago.

(1974), *Regional Planning in Latin America*, Mouton Publishers, The Hague.

*Stokes, C. J. (1970), *Transportation and Economic Development in Latin America*, Praeger, New York.

Strassmann, W. P. (1968), *Technological Change and Economic Development: The Manufacturing Experience of Mexico and Puerto Rico*, Oxford University Press, London.

*Stycos, J. M. (1968), *Human Fertility in Latin America: Sociological Perspectives*, Cornell University Press, Ithaca, New York.

*Taaffe, E. J., Morrill, R. L., and Gould, P. R. (1963), 'Transport Expansion in Underdeveloped Countries: A Comparative Analysis', *Geographical Review*, 53, October, 503–29.

Tavares, M. C., and Castro, A. (1966), 'Economic Planning in Brazil at the Level of the States', Economic Commission for Latin America, 11, 58–80.

Taylor, M. C. (1967), 'Problems of Development in Peru', *Journal of Inter-American Studies*, 9, January, 85–94.

Thiesenhusen, W. C. (1966), *Chile's Experiments in Agrarian Reform*, University of Wisconsin Press, Madison.

(1968), 'Grassroots Economic Pressures in Chile: An Enigma for Development Planners', *Economic Development and Cultural Change*, 16, April, 412–29.

*(1972), 'A Suggested Policy for Industrial Reinvigoration in Latin America', *Journal of Latin American Studies*, 4, May, 85–104.

Thomas, H. (1971), *Cuba: Or the Pursuit of Freedom*, Eyre and Spottiswoode, London.

Thomas, R. N. (1972), 'The Migration System of Guatemala City: Spatial Inputs', *Professional Geographer*, 24, May, 105–12.

*Tinbergen, J. (1961), 'The Spatial Dispersion of Production: A Hypothesis', *Schweizerische Zeitschrift für Volkswirtschaft und Statistik*, 97, December, 412–20.

*Törnqvist, G. (1970), *Contact Systems and Regional Development*, Lund Studies in Geography, B, 35, Lund.

*Torres, F., and Unikel, L. (1970), 'La población económicamente activa en México y sus principales ciudades, 1940–1960', *Demografía y Economía*, 4, 1, 1–42.

Turk, K. L., and Crowder, L. V. (1967), *Rural Development in Tropical Latin America*, Cornell University Press, Ithaca, New York.

Turner, A., and Smulian, J. (1971), 'New Cities in Venezuela', *Town Planning Review*, 42, January, 3–27.

Turner, F. C. (1971), *Catholicism and Political Development in Latin America*, University of North Carolina Press, Chapel Hill.

*Turner, J. (1967), 'Barriers and Channels for Housing Development in Modernizing Countries', *Journal of American Institute of Planners*, 33, May, 167–81.

Turner, J. F. C. (1966), 'Uncontrolled Urban Settlement: Problems and Policies', in Breese, G. (ed.) (1972), 507–34.

United Nations, Department of Economic and Social Affairs (1965), *Planning for Economic Development: Studies of National Planning Experiences*, New York.

*United Nations Economic Commission for Latin America (1965), *El transporte en América Latina*, New York.

*(1966), *The Process of Industrial Development in Latin America*, New York.

*(1967), 'Planning in Latin America', *Economic Bulletin for Latin America*, 12, October, 1–17.

*(1968a), 'The Regional Distribution of Economic Activities, *Economic Survey of Latin America*, 37–56.

(1968b), *Economic Development and Income Distribution in Argentina*, New York.

(1968c), 'The Urbanization of Society in Latin America', *Economic Bulletin for Latin America*, 13, November, 76–93.

*(1969a), 'Industrial Development in Latin America', *Economic Bulletin for Latin America*, 14, Second half of 1969, 3–77.

(1969b), 'Mining in Latin America', *Economic Bulletin for Latin America*, 14, Second half of 1969, 78–109.

(1969c), 'Recent Developments in the Latin American Integration Process', *Economic Bulletin for Latin America*, 14, Second half of 1969, 110–27.

*(1969d), 'Income Distribution in Latin America', *Economic Survey of Latin America*, 1969.

*(1970a), 'Energy in Latin America', *Economic Bulletin for Latin America*, 15, Second half of 1970, 3–93.

(1970b), *Development Problems in Latin America*, University of Texas Press, Austin.

(1971), 'Some Regional Development Problems in Latin America Linked to Metropolitanization', *Economic Bulletin for Latin America*, 16, Second half of 1971, 57–90.

United Nations Educational, Social and Cultural Organisation (1960), *Social Aspects of Economic Development in Latin America*, Geneva.

*United Nations, International Labour Office (1970), *Towards Full Employment*, Geneva.

United Nations, Statistical Office (1960), *Patterns of Industrial Growth 1938–58*, New York.

*(1971), *Demographic Yearbook*, New York.

Utría, R. D. (1972), 'Regional Structure in Latin American Development', in Geisse, G., and Hardoy, J. E. (eds.) (1972), 61–84.

Vallier, I. (1966), 'Church "Development" in Latin America: A Five-Country Comparison', *Journal of Developing Areas*, 1, July, 461–76.

*(1970), *Catholicism, Social Control, and Modernization in Latin America*, Prentice Hall, New Jersey.

*Vapñarsky, C. A. (1969), 'On Rank-Size Distributions of Cities: An Ecological Approach', *Economic Development and Cultural Change*, 17, July, 584–95.

Veliz, C. (ed.) (1965), *Obstacles to Change in Latin America*, Oxford University Press, London.

(ed.) (1967), *Politics of Conformity in Latin America*, Oxford University Press, London.

(ed.) (1968), *Latin America and the Caribbean, a Handbook*, Anthony Blond, London.

*Vernon, R. (1963), *The Dilemma of Mexico's Development: The Roles of* *the Private and Public Sectors*, Harvard University Press, Cambridge, Massachusetts.

*Warren, K. (1973), *Mineral Resources*, Penguin Books, Harmondsworth, Middlesex.

Watters, R. F. (1967), 'Economic Backwardness in the Venezuelan Andes: A Study of the Traditional Sector of the Dual Economy', *Pacific Viewpoint*, 8, May, 17–67.

*Weaver, F. S. (1969–70), 'Backwash, Spread and the Chilean State', *Studies in Comparative International Development*, 1, May.

Webb, K. E. (1972), *Geography of Latin America: A Regional Analysis*, Prentice Hall, New Jersey.

*Weber, A. (1929), *Theory of the Location of Industry*, University of Chicago Press, Chicago.

Weckstein, R. S. (1970), 'Evaluating Mexican Land Reform', *Economic Development and Cultural Change*, 18, April, 391–409.

Weil, T. E., et al. (1970), *Area Handbook for Colombia*, American University, Washington D.C.

*Wilkie, J. W. (1967), *The Mexican Revolution: Federal Expenditure and Social Change since 1910*, University of California Press, Berkeley.

*Williamson, J. G. (1965), 'Regional Inequality and the Process of National Development: A Description of the Patterns', *Economic Development and Cultural Change*, 13, July, 3–45.

*Wilson, G. W. et. al (1966), *The Impact of Highway Investment on Development*, Brookings Institution, Washington D.C.

*Wingo, L. (1967), 'Recent Patterns of Urbanization among Latin American Countries', *Urban Affairs Quarterly*, 2, March, 81–110.

*Winpenny, J. (1971), 'Brazil: The Industrial Sector: Its Situation and Prospects', *Bank of London and South America Review*, 5, November, 642–50.

*Wionczek, M. S. (ed.) (1966), *Latin American Economic Integration: Experiences and Prospects*, Praeger, New York.

(1970), 'The Rise and Decline of Latin American Integration', *Journal of Common Market Studies*, 9, September, 49–66.

Wolf, E. (1959), *Sons of the Shaking Earth*, University of Chicago Press, Chicago.

*Wolfe, M. (1966), 'Rural Settlement Patterns and Social Change in Latin America: Notes for a Strategy of Rural Development', *Latin American Research Review*, 1, 5–50.

Wood, H. A. (1967), 'Regional Planning in Latin America', *Professional Geographer*, 19, September, 272–4.

Wrigley, E. A. (1967), 'Demographic Models and Geography', in Chorley, R. J., and Haggett, P. (eds.) (1967), 189–216.

Young, R. C. (1970), 'The Plantation Economy and Industrial Development in Latin America', *Economic Development and Cultural Change*, 18, July, 342–61.

Zañartu, M., and Kennedy, J. J. (eds.) (1969), *The Overall Development of Chile*, University of Notre Dame Press, Notre Dame, Illinois.

Zipf, G. K. (1949), *Human Behaviour and the Principle of Least Effort*, Addison-Wesley Press, Cambridge, Massachusetts.

Zondag, C. H. (1966), *The Bolivian Economy, 1952–1965: The Revolution and Its Consequences*, Praeger, New York.

Zschock, D. K. (1967), *Manpower Perspective of Colombia*, Industrial Relations Section, Princeton University, Princeton, New York.

(1970), 'Health Planning in Latin America: Review and Evaluation', *Latin American Research Review*, 5, Fall, 35–56.

Zuñiga Trelles, W. (1970), *Perú: agricultura, reforma agraria y desarrollo económico*, Editorial Imprenta Amauta, Lima.

References

1: Orientation and Purpose

1 Kuznets, S. (1966); Clark, C. (1951); Bain, J. S. (1966).
2 Wrigley, E. A. (1967); Hauser, P. M., and Duncan, O. D. (eds.) (1959).
3 Hoselitz, B. F. (ed.) (1960).
4 Lerner, D. (1967).
5 Seers, D. (1963); Galbraith, J. K. (1958); Mishan, E. J. (1967); Myrdal, G. M. (1968), (1970); Adams, J. G. U. (1970).
6 Odell, P. R. (1971); Richardson, H. W. (1969).
7 Bos, H. C. (1965); Tinbergen, J. (1961).
8 Berry, B. J. L. (1966); Soja, E. W. (1968); Board, C., Davies, R. J., and Fair, T. J. D. (1970).
9 Johnson, E. A. J. (1970).
10 Friedmann, J. (1968); Lewis, W. A. (1966); Miller, J. P., and Gakenheimer, R. A. (eds.) (1971); Berry, B. J. L. (1969); Pedersen, P. O. (1970).
11 Johnson, E. A. J. (1970).
12 Darwent, D. J. (1969); Nichols, V. (1969); Lasuen, J. R. (1969).
13 Bird, R. (1963); Lefeber, L. (1958); Wingo, L. (1967).
14 Friedmann, J. (1966); Lewis, W. A. (1966).

2: The International and Historical Setting

1 Humphreys, R. A., and Lynch, J. (eds.) (1965), Furtado, C. (1971), Lambert, J. (1967), Pendle, G. (1963), Stein, S. J. and B. H. (1970), and Hanke, L. (ed.) (1967) are probably the best, but others are listed in the bibliography.
2 Table A.7, *UN World Economic Survey, 1969–70*, New York, 1971.
3 Seers, D., and Joy, L. (eds.) (1971).
4 Seers, D., and Joy, L. (eds.) (1971); Hayter, T. (1971); Griffin, K. B. (1969); Pearson, L. B. (ed.) (1969).

5 UN, Economic Commission for Latin America (1969a).
6 Gibson, C. (1963), 387.
7 ibid., 382.
8 Lambert, J. (1967), 53.
9 Stein, S. J., and B. H. (1970), vii.
10 Frank, A. G. (1968).
11 Scobie, J. R. (1964b); Rippy, J. F. (1944); Vernon, R. (1963); Blakemore, H., and Smith, C. T. (eds.) (1971).
12 Furtado, C. (1971), 11.
13 Dix, R. H. (1967); Payne, J. L. (1968); Fluharty, V. L. (1957).
14 Vernon, R. (1963); Brandenburg, F. R. (1964).
15 Sepulveda Niño, S. (1970).
16 Humphreys, R. A. (1969), 227.
17 ibid.
18 Borah, W. (1963), 373.
19 Lambert, J. (1967).
20 Wolfe, M. (1966).
21 Borah, W. (1963).
22 Lambert, J. (1967), 265.
23 Scobie, J. R. (1964b).
24 Lambert, J. (1967).
25 Myrdal, G. M. (1970).
26 Cole, J. P. (1966).
27 Scobie, J. R. (1964b), 134.
28 UN Demographic Yearbook, 1970 and 1972.
29 Kiser, C. V. (ed.) (1968); Landsberger, H. A. (ed.) (1970); Deutschman, P. J., and McNelly, J. T. (1964); Vallier, I. (1970); Stycos, J. M. (1968).

3: *The Process of Industrial Change*

1 Frank, A. G. (1968); Poppino, R. E. (1968).
2 Leiserson, A. (1966).
3 Furtado, C. (1968), 605–13.
4 Gallo, E., and Katz, J. (1968), 597–604.
5 Grunwald, J. (1970).
6 Furtado, C. (1971).
7 ibid.
8 ibid.
9 Zondag, C. H. (1966).

10 Hurtado Ruiz-Tagle, C. (1966).
11 Furtado, C. (1971).
12 Leiserson, A. (1966).
13 Furtado, C. (1968), 606.
14 UN ECLA (1966), 6.
15 Bergsmann, J. (1970), 22.
16 Furtado, C. (1971), 86.
17 Grunwald, J. (1970), 831.
18 Bergsmann, J. (1970).
19 Gallo, E., and Katz, J. (1968).
20 Bottomley, A. (1965).
21 Scitovsky, T. (1969).
22 Johnson, L. L. (1967a).
23 UN ECLA (1966), 147.
24 Bergsmann, J. (1970).
25 Johnson, L. L. (1967a), 210.
26 King, T. (1970).
27 Bottomley, A. (1965).
28 Gallo, E., and Katz, J. (1968).
29 Winpenny, J. (1971).
30 Dell, S. (1966).
31 Wionczek, M. S. (ed.) (1966).
32 Araujo, O. (1969).
33 Furtado, C. (1968).
34 Hirschman, A. O. (1958).
35 Population censuses of 1940 and 1961.
36 Weber, A. (1929); Smith, D. M. (1971); Estall, R. C., and Buchanan, R. O. (1961).
37 Odell, P. R. (1966).
38 Rocca, C. A. (1970).
39 Galloway, J. H. (1971).
40 Fox, D. J. (1971).
41 Estall, R. C., and Buchanan, R. O. (1961).
42 Weber, A. (1929); Hoover, E. M. (1948).
43 UN ECLA (1969a).
44 King, T. (1970), 59.
45 Colombia, *Anuario General de Estadística*.
46 Fox, D. J. (1971).
47 Dell, S. (1966).
48 Odell, P. R. (1968).

49 Gilbert, A. G. (1970).
50 King, T. (1970); Dillman, C. D. (1970b).
51 Barkin, D. and King, T. (1970).
52 Odell, P. R. (1971).
53 ibid.
54 Hirschman, A. O. (1968b), 15.
55 ibid.
56 Goodman, D. E. (1972).
57 ibid.
58 Weaver, F. S. (1969–70), 240.
59 Lavell, A. M. (1971); Lavell, A. M. (1972).
60 Weaver, F. S. (1969–70).

4: The Pattern of Urbanization

1 UN ECLA (1969a).
2 Blakemore, H. (1971).
3 Childe, G. V. (1941); Pirenne, H. (1925); Mumford, L. (1938).
4 Lerner, D. (1967), 24–5.
5 Hauser, P. M. (ed.) (1957), 8.
6 Hoselitz, B. F. (1955b).
7 Davis, K., and Hertz, H. (1954).
8 Abu-Lughod, J. L. (1965), 343.
9 Griffin, K. B. (1966).
10 Kamerschen, D. R. (1969); Sovani, N. V. (1964).
11 Torres, F., and Unikel, L. (1970).
12 Currie, L. L. (1954).
13 Friedmann, J. (1968), 4.
14 Kahl, J. A. (1968).
15 Friedmann, J. (1968); Currie, L. L. (1966); Delgado, C. (1969); Johnson, E. A. J. (1970).
16 Browning, H. L. (1958), 114.
17 Linsky, A. (1965).
18 Berry, B. J. L. (1961).
19 Vapñarsky, C. A. (1969).
20 Berry, B. J. L. (1969).
21 Davis, K. (1962).
22 Romero, E. (1949).

23 Levin, J. V. (1960); Lieuwen, E. (1961); Frank, A. G. (1968); Furtado, C. (1963).
24 Safford, F. (1967); López, T. A. (1968).
25 Bird, R. (1963).
26 Wingo, L. (1967).
27 Browning, H. L. (1958).
28 Sjoberg, G. (1966), 258.
29 Hoselitz, B. F. (1955b); Spengler, O. (1928).
30 Lewis, W. A. (1966), 72.
31 Griffin, K. B. (1969); Frank, A. G. (1971).
32 Odell, P. R., and Preston, D. A. (1973).
33 See Sjoberg, G. (1966) for a similar argument.
34 Pedersen, P. O. (1970); Hägerstrand, T. (1952).
35 Johnson, E. A. J. (1970).
36 Lewis, W. A. (1966), 73.
37 Arriaga, E. E. (1968).
38 Herrick, B. H. (1965).
39 Flinn, W. L. and Converse, J. W. (1970), 462.
40 Roberts, B. R. (1970); Havens, A. E., and Usandizaga, E. (1966).
41 Nelson, R. R., et al. (1971), 72; Adams, D. W. (1969).
42 Isard, W., et al. (1960); Stewart, J. Q., and Warntz, W. (1958); Zipf, G. K. (1949).
43 Colombia, Departamento Nacional de Planeación (1970).
44 Forni, F., and Mármora, L. (1967).
45 Germani, G. (1963).
46 Lowder, S. (1970), 25.
47 Morse, R. (1971), 23.
48 Margulis, M. (1967); McGreevey, W. P. (1968); Herrick, B. H. (1965).
49 Adams, D. W. (1969), 532.
50 ibid., 532.
51 Roberts, B. R. (1970), 9–10.
52 Lowder, S. (1970).
53 Germani, G. (1963); Herrick, B. H. (1965).
54 Lowder, S. (1970).
55 Browning, H. L., and Feindt, W. (1971).
56 Adams, D. W. (1969), 534.
57 Herrick, B. H. (1965).
58 Lowder, S. (1970).
59 Roberts, B. R. (1970), 17.
60 Germani, G. (1963).

61 Herrick, B. H. (1965).
62 Adams, D. W. (1969), 534.
63 Browning, H. L., and Feindt, W. (1971), 49.
64 Browning and Feindt have interviewed people in both urban and rural areas in their Monterrey study.
65 Balan, J. (1969).
66 ibid., 10.
67 ibid., 12.
68 Havens, A. E., and Usandizaga, E. (1966).
69 Ray, T. F. (1969); Mangin, W. (1967), 68.
70 Jones, E. (1964); Solow, A. A. (1967); Turner, J. (1967); Abrams, C. (1964).
71 Marchand, B. (1966).
72 Preston, D. A. (1969b), 283.
73 Margulis, M. (1970), 144–6.
74 Lowder, S. (1970), 27.
75 Schultz, T. W. (1964).

5: The Rural Sector

1 Furtado, C. (1971).
2 Pearse, A. (1966).
3 ICAD Studies were carried out in Argentina, Brazil, Colombia, Chile, Ecuador, Guatemala and Peru. They have been published separately and are summarized in Barraclough, S., and Domike, A. L. (1966), to which extensive reference is made in this chapter.
4 Barraclough, S., and Domike, A. L. (1966).
5 ibid.
6 ibid.
7 ibid., 50.
8 Colombia, Departamento Nacional de Estadística, Censo de Población, 1964.
9 UN ECLA (1966).
10 Barraclough, S., and Domike, A. L. (1966), 60.
11 Flores, E. (1965); Chonchol, J. (1965); Cline, W. R. (1970).
12 Barraclough, S., and Domike, A. L. (1966).
13 Cline, W. R. (1970).
14 Sternberg, M. (1962).
15 Young, R. C. (1970); Thiesenhusen, W. C. (1972).

16 Pearse, A. (1966), 14.
17 Browning, D. (1971).
18 Barraclough, S., and Domike, A. L. (1966), 46.
19 Pearse, A. (1966), 37–8.
20 Stavenhagen, R. (1968).
21 Preston, D. A. (1970).
22 Paredes Manrique, R. (November 1968).
23 Fundacion IBGE, *Anuario Estatístico de Brasil*, 1969.
24 For a discussion of this problem see Bachmura, F. T. (ed.) (1968) and Wolfe, M. (1966).
25 Davis, L. H. (1970).
26 Wolfe, M. (1966), 22.
27 See Guzmán, G., et al. (1962 and 1964); Fals Borda, O. (1969); Fluharty, V. L. (1957).
28 Wolfe, M. (1966), 39.
29 Gilbert, A. G. (1970); Olden, D. (1971).
30 Colombia, Ministerio de Salud Pública (1970).
31 Wolfe, M. (1966), 22.
32 King, M. H. (1966); Sharpston, M. J. (1972).
33 Pearse, A. (1973).
34 Stavenhagen, R. (1970b); González Navarro, M. (1965).
35 Furtado, C. (1970).
36 Fox, D. J. (1971).
37 Stavenhagen, R. (1970b), 234.
38 ibid., 261.
39 ibid., 268.
40 González Navarro, M. (1965), 228–9.
41 Flores, E. (1965).
42 Stavenhagen, R. (1970b), 251.
43 González Navarro, M. (1965), 221.
44 Furtado, C. (1970), 222.
45 Heath, D. B., et al. (1968). The book includes an English summary of the agrarian reform law.
46 García, A. (1964).
47 Heath, D. B., et al. (1968).
48 Zondag, C. H. (1966).
49 García, A. (1964), 309.
50 Furtado, C. (1970), 225.
51 Heath, D. B., et al. (1968), 54.
52 ibid.

53 García, A. (1964), 313–14.
54 Zondag, C. H. (1966), 188.
55 Heath, D. B., et al. (1968), 376.
56 ibid., 386.
57 Gutelman, M. (1967).
58 ibid.
59 Aranda, S. (1968).
60 Dumont, R. (1970); Boorstein, E. (1968).
61 Feder, E. (1970).
62 Hirschman, A. O. (1965), Chapter Two.
63 Colombia, Ministerio de Agricultura (1971).
64 ibid.
65 Heaton, L. E. (1969), 105–7.
66 Cline, W. R. (1970), 7–8.
67 Parker, F. D. (1964).
68 Browning, D. (1971), 271–2.
69 ibid., 292.
70 Feder, E. (1970).
71 Lehmann, D. (1971).
72 Barraclough, S. (1972).
73 Feder, E. (1970).
74 ibid., 223.
75 *Peruvian Times*; Cotler, J. (1970–71).
76 Quijano, A. (1971), 59.
77 Dumont, R. (1970), 47.
78 Reynolds, C. W. (1971).
79 Lehmann, D. (1971).
80 Smith, T. L. (1969); Eidt, R. C. (1962); Schaedel, R. P. (1965).
81 Scobie, J. R. (1964a), (1964b).
82 Galloway, J. H. (1971); Poppino, R. E. (1968).
83 Morse, R. (1958).
84 Nicholls, W. H. (1969).
85 Parsons, J. J. (1967a).
86 Galloway, J. H. (1971).
87 Nicholls, W. H. (1969), 81.
88 Kleinpenning, J. M. G. (1971b), 287.
89 Fox, D. J. (1971).
90 Bergmann, B. R. (1966).
91 Odell, P. R., and Preston, D. A. (1973).
92 Stewart, N. R. (1965).

93 Dozier, C. L. (1969).
94 Odell, P. R., and Preston, D. A. (1973), 100–102.
95 Galloway, J. H. (1971).
96 Dozier, C. L. (1969), 200.
97 Stewart, N. R. (1965), 154.
98 Odell, P. R., and Preston, D. A. (1973), 104.
99 Dozier, C. L. (1969), 4.
100 Kleinpenning, J. M. G. (1971b).
101 Feder, E. (1970), 216–17.
102 Johnson, E. A. J. (1970).
103 Dumont, R. (1970).
104 Colombia, Ministerio de Educación Nacional (1971).
105 UN ILO (1970); Blaug, M. (ed.) (1969).

6: Transport Development

1 Kansky, K. J. (1963).
2 Soja, E. W. (1968); Gould, P. R. (1960); Gauthier, H. L. (1968).
3 Taaffe, E. J., et al. (1963).
4 Haggett, P. (1965).
5 Scobie, J. R. (1964b).
6 Rippy, J. F. (1944).
7 Dix, R. H. (1967).
8 Contreras, V. (1962).
9 Wilson, G. W., et al. (1966), 155–61.
10 Steiner, H. M. (1966).
11 Brown, R. T. (1966).
12 ibid.
13 Fox, D. J. (1972a).
14 Brown, R. T. (1966); Cole, J. P. (1965).
15 Livesey and Henderson (1969); *Bolsa Review* – various dates; *Peruvian Times*, 16 April 1971.
16 Brown, R. T. (1966).
17 Cole, J. P. (1965).
18 Bergmann, B. R. (1966); Stokes, C. J. (1970).
19 Mario Andreazza quoted in *Time* magazine, September 1971, 36.
20 Kleinpenning, J. M. G. (1971b).
21 ibid.
22 Bergmann, B. R. (1966).

23 Colombia, Ferrocarriles Nacionales de Colombia (1961).
24 Stokes, C. J. (1970).
25 Colombia, COLPUERTOS (1969).
26 Colombia, Ferrocarriles Nacionales de Colombia (1966).

7: Regional Differences in Income and Welfare

1 Keeble, D. E. (1967); Richardson, H. W. (1969).
2 Easterlin, R. A. (1965); Hanna, F. A. (1959); Borts, G. H., and Stein, J. L. (1964).
3 Williamson, J. G. (1965). In his analysis Williamson uses two main measures of inequality (V_w and V_{uw}) both based on the coefficient of variation.

$$V_w = \frac{\sqrt{\sum_i (y_i - \bar{y})^2 . (n_i/n)}}{\bar{y}}$$

where n_i = population of the *i*th region,
n = national population,
y_i = income *per capita* of the *i*th region,
$\bar{y}$ = national income *per capita*.

$$V_{uw} = \frac{\sqrt{\sum_i (y_i - \bar{y})^2/N}}{\bar{y}}$$

where N = number of regions.
4 ibid., 44.
5 Borts, G. H. (1960); Borts, G. H., and Stein, J. L. (1964); Okun, B., and Richardson, R. W. (1961).
6 Myrdal, G. M. (1957).
7 Boeke, J. H. (1953), 4. See also Meier, G. M. (ed.) (1964), Part Two.
8 Boeke, J. H. (1953), 289.
9 Higgins, B. (1956).
10 Bauer, P. T. (1954); Berg, E. J. (1961); Lewis, W. A. (1957); Bauer, P. T., and Yamey, B. S. (1957).
11 Higgins, B. (1956), 112.
12 Lewis, W. A. (1954); Eckaus, R. S. (1955); Ranis, G., and Fei, J. C. H. (1961).
13 Rostow, W. W. (1960); Meier, G. M. (ed.) (1964), Part One.
14 Eckaus, R. S. (1955).
15 Hirschman, A. O. (1958); Myrdal, G. M. (1957).
16 Hirschman, A. O. (1958), 190.

17 Myrdal, G. M. (1957), 34–5.
18 Friedmann, J. (1966).
19 ibid., xv.
20 Meier, G. M. (ed.) (1964); Rostow, W. W. (ed.) (1963).
21 Barraclough, S. (1970b); Frank, A. G. (1970).
22 Cotler, J. (1967–8); González Casanova, P. (1965); Barraclough, S. (1970b).
23 Robock, S. H. (1963); Brazil, Conselho de Desenvolvimento do Nordeste (1959).
24 Baer, W. (1965).
25 Gauthier, H. L., and Semple, R. K. (1971); Graham, D. H. (1970); Almeida Andrade, T. (1971); Williamson, J. G. (1965).
26 Almeida and Williamson produced different results on the V_w measure.
27 Mendoza Berrueto, E. (1969).
28 Wilkie, J. W. (1967), 205.
29 ibid., 272.
30 Barkin, D. (1972b), 112.
31 Lebret Mission (1958); Marabelli, F. (1966); Daza Roa, A. (1967).
32 Daza Roa, A. (1967); Marabelli, F. (1966).
33 Gilbert, A. G. (1970). For a simple explanation of principal components analysis see Rummel, R. J. (1967); King, L. J. (1969).
34 Baer, W. (1964); Baer, W. (1965).
35 Griffin, K. B. (1969).
36 ibid., 64.
37 Johnson, L. L. (1967b).
38 Graham, D. H. (1970) and Almeida Andrade, T. (1971), for example, support this view in the Brazilian case.

8: The Administration of Regional Development

1 UN ECLA (1967).
2 Utría, R. D. (1972), 61.
3 Lieuwen, E. (1961).
4 Friedmann, J. (1966).
5 ibid., 167–8.
6 ibid., 167.
7 Hirschman, A. O. (1965), Chapter One; Robock, S. H. (1963).
8 Blakemore, H. (1971); Berry, B. J. L. (1969); Stöhr, W. (1967); Cotler, J. (1970–71).

9 Hirschman, A. O. (1965).
10 ibid.
11 Mariátegui, J. C. (1952).
12 Dew, E. (1969), 109; Hirschman, A. O. (1965).
13 Dew, E. (1969).
14 ibid., 125.
15 Robock, S. H. (1963); Hirschman, A. O. (1965).
16 Hirschman, A. O. (1965).
17 Barkin, D., and King, T. (1970).
18 Stöhr, W. (1967); Berry, B. J. L. (1969).
19 Chile, ODEPLAN (1965); Colombia, Departamento Nacional de Planeación (1970).
20 Odell, P. R. (1971).
21 Friedmann, J. (1966), 8.
22 ibid.
23 Bor, W., and Smulian, J. (1970).
24 Colombia, Departamento Nacional de Planeación (1970).
25 Hirschman, A. O. (1965).
26 Friedmann, J. (1966), 164.
27 Colombia, Departamento Nacional de Planeación (1970), 340–41.
28 Law 3^{A} 1961 Article 40.
29 International Bank for Reconstruction and Development (1955).
30 Barkin, D., and King, T. (1970).
31 ibid., 107. Such wide powers did not apply to all of the Mexican agencies, however; the Fuerte Commission, for example, was mainly concerned with exploring the possibilities for irrigation and with the avoidance of floods in the lower basin.
32 Hirschman, A. O. (1965); Robock, S. H. (1963).
33 Dinkelspiel, J. R. (1969), 308.
34 Friedmann, J. (1969a), 151.
35 Ludwig, A. K. (ed.) (1969a).
36 Achurra Larrain, M. (1972).
37 Barkin, D., and King, T. (1970).
38 Eckstein, O. (1963), 367.
39 Bos, H. C. (1961), 371.
40 Barkin, D., and King, T. (1970), 244–5.
41 Kleinpenning, J. M. G. (1971a).
42 Friedmann, J. (1966), 169.
43 Robock, S. H. (1963).
44 Posada, A. J. and J. (1966).

45 Hirschman, A. O. (1965), 129.
46 Odell, P. R. (1966).
47 Barkin, D., and King, T. (1970), 245.
48 Dickenson, J. P. (1971), 8.
49 ibid., 8.
50 Kleinpenning, J. M. G. (1971a), 279.
51 Posada, A. J. and J. (1966), Table 6.1.
52 Dinkelspiel, J. R. (1969).
53 Posada, A. J. and J. (1966).
54 Robock, S. H. (1963); Hirschmann, A. O. (1965).
55 Odell, P. R. (1966).
56 Dinkelspiel, J. R. (1969), 309.
57 Dew, E. (1969).
58 Consuegra, J. (1960).
59 Dinkelspiel, J. R. (1969), 314.
60 Robock, S. H. (1963), 104.
61 Dinkelspiel, J. R. (1969), 314.
62 ibid., 311.
63 Daland, R. T. (1967), 204.
64 Barkin, D., and King, T. (1970), 85.
65 Daland, R. T. (1967), 212.
66 Friedmann, J. (1966), 168.
67 Mariátegui, J. C. (1952), 150.
68 Daland, R. T. (1967).
69 Stöhr, W. (1967); Boisier, S. (1970).

9: Spatial Alternatives for the Future

1 Odell, P. R. (1970).
2 Berry, B. J. L. (1966).
3 Skidmore, T. E. (1967), 167.
4 ibid., 168.
5 United Nations, International Labour Office (1970).
6 Cameron, J., and Dodd, W. A. (1970).
7 Johnson, E. A. J. (1970).
8 Bromley, R. J. (1971); Hodder, B. W., and Ukwo, U. I. (1969).
9 Burgos Guevara, H. (1970), quoted in Preston, D. A. (1973), 1.
10 Preston, D. A. (1973).
11 Brown, L. A. (1969); Pedersen, P. O. (1970).

12 Schumacher, E. F. (1965).
13 Currie, L. L. (1954, (1965), (1966); Friedmann, J. (1968), (1971).
14 Friedmann, J., and Lackington, T. (1967).
15 Friedmann, J. (1968).
16 Friedmann, J. (1968).
17 Colombia, Departamento Nacional de Planeación (1972).
18 Gilbert, A. G. (1974) makes more detailed comments on the regional effects of the Plan and on the Government's regional-development policies.
19 UN ECLA (1971), 90.
20 ibid., 89.
21 Bogotá Urban Development Programme financed by the United Nations Development Programme and executed under the control of Llewelyn-Davies, Weeks, Forestier-Walker and Bor. The report was presented in October 1973. The Colombians are planning similar, but smaller, studies for the cities of Cali, Barranquilla and Medellín.
22 Törnqvist, G. (1970).
23 Darwent, D. J. (1969); Hansen, N. M. (1965); Lasuen, J. R. (1969); Nichols, V. (1969).
24 Odell, P. R. (1968).
25 *Bolsa Review*, various dates.
26 Odell, P. R. (1971).

Appendix Two

1 Warren, K. (1973).
2 Grunwald, J., and Musgrave, P. (1970).
3 Odell, P. R. (1970).
4 *Bolsa Review*; Bromley, R. J. (1973).
5 UN ECLA (1970a).
6 Smith, C. T. (1970).

Index